THE LIES THAT BIND

OTHER BOOKS BY KWAME ANTHONY APPIAH

As If: Idealization and Ideals

Lines of Descent: W. E. B. Du Bois and the Emergence of Identity

The Honor Code: How Moral Revolutions Happen

Experiments in Ethics

Cosmopolitanism: Ethics in a World of Strangers

The Ethics of Identity

Thinking It Through: An Introduction to Contemporary Philosophy

In My Father's House: Africa in the Philosophy of Culture

THE
LIES THAT BIND

Rethinking Identity

CREED, COUNTRY, COLOR, CLASS, CULTURE

KWAME ANTHONY APPIAH

LIVERIGHT PUBLISHING CORPORATION

A Division of W. W. Norton & Company

Independent Publishers Since 1923

New York   London

For information about special discounts for bulk purchases, please contact
W. W. Norton Special Sales at specialsales@wwnorton.com or 800-233-4830

Manufacturing by LSC Communications, Harrisonburg
Book design by Kristen Bearse
Production manager: Beth Steidle

Library of Congress Cataloging-in-Publication Data

Names: Appiah, Anthony, author.
Title: The lies that bind : rethinking identity, creed, country, color,
class, culture / Kwame Anthony Appiah.
Description: First edition. | New York : Liveright Publishing Corporation, 2018. |
Includes bibliographical references and index.
Identifiers: LCCN 2018023080 | ISBN 9781631493836 (hardcover)
Subjects: LCSH: Identity (Philosophical concept) |
Group identity. | Identity (Psychology)
Classification: LCC BD236 .A58 2018 | DDC 302.5—dc23
LC record available at https://lccn.loc.gov/2018023080

Liveright Publishing Corporation, 500 Fifth Avenue, New York, N.Y. 10110
www.wwnorton.com

W. W. Norton & Company Ltd., 15 Carlisle Street, London W1D 3BS

1 2 3 4 5 6 7 8 9 0

For my sisters' grandchildren, as they enter the world.

Spes mihi quisque.

Wer bin ich? Der oder jener?
Bin ich denn heute dieser und morgen ein andrer?

Who am I? This one or that one?
Am I then this one today and tomorrow another?

Dietrich Bonhoeffer, "Wer bin ich?"

(1945)

Contents

Introduction

Over the years and around the world, taxi drivers, putting their expertise to the test, have sized me up. In São Paulo, I've been taken for a Brazilian and addressed in Portuguese; in Cape Town, I've been taken for a "Colored" person; in Rome, for an Ethiopian; and one London cabbie refused to believe I didn't speak Hindi. The Parisian who thought I was from Belgium perhaps took me for a Maghrebi; and, wearing a caftan, I've faded into a crowd in Tangiers. Puzzled by the combination of my accent and my appearance, once our ride is under way, taxi drivers in the United States and the United Kingdom regularly ask me where I was born. "In London," I tell them, but that's not what they really want to know. What they mean to ask is where my family came from *originally*. Or, more bluntly: what are you?

The answer to the question of origins—the *where* question if not the *what* question—is that I come from two families in two places pretty far apart. By the time I was born, my mother had lived in London off and on since her childhood, but her real home was far away—in atmosphere, if not in distance—on the edge of the Cotswold Hills, where she had grown up on a farm in a tiny village on the border of Oxfordshire and Gloucestershire. Her grandfather had a genealogist trace his ancestry back through eighteen generations of his forefathers to a Norman knight in the early thirteenth century who lived less than twenty miles from the place where my mother was born some seven hundred years later.

As a result, while my mother was, in a sense, a Londoner when I was born, she was at heart a countrywoman who just happened to work in London . . . though she had spent a fair amount of time living abroad during and after the Second World War, in Russia, Iran, and Switzerland. Not surprisingly, perhaps, given her international experiences, she found a job at an organization in London that was working for racial harmony in Britain and its empire, largely by supporting colonial students. It was called Racial Unity. That was how she met my father, a law student from the Gold Coast. He was an anti-colonial activist, the president of the West African Students' Union, and a representative in Britain of Dr. Kwame Nkrumah, who was to lead Ghana to independence in 1957, just a few years after I was born. You might say she practiced what she preached.

The other side of my family, then, came from Ghana: more precisely from Asante, a region in the heart of the modern Republic of Ghana. My father's lineage, as he taught us, could be traced back to Akroma-Ampim, an eighteenth-century general whose successes in battle had won him the right to a great tract of land on the kingdom's edge. He was a member of the military aristocracy that created the Asante Empire, which dominated the region for two centuries; and his name is one of the names my parents gave me. My father raised us with stories of his family. In a sense, though, it wasn't really *our* family. Just as my mother's people, being patrilineal, thought you belonged to your father's family, my father's, being matrilineal, thought you belonged to your mother's. I could have told those taxi drivers I had no family at all.

This book is full of family stories because I want to explore the ways in which narratives like these shape our sense of who we are. Each person's sense of self is bound to be shaped by his or her own background, beginning with family but spreading out in many directions—to nationality, which binds us to places; to gender, which

connects each of us with roughly half the species; and to such categories as class, sexuality, race, and religion, which all transcend our
local affiliations.

I've set myself the task in this book of discussing some of the ideas
that have shaped the modern rise of identity and trying to see some
of the mistakes we regularly make about identities more clearly. Philosophers contribute to public discussions of moral and political life,
I believe, not by telling you what to think but by providing an assort-
ment of concepts and theories you can use to decide what to think
for yourself. I will make lots of claims; but however forceful my language, remember always that they are offered up for your consider-
ation, in the light of your own knowledge and experience. I'm hoping
to start conversations, not to end them.

What I won't offer is an explanation of why identity talk has
exploded through my lifetime—a fascinating question, but one for
intellectual and social historians. Instead, I'm going to take the modern prevalence of ideas about identities as a given but challenge some
of our assumptions about them. I aim to persuade you that much of
our contemporary thinking about identity is shaped by pictures that
are in various ways unhelpful or just plain wrong. Getting to pictures
that are more helpful and closer to the truth won't *settle* any political
questions. But I think it can make our discussions more productive,
more reasonable, even, perhaps, a little less antagonistic. That, at any
rate, is my hope. Sensible discussions about matters that profoundly
engage our passions are essential if we are to live together in concord.

For much of my adult life, three features have mattered most when
I meet someone for the first time: I am a man, I am not white, and
I speak what used to be called the Queen's English. These are mat-
ters of gender, race, class, and nation. It is a natural enough thought
nowadays that these are all characteristics of the same general kind.
They are, as we now say, matters of identity. And we all assume that

identities like these will shape not just other people's responses to me but also my thoughts about my own life.

Five of the chapters that follow are focused on one species of identity: creed, country, color, class, and culture. But it will help to say something right at the start about the most obvious of the questions raised by this disparate list; namely, what on earth do they all have in common? How, in short, do identities come into being? My own thinking about these matters has led me over the years to an answer that has guided me in the explorations that follow. It is one philosopher's answer to a double question: what are identities and why do they matter? That will be the task of the first chapter—to explore the manifestations, the mechanisms, and the motives of the multiple systems of classification human beings employ.

Some collective identities being highly situational, "we" in this book typically means my readers and I, all of us connected in some way with patterns of ideas to be found among educated people in every continent. For the intellectual temptations I am trying to combat are temptations I have experienced regularly myself. Because I imagine readers in many places, I have sometimes explained what some of them will already know: what "confirmation" is to an Anglican, who a Hindu god is, what "Sunnah" means to Muslims. In a book about a wide range of identities, it's natural to expect a wide range of fellow readers, who will have different experiences and be knowledgeable about different things.

My main message about the five forms of identity that take us from Chapter Two to Chapter Six is, in effect, that we are living with the legacies of ways of thinking that took their modern shape in the nineteenth century, and that it is high time to subject them to the best thinking of the twenty-first. The European and American intellectuals who founded modern anthropology in the later nineteenth century tended to think of religion as centrally about the things we believe; and that idea has percolated into the general culture. But I'm going to argue that at the heart of religious life across space and time are matters other than creed. And, once you see that creeds are not so central, you'll also have to accept that scriptures—as sources of belief—matter less than many people think.

When it comes to modern states, shaped by a form of nationalism that also arose through the nineteenth century, law and common sense suggest that peoples have a right to determine their own fates. We speak of self-determination and autonomy, about independence and freedom. But, as I'll argue, there's something wrong with our models here, too, starting with the answers we've given to a fundamental question: what makes a bunch of people into a nation?

Race has been a source of trouble in human affairs since the contours of the modern ways of thinking about it became dimly visible in the rise of new scientific ideas about human beings as parts of the natural world. These ideas grew explosively in the nineteenth century, as did the cultural authority of biology, the new science of life. Much of the elaborate scientific superstructure that grew up around race was dismantled in the past century, as anthropologists and biologists worked out the implications of Darwin's and Mendel's ideas, and discovery upon discovery was made in evolutionary theory, population biology, and genetics. But the world outside the sciences hasn't taken much notice. Too many of us remain captive to a perilous cartography of color.

The issue with class, which I discuss in Chapter Five, is not so much that we have a picture of it that is mistaken as that we operate with a set of pictures that is incoherent and inconsistent. And the most influential solution we've devised to the problems posed by class may, like the leeching and cupping of eighteenth-century physicians, worsen the condition it means to remedy.

I won't try to summarize the multiple mistakes we make about our broader cultural identities, not least the very idea of the West. So let me just say here that they're manifest in the temptation to imagine that people's origins make them either inheritors of, or outsiders to, Western civilization.

Throughout the book we'll see how gender—which must be the oldest form of human identity—subtends and shares the problems of other identities. Thinking more clearly about gender, the project of feminist philosophy for more than a generation, helps us think about other identities. That's why gender is central to the first chapter, which lays out some of the general picture of identity I rely on. But every identity has its own distinctive misconceptions.

In each of my five test cases, we fall into an error I'll describe in the first chapter: of supposing that at the core of each identity there is some deep similarity that binds people of that identity together. Not true, I say; not true over and over again. How plausible I can make this thought will depend upon arguments, but also upon details and upon the scores of stories that illustrate my claims. There's no dispensing with identities, but we need to understand them better if we can hope to reconfigure them, and free ourselves from mistakes about them that are often a couple of hundred years old. Much of what is dangerous about them has to do with the way identities—religion, nation, race, class, and culture—divide us and set us against one another. They can be the enemies of human solidarity, the sources of war, horsemen of a score of apocalypses from apartheid to genocide. Yet these errors are also central to the way identities unite us today. We need to reform them because, at their best, they make it possible for groups, large and small, to do things together. They are the lies that bind.

ONE

CLASSIFICATION

Why am I me?

Stendhal,
Le rouge et le noir (1830)

TALKING IDENTITY

Until the middle of the twentieth century, no one who was asked about a person's identity would have mentioned race, sex, class, nationality, region, or religion. When George Eliot writes in *Middlemarch* that Rosamond "was almost losing the sense of her identity," it's because Rosamond is faced with profoundly new experiences when she learns that Will Ladislaw, the man she thinks she loves, is hopelessly devoted to someone else.[1] Identity here is utterly particular and personal. The identities we think of today, on the other hand, are shared, often, with millions or billions of others. They are social.

One looks in vain for talk of such identities in the social science of the early twentieth century. In *Mind, Self, and Society*, published in 1934, George Herbert Mead outlined an influential theory of the self as the product of an "I" responding to the social demands of others, which, once internalized, formed what he called the "me." But in that great classic of early twentieth-century social thought, you'll never find the word "identity" used in our modern sense. Talk of identity really takes off in developmental psychology after the Second World War, with the influential work of the psychologist Erik Erikson. In his first book, *Childhood and Society*, published in 1950, he uses the term in more than one way; crucially, though, he recognizes the importance of social roles and group memberships in shaping one's sense of self, which he called, in psychoanalytic language, an "ego identity." Later on, Erikson explored the crises of identity in the lives of Martin Luther and Mahatma Gandhi, and published books with titles like

Identity and the Life Cycle (1959), *Identity: Youth and Crisis* (1968), and *Dimensions of a New Identity* (1974).

Erikson, who grew up in southwest Germany, told a tale of his own origins that sits right at the heart of our contemporary notions.

> My stepfather was the only professional man (and a highly respected one) in an intensely Jewish small bourgeois family, while I (coming from a racially mixed Scandinavian background) was blond and blue-eyed, and grew flagrantly tall. Before long, then, I acquired the nickname "goy" in my stepfather's temple; while to my schoolmates, I was a "Jew."

I'm guessing that, while his Jewish confreres did use the Yiddish word for a gentile, those German kids didn't always use a word as polite as "Jew." His biological father had been a Dane named Salomonsen; his adopted father's name was Homburger. But at some point he took the last name of Erikson, which, as his daughter once observed drily, suggested that he was father to himself. In a sense, then, he was his own creation.[2] Identity, we can surely conclude, was a fraught issue for him personally.

In his first book, Erikson offered a theory as to why, as he put it, "we"—and given our subject, it's worth noticing that he seems to mean "we Americans"—"began to conceptualize questions of identity." He thought that identity had become a problem in the United States because the country was "trying to make a super-identity out of all the identities imported by its constituent immigrants"; and, he continued, "we do so at a time when rapidly increasing mechanization threatens these essentially agrarian and patrician identities in their lands of origin."[3] It's a good story. But I do not believe it. As we shall see throughout this book, identity, in our sense, was a problem long before we began to talk about it in this modern way.

If Erikson, weaving between personal and collective forms of identity, gave the term broad currency, the influential American sociologist Alvin W. Gouldner was among the first to offer a detailed definition of social identity as such. "It seems that what is meant by a 'position' is the social identity which has been assigned to a person by members of his group," he wrote in a 1957 essay. And he proposed an account of what this means, practically, in social life. First, he thought, people "observe or impute to a person certain characteristics," which allows them to "answer the question 'Who is he?'" Next, "these observed or imputed characteristics are ... interpreted in terms of a set of culturally prescribed *categories*."

> In this manner the individual is "pigeonholed"; that is, he is held to be a certain "type" of person, a teacher, Negro, boy, man, or woman. The process by which the individual is classified by others in his group, in terms of the culturally prescribed categories, can be called the assignment of a "social identity." The types or categories to which he has been assigned *are* his social identities. . . . Corresponding to different social identities are differing sets of expectations, differing configurations of rights and obligations.[4]

As you'll see, I think that Gouldner got a lot right.

Appeals to identity swelled through the sixties and, by the end of the seventies, many societies had political movements grounded in gender and sexuality, race, religion, and ethnicity (even as class politics frequently receded into the background). In more than a few places, regionally based movements that sought to undo often long-established states spoke the language of national identity. In Europe alone, there's Scottish, Welsh, Catalan, Basque, Padanian, and Flemish nationalism; near the end of the twentieth century, Yugoslavia collapsed into a collection of distinct countries; there are rumblings in Brittany, Corsica, and Normandy . . . and that's far from a complete list.

A LITTLE THEORY

I have been writing and ruminating on questions of identity for more than three decades now. My theoretical thinking about identity began, actually, with thoughts about race, because I was genuinely puzzled by the different ways in which people in different places responded to my appearance. That wasn't so much the case in Asante, where, so it seemed to me, one local parent was usually enough to belong. Jerry Rawlings, Ghana's head of state from 1981 to 2001, had a father from Scotland; he wasn't chosen by the people originally—he came to power twice through coups d'état—but his fellow countrymen eventually elected him to the presidency twice. Unlike my three sisters, born, like my father, in Asante, I have never been a Ghanaian citizen. I was born in England, before Ghana's independence, with an English mother, and showed up in Asante at the age of one. So I'd have had to apply for Ghanaian citizenship, and my parents never applied for me. By the time it was up to me, I was used to being a Ghanaian with a British passport. My father, as president of the Ghana Bar Association, was once involved in writing one of our many constitutions. "Why don't you change the rules, so that I can be both Ghanaian and British?" I asked him. "Citizenship," he told me, "is unitary." I could see I wasn't going to get anywhere with him! But, despite my lack of that legal connection, sometimes, when I do something noteworthy, I am claimed, at least by some, for the place that is home to half my ancestry.

The story in England was complex, too. In my grandmother's village, Minchinhampton, in Gloucestershire, where I spent much time in my childhood, those we knew never appeared to doubt our right to be there. My aunt and uncle lived in this picturesque market town in the West of England, too. My aunt had been born there. My grandfather had spent time as a child at a house in the valley, which belonged to his uncle, whose mill had once woven cloth for the tunics of British soldiers and green baize for billiard tables. My great-grandfather, Alfred Cripps, had briefly served as the member of parliament for Stroud, a few miles to the north, and *his* great-grandfather, Joseph Cripps, had represented Cirencester, a few more miles east, for much of the first half of the nineteenth century. And there were Crippses in that area—some buried in Cirencester churchyard—dating back to the seventeenth century.

But the skins and the African ancestry I shared with my sisters marked us out as different, in ways we weren't always conscious of. I recall going to a sports day, a few decades ago, at a school in Dorset I'd attended as a preteen, and coming upon an elderly man who had been headmaster in my day. "You won't remember me," I apologized, as I introduced myself to him. Hearing my name, he brightened and took my hand warmly. "Of course I remember you," he said. "You were our first colored head boy." When I was young, the idea that you could be properly English and not white seemed fairly uncommon. Even in the first decade of the twenty-first century, I remember the puzzled response of an older Englishwoman who had just heard a paper on race I gave at the Aristotelian Society in London. She just didn't understand how I could really be English. And no talk of thirteenth-century ancestors in Oxfordshire could persuade her!

In America, once I got there, things seemed at first relatively simple. I had an African father and so, like President Obama later, I was black. But the story here, too, is complicated . . . and has changed over the years, in part because of the rise of the idea of mixed-race people as an identity group. Color and citizenship, however, were quite separate matters: after the Civil War no sensible person doubted you could be black and American, at least so far as the law was concerned, despite a persistent undercurrent of white racial nationalism. I'll say more about the ideas of race that shaped these experiences later, but I hope it's clear why I might have ended up puzzled about how to make sense of them.

When I turned, over the years, to thinking about nationality and class and culture and religion as sources of identity, and added in gender and sexual orientation, I began to see three ways in which these very disparate ways of grouping people do have some important things in common.

LABELS AND WHY THEY MATTER

The first is obvious: every identity comes with labels, so understanding identities requires first that you have some idea about how to apply them. Explaining to someone what Ewes or Jains or *kothis* are begins with some suggestion as to what it is about people that makes each label appropriate for them. That way, you could look for someone of that identity, or try to decide, of someone you'd met, whether the label applied.

So, the label "Ewe" (usually pronounced eh-vey or eh-wey) is an ethnic label, what social scientists call an "ethnonym"; which means that if your parents are both Ewe, you're Ewe, too. It applies, in the first place, to people who speak one of the many dialects of a language that is called "Ewe," most of whom live in Ghana or Togo, though there are some in many other parts of West Africa and, increasingly, around the world. As is typical of ethnic labels, there can be arguments about whether it applies to someone. If only one of your parents is Ewe and you never learned any of the many dialects of the Ewe language, are you Ewe? Does it matter (given that the Ewe are patrilineal) if the parent was your mother rather than your father? And, since Ewe belongs to a larger group of languages (usually called "Gbe" because that's the word for language in all of them) that shade off into one another, it's not easy to say exactly where the boundaries between Ewe people and other Gbe-speaking people lie. (Imagine looking for the boundaries of Southern speech in America or a cockney accent in London and you'll grasp the difficulty.) Nevertheless, large numbers of people in Ghana and Togo will claim that they're Ewe and many of their neighbors will agree.

That's because of the second important thing identities share: they matter to people. And they matter, first, because having an identity can give you a sense of how you fit into the social world. Every identity makes it possible, that is, for you to speak as one "I" among some "us": to belong to some "we." But a further crucial aspect of what identities offer is that they give you reasons for doing things. That's true about being a Jain, which means you belong to a particular Indian religious tradition. Most Jains are the children of two Jains (just as most Ewes are the children of two Ewes), but there's much more to it than that. And anyone can join who is willing to follow the path set by the *jinas*, souls who have been liberated by conquering their passions and can spend a blissful eternity at the summit of the universe. Jains are typically expected to heed five *vratas*, which are vows or forms of devotion. These are: nonviolence, not lying, not stealing, chastity, and nonpossessiveness. (Like taboos, which are also central to many identities, the *vratas* define who you are by *what* as well as *who* you are *not*. There's a lot of "Thou shalt not's" in the Ten Commandments, too.)[5]

The detailed content of each of these ideals depends, among other things, on whether you are a layperson on the one hand, or a monk or nun on the other. The general point, though, is that there are things people do and don't do *because they are Jains*. By this, I mean only that they themselves think from time to time, "I should be faithful to my spouse . . . or speak the truth . . . or avoid harming this animal . . . because I am a Jain." They do that, in part, because they know they live in a world where not everyone is a Jain, and that other people with other religions may have different ideas about how to behave.

Though there are Ewe religious traditions (lots of different ones), being Ewe isn't, by contrast, a religious identity, and doesn't come with the same sort of specified ethical codes. Ewes can be Muslim, Protestant, or Catholic, and many practice the traditional rites that go by the name of voodoo. (Like the Haitians, they borrowed this word from the Fon peoples, who are their neighbors. It means "spirit.") But, all the same, Ewe people sometimes say to themselves, "As an Ewe, I should . . ." and go on to specify something they believe they should do or refrain from doing. They do things, in short, because they are Ewe. And this, too, depends, in part, on their recognition that not everyone is Ewe, and that non-Ewes may well behave differently.

People who give reasons like these—"Because I'm a this, I should do that"—are not just accepting the fact that the label applies to them; they are giving what a philosopher would call "normative significance" to their membership in that group. They're saying that the identity matters for practical life: for their emotions and their deeds. And one of the commonest ways in which it matters is that they feel some sort of solidarity with other members of the group. Their common identity gives them reason, they think, to care about and help one another. It creates what you could call norms of identification: rules about how you should behave, given your identity.

But just as there's usually contest or conflict about the boundaries of the group, about who's in and who's out, there's almost always disagreement about what normative significance an identity has. How much can one Ewe or one Jain legitimately ask of another? Does being Ewe mean you ought to teach the Ewe language to your children? Most Jains think that their religion requires them to be vegetarian, but not all agree that you must also avoid milk products. And so on. While each Ewe or each Jain will have done things because of their identity, they won't always do the same things. Still, because these identities sometimes help them answer the question "What should I do?" they're important in shaping their everyday lives.

One further reason that's true is the third feature all identities share: not only does your identity give *you* reasons to do things, it can give others reasons to do things *to* you. I've already mentioned something people can do to you because of your identity: they can help you just because you share an identity with them. But among the most significant things people do with identities is use them as the basis of hierarchies of status and respect and of structures of power. Caste in South Asia means some people are born into a higher status than others—as Brahmins, for example. These are members of the priestly caste, who are "polluted" by contact with members of castes that are regarded as lower. In many places in the world one ethnic or racial group regards its members as superior to others, and assumes the right to better treatment. The English poet Shelley, in "Ozymandias," refers to the "frown / and wrinkled lip and sneer of cold command" on the stone face of the sculpture of a long-dead Pharaoh. The royal ancestry of this "king of kings" would have meant that he was used to obedience. Dominant identities can mean that people will treat you as a source of authority; subordinate identities can mean you and your interests will be trampled upon or ignored.

And so an important form of struggle over identity occurs when people challenge the assumptions that lead to unequal distributions of power. The world is full of burdensome identities, whose price is that other people treat you with disrespect. *Kothis* in India know this very well. They are people who, though assigned a male identity at birth, themselves identify as feminine, and experience erotic attraction to men who are more typically masculine. And *kothis* have been subjected over the years to insult and abuse, and to rejection by their families; many of them have been forced by their marginal position into sex work. In recent years, emerging ideas about gender and sexuality—about homosexuality, intersexuality, and transgender identity, and about the complexity of the connection between biological sex and human behavior—have created movements that seek to alleviate the social exclusion of people whose gender and sexuality fall outside traditional norms. The Indian Supreme Court has even declared that individuals are entitled to be recognized as male, female, or third-gender, as they themselves decide.

Once identities exist, people tend to form a picture of a typical member of the group. Stereotypes develop. They may have more or less foundation in reality, but they are almost always critically wrong about something. *Kothis*, some Indians think, really want to be women: they are, many people suppose, what Europeans and Americans would now often call "transsexual." But that's not necessarily so. Ewes, other Ghanaians fear, are particularly likely to use "juju"— witchcraft or "black magic"—against their enemies. But witchcraft is traditional all over Ghana, so this isn't, actually, much of a distinction. (I once wrote an account of my father's funeral, in the course of which I discussed how we had to deal with the threat of witchcraft in our family. We, as you know, were Asante, not Ewe.)[6] People believe that Jains are so obsessed with nonviolence that they insist on covering their faces with white cloth to avoid killing insects by ingesting them. In fact, most Jains don't wear the *muhapatti*, as the white cloth is called, and its use has a variety of rationales that have nothing to do with saving the lives of insects.

In sum, identities come, first, with labels and ideas about why and to whom they should be applied. Second, your identity shapes your thoughts about how you should behave; and, third, it affects the way other people treat you. Finally, all these dimensions of identity are contestable, always up for dispute: who's in, what they're like, how they should behave and be treated.

WOMAN, MAN, OTHER?

———

This picture of identity is, in effect, a generalization of ways of thinking about gender that have been pioneered by feminist scholars. Feminism made use of theoretical ideas in the pursuit of women's equality and liberation from old patterns of oppression. All human societies have some form of gender system—some way of thinking about the significance of the distinction between men and women. But feminist theories allow us to see what all the multitudinous systems of gender have in common while, at the same time, allowing us to keep track of their differences.

Let's rehearse some details. The vast majority of human bodies can be recognized as belonging to one of two biological kinds. Simply examining the genitalia—the organs of sexual reproduction—will usually allow you to see that someone is biologically male (because he has a penis, scrotum, and testicles), or biologically female (because she has a vagina, labia, uterus, and ovaries). In adults, you may be able to make the discrimination at a glance: the breasts of the biological females will grow at puberty, facial hair will develop in the males, their voices will deepen, and so on. Chromosomal analysis will also usually allow you to discover that the males have an X and a Y chromosome and the females two X's. Knowing all this, ordinary people and medical experts alike can apply the labels "woman" and "man."

But these turn out to be only two of the great variety of regularly occurring combinations of sex chromosomes and sexual morphology. In the standard case, the sex organs of human males and females initially develop in the same way in the embryo, and in the early stages the structure that will eventually become either an ovary or a testis is called the "indifferent gonad." In the typical male fetus, genes on the Y chromosome trigger changes that produce the male testis, and thus the production of hormones that influence the development of other sex-related structures. Absent this stimulus, the indifferent gonad turns into an ovary. It's the presence of the Y chromosome, then, that makes you a male.

That's the basic story. But there are many variations. One possibility is that, despite the presence of a Y chromosome, female external genitalia emerge. This can happen for a variety of reasons, one of which is androgen insensitivity syndrome (AIS), which means that your cells are not normally sensitive to male sex hormones. XY people with AIS can have either male or female external genitalia, or something in between, but the females aren't fertile because they have testes in place of ovaries.

There are other ways in which a mismatch between external appearance and your sex chromosomes can develop. Maternal androgens can turn the genitalia in the male direction, producing someone who is XX but externally male. So a fertilized human egg that is clearly XY can end up producing someone who looks like a woman and one that is XX can produce someone who looks like a man. And there are various other possible combinations: penis and ovaries, vagina and abdominal testes, external genitalia that are intermediate, and so on.

And that's all assuming you start out with two sex chromosomes. In fact, there are some people who are XO, having just one X chromosome. This is Turner syndrome, and people who have it have the bodies of women, though they're usually infertile and often shorter than average. (You need at least one X chromosome to survive—the Y chromosome is much smaller than the X and lacks some of the genes on the X that are essential for human life—which is why there are no OY males.) People with Turner syndrome sometimes have medical problems; but among the best-known people with the condition are a world champion gymnast, Missy Marlowe, who has been a spokesperson for the Turner Syndrome Society, and the Oscar-winning actress Linda Hunt.

Then there are people with an extra X chromosome—XXY or XXX—and, rarely, even more. Because in normal female cells only one of the X chromosomes is active (the other existing in a contracted and largely inactive form called a "Barr body"), these extra X's don't usually make a huge difference: if you have a Y chromosome, you'll look male; if you don't, you'll look female. While all these variations are rare, they do mean that even at the level of physical morphology, there just isn't a sharp division of human beings into two sexes.

All societies start with this spectrum of morphological possibilities. They are a basic part of our human biology. Because the intermediate cases are statistically rare, many people in smaller communities may never interact with anyone but XY males and XX females, with a sexual morphology in the standard range. Given this variability, it's not surprising that different societies have come up with different ways of assigning people to a gender. In many places, surgeons have often tried to "tidy up" the genitalia of babies born with nonstandard sexual bodies, soon after birth. So they've sought to bring everybody into a binary system, in which everyone is more or less clearly male or female. Not everyone agrees that this is a good idea.

In India, *kothis* have long been treated as neither men nor women; and *kothi* interacts with another form of South Asian gender identity, whose label is *hijra*.[7] *Hijras*, as a committee of Indian government experts put it in 2014, "are biological males who reject their 'masculine' identity in due course of time to identify either as women, or 'not-men,' or 'in-between man and woman,' or 'neither man nor woman.'"[8] But *hijras* have a long tradition of living as a community with rites of entry, dressing in women's clothes, and wearing women's makeup. *Kothis*, on the other hand, generally cross-dress only in private or when socializing with one another. Many don't cross-dress at all. Sometimes *hijras* have sought gender-reassignment surgery; in the past, many underwent castration. Notice that neither of these terms corresponds to our terms "transgender" or "homosexual," since (to mention only one difference) the South Asian categories don't cover what we would call either F-to-M transsexuals or lesbians.

Anjum, one of the protagonists of Arundhati Roy's extravagantly rambling novel *The Ministry of Utmost Happiness,* is what would once have been called a hermaphrodite: she is raised as a boy named Aftab because her mother seeks to conceal the fact that she has both male and female sexual organs.[9] But the boy, Aftab, doesn't want to be a boy, though he doesn't yet know what he *does* want to be. And then, one spring morning,

Aftab saw a tall, slim-hipped woman, wearing bright lipstick, gold high heels and a shiny green satin salwar kameez, buying bangles from Mir the eagle-seller. . . . Aftab had never seen anyone like the tall woman with the lipstick. . . .

He wanted to be her.[10]

Aftab follows this colorful *hijra* home to the Khwabgah—the town house where the *hijras* of her part of Delhi live—and finds there a whole community of people to whom she somehow knows she belongs. Being *hijra* is more than having a male body and feminine style: as we learn through the novel, *hijras* have a role in Indian life, and so identifying as one entails more than just dressing up. I am relaying the account of a fictional character; but Anjum, I'm told, is based on a real person.

On the other side of the globe, too, some of the Indian tribes of North America once recognized a variety of genders. The Navajo, in the nineteenth century, for example, called intersexes who were masculine *dilbaa*, and those who were feminine *nádleehí*.[11] They took up special roles in religious life. More recently, many American Indian activists have come to use the neologism "Two Spirit" to speak of those who do not fit easily into the categories of man and woman, in one way or another. The term reflects the fact that people who were neither men nor women, but had something—a spirit—from each, played special religious roles in many American Indian societies. And this is how a lot of contemporary American Indians, whom many other Americans would call lesbian, gay, or trans, now choose to identify themselves.

What feminist theorists taught us to see was that when we speak of men and women, or of other genders, we're not talking just about bodies. In calling a child a girl or a boy—in applying that label—every society is assuming more than that the child has a certain sexual morphology. And so we distinguish now between sex (the biological situation) and gender (the whole set of ideas about what women and men will be like and about how they should behave). Some research-ers have argued that one out of every hundred children is intersex in some way.[12] In a world of more than 7 billion people, 1 percent of the population is a whole lot of individuals. So midwives and obste-tricians and others who witness many births may well come across such cases from time to time and have to decide what (if anything) they should do about them. But even in a world of XX females and XY males, gender would impose a great deal of structure on thinking about what women and men are, or should be, like.

Why? Because identities, as I said, involve labels and stereotypes. That is obvious in the case of gender. If you're labeled a man, in most societies, you are supposed to be sexually interested in women, to walk and use your hands in a "manly" way, to be more physically aggressive than women, and so on. Women should be sexually inter-ested in men, walk and talk in a feminine way, be gentler than men, and all the rest. I have been using the words "male" and "female" to talk about bodily differences: but we need words to mark these other forms of difference built upon that foundation. So I'm going to con-tinue using "masculine" and "feminine" to talk about the forms of thought, feeling, and behavior that our pictures of gender lead us to expect in men and in women, respectively. Men are—and are sup-posed to be—well, masculine. Men should lead, women should fol-low; women obey, men command. And that "supposed to be" and those "shoulds" are both descriptive (this is what we expect men and women to be like) and normative (this is what we think is right). But, once more, people disagree about these traditional claims about what men and women—and people who think they are neither—should be like. And these notions clearly vary across time and space; many con-temporary New Yorkers will assume that a woman might be tough as nails and that a man could be, in Shakespeare's phrase, "as mild and gentle as the cradle-babe."

Labels, stereotypes, and ideas about how you should behave: these, I said, are there in every identity. And gender has the last of the traits

I mentioned, too; it involves ideas not just about how you should behave, but also about how others should behave toward you. In the old days, there was a gentlemanly code (reflecting hierarchies of power) of opening doors and holding out chairs and paying for meals, and such. New norms of treatment have emerged, some relating to how women interact with one another, or how men interact with men, some relating to how women and men interact. Next time you're in a crowded elevator in a modern cosmopolitan city, watch to see whether the men stay back to let the women exit first. Now imagine the life of a woman who insists, in the name of challenging older stereotypes, on refusing such offers. Identities, in this way, can be said to have both a subjective dimension and an objective one: an identity cannot simply be imposed upon me, willy-nilly, but neither is an identity simply up to me, a contrivance that I can shape however I please.

The shape of one identity can also be contoured by your other identities. To be an Ewe woman is not just a matter of being a woman *and* being an Ewe, in some easy act of addition. An Ewe woman faces certain expectations—expectations to meet and expectations to be met—that are peculiar to Ewe womanhood. To be Chinese and gay means something different if you're a native of San Francisco than it does if you're a native of Zhumadian, in China's Henan Province, where, not long ago, a hospital institutionalized a man for "sexual preference disorder" and forced him to undergo conversion therapy. The social import of an identity can vary with wealth, age, disability, weight, employment status, and any other social coordinate you might think of. In political contexts, though, an identity group can be avowedly global ("Workers of the world, unite!"; "Women of the world, rise up!"), sometimes with older forms of identity melded into larger, newer composite ones (people of color; LGBTQ). Identity is here enlisted for purposes of solidarity. To be sure, being a member of an identity group that is, in certain respects, subordinated doesn't necessarily make you sympathetic toward another (black Americans,

often for religious reasons, are more likely to oppose same-sex marriage than whites), and sometimes the fiercest antipathy toward an
identity group (as with squabbles among religious sects over "her-
esies") emanates from an intimately adjacent one.

These complex interactions between identities—which we see
in the case of *kothis*, say, where ideas of sexuality and gender both
matter—are one reason that Kimberlé Crenshaw, a feminist legal
theorist and civil rights activist, introduced the idea of *intersectionality*. She wanted to talk about the ways in which our many
identities interact to produce effects that are not simply the sum of
each of them. Being a black lesbian is not a matter of combining
African-American, female, and homosexual norms of identification: LGBTQ norms of identification can depend on your race and
your gender. Nor are the negative social responses to black lesbians
simply a combination of the racist and homophobic responses that
also affect black gay men and the sexist responses experienced
by middle-class white women.[13] Racism can make white men fear
black men and abuse black women. Homophobia can lead men in
South Africa to rape gay women but murder gay men. Sexism in the
1950s kept middle-class white women at home and sent working-
class black women to work for them. Examples of intersectionality
proliferate.

The fact of intersectionality raises a problem for one of the ways
people bring their identities to bear nowadays. Say that Joe, who's a
white man, claims to speak *as a man*, or *as a white person*. What does
that mean, beyond the fact that he's speaking *and* he's male or white?
Having an identity doesn't, by itself, authorize you to speak on behalf
of everyone of that identity. The privilege of representing a group
has to be granted somehow. So, absent evidence that he's somehow
been given or otherwise earned the authority, it can't mean that Joe is
speaking for all white people or for all men. You might think that he
has at least the authority of experience to speak about what it's like to
live as a white man. Is that something that a white man can discuss

with special knowledge, just because he's been through it? Not if we take the point about intersectionality. For, to the extent that how people treat you affects your experience, intersectionality makes it likely that there will be differences in the experience of, say, gay white men and straight white men; and, if Joe had grown up in Northern Ireland, as a gay white Catholic man, his gay white Protestant male friends might well have rather different experiences, too. And, once you think about it a little, you can see that, while your identity affects your experience, there's no guarantee that what you've learned from it is going to be the same as what other people of the same identity have learned.

Yet the familiar fact that our identities are multiple and can interact in complicated ways is consistent with a pretty frugal account of what, conceptually, any identity consists in: taking a label and a picture of how to apply it that entrains norms about how people who have the label should behave and how they should be treated.

HABITUS

None of that is new, of course. "Woman," "Ewe," "Jain," "*kothi*," "*hijra*," were like that long before scholars started talking about social identities. From Shakespeare to Gilbert and Sullivan, there's a long history of pride in being English that echoes portentously from Henry V's speech at Harfleur addressing his troops as "good yeoman, whose limbs were made in England," to the more comical strains of *H.M.S. Pinafore*, where the Boatswain affirms that Ralph, the humble cabin boy,

> . . . has said it
> And it's greatly to his credit,
> That he is an Englishman.

As a teenager, I delighted in a satiric recording by Michael Flanders and Donald Swann who insisted, "the English are best," and sang cheerfully that they "wouldn't give tuppence for all of the rest!" What's new is thinking of these diverse sorts of labels—Englishman, woman, *kothi,* and so on—as things of the same kind. The rise of identity is the rise of that thought.

Once you think that thought, you can ask questions about the social and psychological significance of identities. And a great deal of modern psychology and sociology has been about just that. To complete my sketch of a theory of identity, I want to point to three important discoveries that have emerged in the course of such research.

The first is about how central identity is to the way we deploy our bodies. The French sociologist Pierre Bourdieu put it this way. Each of us has what he called a *habitus*: a set of dispositions to respond more or less spontaneously to the world in particular ways, without much thought. Your habitus is trained into you starting from childhood. Parents tell you not to speak with your mouth full, to sit up straight, not to touch your food with your left hand, and so on, and thus form table manners that are likely to stick with you all your life.[14] Once they are inculcated, these habits aren't consciously associated with an identity: middle-class English people don't consciously decide to hold their knives in their right hands in order to act English, any more than Ghanaians use only their right hands to eat in order to display that they're Ghanaian. But these habits were nevertheless shaped by their identities.

Bourdieu held a prestigious chair at Paris's Collège de France and had a career in the heart of the French academic elite, but he grew up in a village in southwest France, the son of a farmer turned postman, and retained a critical distance from the social codes that surrounded him as an adult. He saw the habitus as grounded in the distinctive way in which a person used his or her body, what he called the "bodily hexis," "a durable way of standing, speaking, walking, and thereby of feeling and thinking."[15] (I wouldn't bother to introduce this horrible jargon if it weren't going to be useful later!) But it also includes

modes of speech, such as what he once called the French "intellectuals' new style of speech—a little hesitant, even mumbling, inter-
rogative ('non?') and faltering," that had replaced "the old professorial
style (with its long sentences, imperfect subjunctives, etc.)"[16]

You learn how to dress as a man or as a woman in ways that are
shaped by the clothes you are given as a child, which themselves are
selected because of your gender. You learn how to walk, in part, by
watching other boys or girls walking. If a man wears makeup—as
the Prophet Muhammad wore kohl around his eyes and Maasai men
paint their faces with ochre—he'll wear it in the way other men do;
in most societies, women wear different styles of makeup from men.
But none of this is particularly conscious: when I buy a jacket, I'm not
thinking, "Must dress like a man." When I walk, I don't consciously
reflect that I'm not walking like a woman. Nevertheless, my clothes
and my gait reflect my gender and the models of masculinity I have
relied on. As Aftab/Anjum reminds us, it is through our identifica-
tions that we recognize our models.

Gender norms are enforced in myriad ways. I recall a lesson
delivered, when I was eight or nine, by the decidedly old-fashioned
headmaster of a school I then attended. His name was Reverend
Hankey (you can imagine what a group of prepubescent boys made
of that) and one day he gave us a stern lecture that there was to be no
roughhousing—"ragging" he called it, in the argot of the day—in the
combination room where we hung out between classes. A few days
later, he came into the room and found me sitting on the chest of a
fellow student, who, if memory serves me right, we called "Piggy,"
because his family name was Hogsflesh. I was tickling Piggy as he
struggled to escape. We were summoned to the headmaster's office,
where my fellow ragger went first. I heard the sound of four whacks
on his bottom with a bamboo cane. So I girded myself up for the
same. But after the third whack, Reverend Hankey stopped. "I'm giving you one less than Hogsflesh," he pronounced solemnly. "I said
no ragging. But if you are going to rag, it's better to be on top." (The

school, if not Reverend Hankey's ideals of masculinity, dissolved a few years later.)

Girls in Japan see other girls covering their mouths when they laugh. They do likewise. If they don't, they are corrected. But because of this, some gay men in Japan also cover their mouths when they laugh, and this reflects the fact that they identify to some degree with women. Because the ways in which men and women dress and walk in different social groups are different, you end up walking and dressing in ways that reflect your identity, not just your gender but your class and your ethnicity. The swagger of some inner-city African-American men is as much a reflection of class as of race and gender. The *Encyclopedia of African American Popular Culture* meticulously describes the style of the "pimp walk" as a "demonstration of cool masculinity . . . a cocksure combination of leisurely strutting, black aesthetics and public performance . . ."[17] A woman who walked that way would strike others as strange; and most patients would be skeptical of doctors who walked that way, whatever their race or social origins.

Among the most significant elements of your bodily hexis, Bourdieu thought, were habits of using your mouth; people acquire a distinctive accent, a recognizable way of speaking, that reflects dimensions of their social identity.[18] An accent can distinguish a class or even a profession, as does the speech of the ludicrous cavalry officer, Wellesley Ponto, in Thackeray's 1848 *Book of Snobs*. Thackeray describes him as "a gaunt and bony youth," who explains frankly why he needs his father to pay off the debts he has acquired living up to the style of his more prosperous fellow officers.

"Gad!" says he, "our wedgment's so doothid exthpenthif. Must hunt, you know. A man couldn't live in the wedgment if he didn't. Mess expenses enawmuth."

Thackeray was satirizing such people, but the accent was real. And the drawl and the lisp were meant to express an aristocratic indifference to haste and a languorous unwillingness to waste energy in conversation. The stiff upper lip here was not just figurative. Bourdieu in his work offered another example of a connection between the overall habitus of one class and another, in a fascinating discussion of the distinction between two words in French that can both refer to the mouth, *bouche* and *gueule*. The sociologist John Thompson summarizes the analysis very nicely:

> In French there is a distinction between a closed, pinched mouth (*la bouche*) and a large open mouth (*la gueule*). Individuals from working-class backgrounds tend to draw a socially and sexually overdetermined opposition between these terms: *la bouche* is associated with the bourgeois and the feminine (e.g., tight-lipped), whereas *la gueule* is associated with the popular and the masculine (e.g., "big mouth," "loud mouth").

As a result, speaking like a bourgeois can seem to a working-class Frenchman to betray his masculinity.[19]

Most of us do not think of our accent as something we consciously chose, nor do we usually reflect upon the fact that the reason we speak the way we do reflects many dimensions of identity beyond the region and the class we come from. Our accent is part of our habitus, one of the routine ways in which we use our bodies. I mentioned in the introduction that my English accent has sometimes puzzled taxi drivers, in part because they're not used to brown-skinned people sounding like members of the English upper middle classes; but, like most people, I speak in the way my school friends spoke when I was growing up. It's unusual to acquire the fluency of a native speaker in a new language as an adult. But a Ghanaian man I know, who has lived in Japan for a long time, told me that he once approached a Japanese woman who was having trouble with a bicycle with a flat tire. When he first started speaking to her, she didn't look up. His Japanese sounded quite normal to her. When she finally glanced up at him, he could see a look of astonishment cross her face. She hadn't expected to see a black-skinned foreigner. (For the record, the story turns out well: she's now his wife.)

Habitus and identity are connected by the fact that we recognize certain forms of behavior—accents, but also ways of walking, styles of dress—as the signs of certain forms of identity and that our identities shape our habitus unconsciously. I've said that identities matter because they give us reasons to do things, reasons we think about consciously. But the connection between identity and habitus means that identities matter in unreflective ways as well. The distinguished American social psychologist Claude Steele describes how a young black graduate student at the University of Chicago, troubled by the fearful responses of white people, takes to whistling Vivaldi as he walks down the street. The student signals his knowledge of "high culture," and white people (who might not know it's Vivaldi), recognize this is classical music. "While hardly being aware of it," Steele writes, they drop "the stereotype of violence-proneness. . . . Fear fades from their demeanor."[20] Sociolinguists have catalogued the many ways in which people adjust their verbal style in response to the social identities of people they're talking to, again while hardly being aware of it. I've been told that I adjust my accent in an American direction when I'm telling New York taxi drivers where I want to go. It doesn't matter that I apparently have a terrible American accent. I'm trying—without consciously meaning to—to make myself easier to understand for people who are often, like me, immigrants, and are working to understand the local dialect of English.

ESSENTIALISM

The second important psychological truth also comes with a fancy name: essentialism. Psychological research has revealed that, long before anyone instructs children to group people into categories, they're programmed to do it anyway. By the age of two, children distinguish between males and females and expect them to behave differently. And once they classify people, they behave as if each person in the group shares some inner something—an essence—that explains why they all have so much in common. "Essentialism is the view that certain categories have an underlying reality or true nature that one cannot observe directly," the developmental psychologist Susan Gelman says, "but that gives an object its identity, and is responsible for other similarities that category members share."[21] Children everywhere are full-fledged essentialists by the time they are four to six years old.

It's not that they don't notice the superficial, visible features of people. Far from it. The color of hair and skin and other aspects of physical appearance play a role in determining what sorts of people are grouped together. I know of a distinguished black New York literary agent who finds children in the elevator of her building reaching out to her for a hug: in their world black women are nannies, and nannies are there for the hugging. What essentialism means is that children assume that these superficial differences—the ones that lead to applying the label—reflect deeper, inward differences that explain a great deal of how people behave.

Research with young children suggests that one of our most basic strategies for making sense of the world is to form the sorts of generalizations that linguists call "generics"—generalizations like "Tigers eat people," and "Women are gentle." It also turns out that it's very hard to say what makes generics true. They're not equivalent to universal claims like "All tigers eat people." After all, most tigers have not eaten a person; in fact, very, very few have. As for whether women are gentle: well, which women? Certainly not the fierce Amazon regiment (whom the Fon charmingly called "our mothers,") that served the nineteenth-century kings of Dahomey. So the generic claim that "Women are gentle" doesn't mean *all* women are gentle; and "Tigers eat people" doesn't mean that *most* tigers eat people. In fact, as my friend the philosopher Sarah-Jane Leslie has pointed out, an epidemiologist can sincerely say, "Mosquitoes carry the West Nile virus," while knowing that 99 percent of them *don't* carry it.

Generics work by a basic kind of association of ideas. So thinking "Tigers eat people" means that, faced with a tiger, your default response is going to be to think about its eating someone—perhaps even you. "Mosquitoes carry the West Nile virus" will have your doctor checking your temperature when she sees your mosquito bites.[22] As these examples suggest, one thing that makes it more likely that we'll accept a generic is if the property it mentions is one that we have a reason to be concerned about: like people-eating or pathogen-spreading.

But it also helps if we think of the class (tigers, women, mosquitoes) as a kind, as a group of organisms with a shared essence. And getting children to think of a group of *people* as a kind is very easy. The psychologist Marjorie Rhodes and her colleagues did the following simple experiment. They showed four-year-olds pictures of a fictional kind of person they called a Zarpie. The pictures were male and female, black, white, Latino, and Asian, young and old. With one group of kids, the experimenters made lots of generic remarks about these imaginary people—"Zarpies are scared of ladybugs," and the like. With another group of kids, they avoided generics. ("Look at this Zarpie! He's afraid of ladybugs!") A couple of days later they showed the kids a Zarpie and said that he made a buzzing sound. It turned out that the kids who'd heard a lot of generics about Zarpies were much more likely to believe that *all* Zarpies made buzzing sounds. Generic talk encouraged them to think of Zarpies as a kind of person. And once kids think of Zarpies as a kind of person, they're more likely to infer that the behavior of one Zarpie reflects the nature of all Zarpies, that buzzing flows from the Zarpie essence.[23]

Let's put the lessons of the last two paragraphs together. I can get you to think of people—even a group of diverse-looking people of both sexes and all ages—as a kind, by making generic remarks about them. And you're more likely to accept a generic claim about a group if what it says is something negative or worrying. We humans are more likely, then, to essentialize groups about which we have negative thoughts; and more likely to have negative thoughts about groups we've essentialized. There's an unfortunate vicious circle for you. (The next time someone tells you that "Muslims are terrorists," you might want to bear that in mind.)

The plain fact is that we're really good at conjuring up Zarpies, and viewing them with suspicion. Take the Cagots, of the French and Spanish Pyrenees. Though they largely melted away in the nineteenth century, through migration and assimilation, the Cagots were, for a millennium, treated as pariahs, relegated to disfavored districts, even forced to use separate doors in churches, where they received the Communion wafer at the end of a stick. Because contact with the Cagots was contaminating, they were severely punished for drinking from the same water basin as others, for farming, or even for walking barefoot on the streets. Songs about them—one, recorded in the mid-nineteenth century, goes: "Down with the Cagots, / Let's destroy them all! / Let's destroy the Cagots, / And down with them all!"— made it clear how you should regard them, but didn't tell you why. What distinguished them from their neighbors? Not their appearance. (That's why they were forced to identify themselves with badges pinned to their clothing, often duck or goose feet, or fabric facsimiles.) Not their family names. Not their language. Not their religion. The real mystery of the Cagots, Graham Robb concludes in his history of France, "was the fact that they had no distinguishing features at all."[24]

In large ways and small, essentialism shapes our public history, and it shapes our personal histories as well. It's there in the responses of some white people to Claude Steele's black graduate student on the streets around the University of Chicago. It's evident, too, in the ways we are prone to assume, in the domain of gender, that "boys will be boys" and men, men. We expect all kinds of gendered behavior in ways that suggest that there is an inner something that not only explains why (as we might imagine) men look like one another and behave in similar ways. And when we first discover some who don't—men who don't desire women, for example—we can be taken aback. Our next step is usually not to abandon the thought that men desire women, but to note an exception, while sticking to the old generalization. Only later are we likely to adopt a new category, gay men, that allows us to return to the old generalization, now about a new group, straight men. (So our second step is likely to be presupposing that everyone is either gay or straight, which turns out not to be exactly true either.)

In the course of this book, we'll encounter this most basic of our cognitive habits over and over again. So it's worth insisting from the start that essentialism about identities is usually wrong: in general, there isn't some inner essence that explains why people of a certain social identity are the way they are. We've seen already that there's more than one way to come to be a man or a woman. The story of why Ewes speak Ewe or Jains practice their religion doesn't begin with a shared inner something that explains why they do those things. And most of the things that most people do aren't done *because* they are women or men, of this or that ethnicity or race or religion. Like the imaginary Zarpies, most groups of real people, defined by the large-scale identities that shape our social world, are enormously diverse.

THE FOUR-DAY-OLD TRIBE

The last lesson in the psychology of identity I want to mention was demonstrated in an experiment that took place over a few days in the beautiful, hilly woods of the San Bois Mountains of Oklahoma, in 1953. That summer, a team of researchers assembled two groups of eleven-year-old boys at adjoining but separate campsites, in a place called Robbers Cave State Park. The boys were from the Oklahoma City area. They hadn't met before, but they came from similar backgrounds—they were Protestant, white, and middle-class. All this was by careful design. The researchers were studying the formation of what social psychologists call in-groups and out-groups—the way that tension developed between them and the way it might be alleviated—and the Robbers Cave experiment is a classic piece of social science.

The camp area was remote and densely wooded; the boys had been there for about a week before they learned that there was another camp of boys nearby. The two groups then challenged each other to competitive games, like baseball and tug-of-war. In the next four days, a couple of things happened. The groups gave themselves names—they were the Rattlers and the Eagles—and a fierce antagonism arose between them. Flags were torched; cabins were raided; rocks were collected as weapons for an anticipated attack.[25]

Notice that the boys felt no need for a collective name until they learned about the presence of those other boys on the campgrounds. But, as our theory predicts, to form identities they needed labels. Among the Rattlers, an ethos of "toughness" developed, after they discovered one of the higher-status boys in the group had incurred a minor injury without mentioning it to anyone; being toughs, they also started to curse. The Eagles, having defeated the foul-mouthed Rattlers in a baseball game, decided to distinguish themselves by *not* cursing. These quasi-cultural differences could be recognized in the way each group talked about itself and the other group: the scrappy, macho Rattlers regarded the Eagles as "sissies" and "little babies"; the pious and clean-living Eagles considered the Rattlers to be "bums."[26] Labels came first, then, but essences followed fast. The boys didn't develop opposing identities because they had different norms; they developed different norms because they had opposing identities. As far as identity goes, it turns out a lot can happen in four days.

Our third psychological truth, then, is just that we humans ascribe a great deal of significance to the distinction between those who share our identities and those who don't, the insiders and the outsiders, and that we do this with identities new (like Rattlers or Eagles) and long-established, large and small, superficial and profound.

There's a whole list of psychological tendencies that go with this distinction between in-groups and out-groups. It may seem obvious, for example, that people tend to favor those of their own identity and to look down on out-group members. But given the scale of many groups, this should be more surprising than it is. Why would a Hindu give preference to another Hindu he does not know over a Muslim neighbor? There are a billion Hindus, and you have only a few hundred neighbors. And yet, everywhere in the world, we take this sort of partiality for granted.

There's a commonsense way of talking about all this. We're *clannish* creatures. We don't just belong to human kinds; we prefer our own kind and we're easily persuaded to take against outsiders. Evolutionary psychologists think these tendencies were once adaptive; they helped people survive by creating groups they could rely on to deal with the hazards of prehistoric life, including the existence of other groups competing for resources. Something like that is probably right. But whatever the explanation, it seems pretty clear that we're not just prone to essentialism, we also have these clannish tendencies, and each of us has a habitus shaped by our various identities.

The little theory of identity I just sketched and those three psychological observations helped me as I set out to think about the particular forms of identity that are the main subjects of this book. Having these ideas at hand will help us chart our way through religion, nation, race, class, and culture as sources of identity. I'm going to start with religion, because many modern religious identities connect us with some of the oldest human stories. You could debate whether, in that sense, religious identities are older than national, racial, and cultural ones; what's certain is that all of these modern forms of identity connect with religion.

In the chapters that follow, I'll be exploring a variety of ways in which identities can go awry, and can be enlisted for ill. So let me offer this stipulation as we set out: however much identity bedevils us, we cannot do without it. You'll recall the old joke. A man goes to see a psychiatrist. He says, "Doctor, my brother's crazy—he thinks he's a chicken." The psychiatrist says, "Well, why don't you bring him in?" And the fellow replies, "Oh, I would, but we need him out there laying the eggs." Social identities may be founded in error, but they give us contours, comity, values, a sense of purpose and meaning: we need those eggs.

TWO

CREED

Did he find four separating forces between his temporary guest and him?

Name, age, race, creed. . . .

What, reduced to their simplest reciprocal form, were Bloom's thoughts about Stephen's thoughts about Bloom and about Stephen's thoughts about Bloom's thoughts about Stephen?

He thought that he thought that he was a jew whereas he knew that he knew that he knew that he was not.

James Joyce, *Ulysses*
(1922)

PREACHMENTS AND PRACTICES

———

When my parents, born thousands of miles apart, got married in the 1950s, many people warned them that their "mixed marriage" was going to be difficult. My parents agreed. But not because, as those people supposed, my mother was white, my father black. You see, my father was a Methodist and my mother an Anglican. And since the mid-eighteenth century, that distinction has been posing real challenges. John Wesley, the Anglican cleric who cofounded Methodism with his brother Charles, once said, rather starkly: "I fear, when the Methodists leave the Church, God will leave them."[1] I can report that this remark does not come up very often in conversation among Ghanaian Methodists; the Methodists left the Church of England anyway.

My parents were members of two different Christian churches for the rest of their lives. But they lived together in Kumasi, the town in Ghana I grew up in, until my father died; and my mother was buried beside him a decade and a half later. One reason their marriage worked, I think, was that they were each sustained by their slightly different variants of the Christian faith. What some counted a burden, they counted a blessing. Because Christianity wasn't something they practiced only on Sundays: it infused their lives. And in that way it was like many other religious traditions over the millennia.

Take Judaism, the eldest of the Abrahamic creeds. For thousands of years, prayers, rituals, sacred texts, dietary laws, and other regulations have played a central role in defining a Jewish community and distinguishing it from the people among whom the Jews have lived. They were a people—a group defined by shared ancestry, real or imagined—who shared what we would call a religion. The Jews of Alexandria in the first century BCE looked different from their neighbors because of the ways they dressed their hair and their beards, the clothes they wore, the way they prayed. They had their own bodily hexis and habitus. They also ate different things and were guided by different scriptures. Neither they nor their neighbors could have drawn a sharp line between Jewish custom and Jewish religion. Judaism, as Mordecai Kaplan (the founder of modern Jewish Reconstructionism) insisted, is the folk religion of the Jewish people. And the notion here that identity might precede doctrine is actually a startling one. There's a reason that we refer to religious identities with words like "faith," "confession," or, indeed, "credo," from the Latin for "I believe." It's that we've been taught to think of religion principally as a matter of beliefs.

I want to argue that this simple idea is deeply misleading, in ways that can make interreligious comity seem both harder and easier than it really is. I want to persuade you that religion is *not*, in the first instance, a matter of belief.

Every religion can be said to have three dimensions. Sure, there is a body of belief. But there's also what you do—call that practice. And then there's who you do it with—call that community, or fellowship. The trouble is that we've tended to emphasize the details of belief over the shared practices and the moral communities that buttress religious life. Our English word "orthodoxy" comes from a Greek word that means "correct belief." But there's a less familiar word, "orthopraxy," that comes from another Greek word, πρᾶξις (*praxis*), which means "action." Orthopraxy is a matter not of *believing* right but of *acting* right.

Consider those Jews of Alexandria. Already more than 2,000 years ago, it was possible to belong to this community without believing in God: Philo of Alexandria, a Jewish philosopher who lived in the first century BCE, discusses atheism. True, he was against it. But he was contesting a position that was tempting some in his own community.[2] (These days, of course, people readily think of themselves as Jewish without believing in the Jewish god.) Amartya Sen, the great Indian economist and philosopher, once told me how, as a child, he went to ask his grandfather about Hinduism. You're too young, he was told, come back when you're older. So he came back as a teenager to try again. But he had to begin by warning his grandfather that he had decided in the interim that he didn't believe in the gods. There you are, his grandfather replied, you belong to the *atheist* branch of the Hindu tradition.

We can approach the matter from the other direction. In the twelfth century, Maimonides, the greatest medieval Torah scholar, decocted the essence of Judaism into Thirteen Principles: tenets such as "the unity of God," the existence of prophecy, the divine origins of the Torah. Suppose you sit by yourself in your study and persuade yourself of all these principles. You would not thereby become Jewish. These abstract beliefs mean very little if you lack a direct relationship to traditions of practice, conventions of interpretation, communities of worship.

What's easy to miss is that an avowal of faith is a performance as much as it is a proposition. The Athanasian Creed tells of "one God in Trinity and Trinity in unity." Who knows what this has meant to individual believers around the world? It's a pledge of allegiance: the act of affirmation matters independently of what philosophers would call its "propositional content." Could most Christians explain, for that matter, precisely what it means for the Holy Spirit to "proceed from the Father and the Son," as the Nicene Creed insists?

Scriptures survive in part precisely because they aren't just lists of beliefs or instructions on how to live. But even religious documents that are meant to define those beliefs that mark off one sect from another usually require interpretation, as I learned from my Anglican mother. She told me that when she was preparing for confirmation, the ceremony that marks the transition to full adult membership of the Anglican Church, she mentioned to her father that she was having difficulty with some of the Thirty-Nine Articles of faith that have defined the distinctive traditions of the Anglican Church since the reign of Elizabeth I. "Well," Grandfather said, "I have a friend who can help you with that." That friend was William Temple, then the Archbishop of York, and later the Archbishop of Canterbury, spiritual head of the Anglican Church. My mother went to see him. As they scrutinized the Articles, every time my mother said that something was hard to believe, the archbishop agreed with her. "Yes, that *is* hard to believe," he would say. She went home and told her father that if you could be an archbishop with her doubts, you could surely be an ordinary Anglican.

What she was affirming when she affirmed the Thirty-Nine Articles mattered to her; what mattered to the Church, first and foremost, was that she affirmed them. In the world of identity, utterances have functions, separate from their meanings. "Colorless green ideas sleep furiously," a sentence the linguist Noam Chomsky devised as an example of something grammatically well formed but nonsensical, could function as a credo for some sect, baffling to the novitiate, but prodding the cohort of adepts closer to ineffable revelation. Some traditions of contemplative practice alight on koans (what is the sound of one hand clapping?) or other forms of esoteric knowledge that can be fully understood only when we have reached a higher state of enlightenment and advanced into a more privileged circle. And the Druze cherish doctrines about the ultimate nature of God and reality that most Druze are not privy to. ("Esoteric" originally meant "reserved for an inner circle.") Beliefs that you don't personally possess—not because you reject them, but because you cannot even access them—can thus be central to your religion.

Gore Vidal took note of this tendency in *Julian,* a wonderful novel about the last of the pagan Roman emperors, Julian the Apostate, who lived in the middle of the fourth century CE. In it, we're told of "those temples at Rome where certain verses learned by rote are chanted year in and year out, yet no one, including the priests, knows what they mean, for they are in the early language of the Etruscans, long since forgotten."[3] But that doesn't render the rites meaningless, as Vidal's character apparently thought: many of us have witnessed the power of ceremonies in a language we do not know. Jews use an Aramaic version of a prayer called the Kaddish when they are in mourning, in communities that haven't used Aramaic for more than a millennium. Hearing it recited at a funeral is a powerfully moving experience, even if you have no idea what it means. Many older Catholics, including many who don't know Latin, still miss the glories of the old Tridentine Latin mass, whose use was discouraged after the Second Vatican Council in the early 1960s. Whatever that's about, it's not about doctrine: for doctrine, by definition, survives translation from one language to another. Which also means that if, as many Muslims believe, the Quran is untranslatable, its value must lie in something more than the doctrines it contains.

I distinguished among belief, practice, and community. But, in obvious ways, each interpenetrates the others. The declaration of a belief, as I said, is a form of practice. Some beliefs (not least ethical precepts) enjoin certain practices, while the meaning of a practice can be shaped by the beliefs that it entrains. (If someone takes a knife to you, her beliefs help determine whether it's assault or surgery.) And, of course, communities define themselves by and through beliefs and practices. That's one reason that differences in beliefs define sects—but they don't create them, in any straightforward way. When you talk to individual Christians or Muslims or Buddhists or Jews, you are going to find differences even within the sects, as my mother disagreed with some of the members of her tiny church in Kumasi. People may join churches and temples and mosques and announce sectarian identities, but when it comes to the fine points of belief, it can sometimes seem that each of us is a sect of one. Every church has areas of permissible differences, then. Sometimes these can be cast as distinctions of emphasis, and, when they come with constituencies, they can be nested within a religion, the way different religious orders—Franciscan, Benedictine, Dominican, Jesuit, and so on—are incorporated within the Catholic Church. Which differences exile its followers from the in-group is, in a real sense, a political matter, not simply a theological one. Heretics aren't killed because they differ in arcane theological details; they're killed because they reject, and threaten, the authority of their theocratic rulers.

At the same time, minor variations in practice can enable you to recognize others as members of your particular denomination or form of worship—or as interlopers from another. Consider what Muslims do with their forefinger during the *tashahhud*. (Observant Muslims pray five times a day, and the *tashahhud* is the portion of this prayer in which you face Mecca on your knees.) When you're kneeling for the *tashahhud*, you offer praise to God and peace to the Prophet, and you bear witness that there is no god but Allah, whose servant and messenger is Muhammad. Sunnis tend to lift their index finger during the *tashahhud*; Sunni clerics class this with actions that are recommended (*mustahabb*), not compulsory. The general thought is that the pointing indicates the greatness of the one you are addressing. Yet how and when people point differs from one school to another, even from one congregation to another.

Some Muslims, with the support of the Hanafi School of Islamic jurisprudence, think that when you say (in Arabic) "there is no God except Allah," you should raise your forefinger when you say "no," and lower it when you say "except Allah." Some, with support from the Shafi'i School, raise their forefinger when they say "except Allah." Others keep the finger engaged throughout the prayer. But what exactly should you do with the raised forefinger? Some move it left and right, or keep it raised and still, or move it up and down. And among those who move it up and down, there is the issue of how much movement is appropriate. Some clerics disapprove of wide angles, and think that the finger should be moved up and down in a subtler wobble, the whole consistent with an upward tilt. In sorting through these options, there are various sacred texts to consult and interpret and weigh, but there are also continuities of practice within communities. A modern ruling, issued by the Saudi-based Standing Committee for Scholarly Research and Issuing Fatwas, warns that this matter "should not lead to dispute and division," which suggests that it can, and has.[4] These niceties of bodily hexis help mark out which community of worship you belong to. They help establish subdivisions, gradients, of religious identity—the sort of subdivisions that don't much matter, until they do.

Differences of practice like these are not uniquely Muslim, by any means: wikiHow offers instruction on how Christians may cross themselves, making the sign of the cross on their bodies, in the Western and Eastern traditions of the Church. But you'll need more than a single website to discover *when* you should cross yourself according to the various traditions that permit or require it. And Protestants, other than some Anglicans, Methodists, and Lutherans, tend not to do it at all.

Human beings are prone to making new religious communities, as they are to defining their own by contrast to other ones. *You're not doing it right* is a powerful sentiment. There's an old joke about a Jewish man shipwrecked on a desert island. Over the decades he builds three buildings. When he's found, his rescuers ask him what they are. "This is my house. This is the synagogue I go to. And this," he says finally, "this is the synagogue I *don't* go to."

THE ONE AND THE MANY

If by a religion you meant a single coherent set of doctrines, precepts, and practices, then none of the familiar global religions—nor any of the local folk religions of a thousand societies around the world—would be one religion. It would, at the limit, be a plenitude of religions in every moment, new ones hatching every day. Together Buddhists, Christians, Jews, Hindus, Muslims, and Taoists make up some two-thirds of the world's population; but they are fissured into vast numbers of sects.

For that matter, you may not realize how much your religion has drifted from the religion of those you view as your congregational predecessors; religious practices over time are, in a familiar way, like all traditions, a bundle of continuities and discontinuities. The tendency of religions to schism means that there are always disagreements about who's in and who's out. It's easy to find Jewish- or Christian-identified sects that are so heterodox as to raise questions about their identification. So, for example, despite the fact that they called themselves the "Church of Jesus Christ of Latter-day Saints," the Mormons were widely regarded as non-Christian in the past, in part because they *didn't* believe in the Trinity and *did* believe that God has a physical (though eternal and perfect) body. We can be confident, as well, that many ultra-Orthodox Jews regard much of modern Judaism as simply not Jewish at all.

Sometimes it would be better if others *didn't* regard you as belonging. Muslim clerics tend to regard members of the Bahá'í faith—which arose in nineteenth-century Iran, and was at first seen as an Islamic sect—as apostates or heretics, whereas the Bahá'í regard themselves as members of a distinct religion. Iran's current persecution of the Bahá'í presupposes that they are, in a sense, bad Muslims. In cases like this where a state persecutes those it takes to be dissident members of the official religion, it is often safer to be entirely out than halfway in. Ahmadis in Pakistan, who do think of themselves as Muslims, are legally prohibited from calling themselves Muslims; Christians, on the other hand, are allowed to worship largely unmolested. In Lahore, in 1953, hundreds, and perhaps thousands, of Ahmadis were murdered in riots; in 2010 nearly a hundred were murdered there again by the Punjabi Taliban; in 2016 there was an attack on an Ahmadi mosque on the Prophet's birthday.

(Christians were attacked by Taliban splinter groups a few months earlier; but they got sympathy and support from many in the Sunni majority.) Nor are such arguments confined to the smaller religious movements. Profound disagreements about the coherence of religious identity arise for Hinduism, which is, on one accounting, the world's third-largest religion.

The word "Hinduism" emerged in the nineteenth century, and some scholars argue that the religion did, too. They say that British colonials, taken aback by the pagan profusion of cults and gods they encountered, sought to compact a religious diversity into a single, subsuming entity. Being literate Christians, they looked for sacred texts that might underlay this imputed tradition, enlisting the assistance of the Sanskrit-reading Brahmins. A canon and an attendant ideology was extracted, and, with it, Hinduism. Other scholars question this history, insisting that a self-conscious sense of Hindu identity preceded this era, defined in no small part by contrast to Islam.[5] (A similar story can be told about other "world religions.") We shouldn't expect to resolve this dispute, which involves the weightings we give to points of similarity and points of difference. And scholars on both sides of this divide acknowledge the vast pluralism that characterized, and still characterizes, the beliefs, rituals, and forms of worship among the South Asians who have come to identify as Hindu.

You can see why it's hard to make sense of the idea that Hinduism is a single coherent whole, once you recognize the scale and multifariousness of the Sanskrit religious writings that might now be regarded as its scriptures. The longest of these is the religious epic, the *Mahābhārata*, which clocks in at some 1,800,000 words (ten times the length of the *Iliad* and the *Odyssey* combined). Then there's the *Ramayana*, which recounts the heroic attempts of Prince Rama to rescue his wife from a demon king. It has 24,000 or so verses: about as many as there are in the Hebrew Bible. The Vedas, which are the oldest Sanskrit scriptures, include hymns and other magical and liturgical literature; and the *Rig-Veda*, the oldest, consists of nearly

11,000 lines of hymns of praise to the gods. How many gods? Well, there's Brahma, the Creator; Vishnu, the Preserver; and Shiva, the Destroyer. Next, among the most popular, we might mention Shiva's eldest son, Ganesha, represented with an elephant head; Rama, who is an incarnation of Vishnu; Krishna, who is associated with the teachings of the *Mahābhārata*; and Saraswati, Brahma's wife, goddess of learning. That's only the beginning, though, and a popular Indian saying announces that there are 33 crores (that's 330 million!) gods. And I haven't begun to mention the hundreds of festivals and thousands of rituals that take place in the hundreds of thousands of temples scattered across the Indian subcontinent.

In critical ways, the story of Hinduism reflects a larger pattern. Despite the antiquity of the word *religio* (which Lucretius famously condemned in the *De rerum natura* more than 2,000 years ago), the modern concept of religion—as a class that includes, say, Islam, Christianity, Taoism, and Buddhism—gained currency only in the nineteenth century.[6]

SCRIPTURAL DETERMINISM

Given the variegated nature of religions as they're actually practiced, it has been tempting to try to establish the essential unity of religions through a shared taproot other than practice: and (in the religions of literate peoples) the most accessible candidate for such a taproot is the body of texts that our religionists hold sacred. Earlier, I suggested that we distort the nature of religious identity by a narrow fixation on faith. This fallacy is entwined with another: that of scriptural determinism, which, in its simplest version, involves the claim that our religious beliefs repose in our sacred texts—that to be a believer is to believe what's in the scriptures, as if one could decant from them, like wine from an urn, the unchanging nature of a religion and its adherents.[7]

Many contemporary people, at least in the circles I move in, don't know very much about any scriptural tradition. In England or Canada or Australia, you can be an Anglican for weddings and funerals and not very much else. (In that very English film *Four Weddings and a Funeral,* by far the longest reading at any of the five ceremonies is of an elegy by the poet W. H. Auden.) Once, male Jews would have studied the Torah regularly; nowadays many do not really study the single portion you interpret when you go through your bar mitzvah and are called to the Torah as you pass from boy to man. (The non-Orthodox celebration of a girl's coming of age in a bat mitzvah moved closer to the forms for boys in the later twentieth century, but this doesn't mean that most modern Jewish women have a deep knowledge of the Torah either.) British or American Hindus, like many Hindus in South Asia, aren't very likely to know Sanskrit, or to be able to tell you more than a few of the thousands of tales in the rich body of ancient Hindu religious writings. Devout Muslims may study the Quran, but most are not schooled in interpreting the transcribed oral traditions—the hadith—that report the doings and sayings of the Prophet and define the Sunnah, the example given by the life of the Prophet and his companions. So it may be worth pointing out some of the features that are common to these scriptural writings, since the determinist argument requires us to evaluate claims about their interpretation.

Let me take, more or less at random, the opening passage of Isaiah, a book that many Christians are at least vaguely aware of, however little time they spend in church, because of the resonant passages that are read in services at Christmas. "The people that walked in darkness have seen a great light." "Wonderful, Counseller, The mighty God, The everlasting Father, The Prince of Peace." (You might also recognize these words from Handel's *Messiah*: "And there shall come forth a rod out of the stem of Jesse . . .") These phrases echo in my memory from a score of candlelit evenings when I was young, as I listened enthralled by the mystery of the incarnation . . . and excited at the prospect of presents from Santa Claus in the morning.

Here's how that book begins:

> The vision of Isaiah the son of Amoz, which he saw concern-
> ing Judah and Jerusalem in the days of Uzziah, Jotham, Ahaz,
> and Hezekiah, kings of Judah. Hear, O heavens, and give ear, O
> earth: for the Lord hath spoken, I have nourished and brought
> up children, and they have rebelled against me. The ox knoweth
> his owner, and the ass his master's crib: but Israel doth not
> know, my people doth not consider.

Much of scripture is written in arcane language like this—language
that is, indeed, poetical and metaphorical, but, at the same time, simply obscure. Much consists of narratives: some ostensibly historical,
some, like the parables told by Jesus in the New Testament, overtly
fictional. And while the students of scripture spend much time drawing consequences from these stories, the stories themselves do not,
like Aesop's fables, announce their moral at the end. In the New Testament parable of the Good Samaritan, for example, a man is robbed
and left for dead beside the road. A priest and a Levite (a member of
a Jewish tribe dedicated to assisting in worship in the Temple) walk
right by. A Samaritan, a member of a group despised by ordinary
Jews, stops to provide help. Jesus tells this story in answer to a question from a Pharisee about what it is to be a good neighbor. But he
doesn't tell us *why* the Samaritan is a model of a good neighbor. He
simply says that the man he is talking to should "go and do likewise."
How can we apply that thought to our busy lives here in the twenty-
first century? Does it mean that each of us should be looking after a
family of Syrian refugees?

Not all scripture is elliptical in this way. With our Alexandrian
Jews in mind, we might turn to something that looks altogether cut
and dried: kashrut, the dietary codes that spelled out for them what's
kosher and what's unclean. This would seem the ultimate case of
"Read the manual, stupid." The relevant passages from the Torah are

either specific rules or even more specific lists of foods. For example, the fish you eat must have scales: check. But what about fish that have *weird* scales? Swordfish have scales that change as they age; and sturgeon have ganoid scales, which can't be removed without tearing the skin, instead of the more typical ctenoid and cycloid scales. Rabbinic authorities disagree about the status of these fish. The Hebrew Torah, in its authoritative Masoretic version, helpfully lists the specific birds it forbids. But these aren't bird names you'll find in your *Field Guide to Birds*. One bird name actually translates as "vomiting." Is that a pelican? That's one guess, but we're not sure. Another bird name means "purple." Is that a flamingo? A purple swamp hen? Nobody knows. Moving beyond birds, there's the prohibition on the *anaqah*, which means "groaners." Some think those are geckos. Others say ferrets. It's the most straightforward part of the Pentateuch, and it's a blizzard of uncertainties. People seek the clarity of "Eat This, Not That." Instead, we could be explicating a Mallarmé poem.[8]

Frequently, the stakes are greater than whether sturgeon will be on the menu. What to do with the fact that, while Judaism is monotheistic, the Torah is filled with references to other gods (typically in the course of extolling Yahweh as being above them)? Some Christians think that Jesus really was, in some sense, God, the creator of the universe who spoke to Moses out of a burning bush. Others think he was just a very special human being. Both can cite scripture to support them. In the Gospel According to St. John, the risen Christ tells his mother, "I ascend unto my Father, and your Father; and to my God, and your God." Sounds like he's saying he's *not* God." But a few chapters earlier, he says to his disciples at the Last Supper, "He that hath seen me hath seen the Father." Sounds like he *is* the Father.

Another venerable Christian dispute involves the question of what will justify our salvation: good works or faith alone? Ephesians tells us, "For by grace ye are saved through faith: and that not of yourselves: it is the gift of God: Not of works, lest any man should boast." But James tells us, "Faith without works is dead"; and St. Paul in

Romans says that God "will render to every man according to his deeds." You can build a case in either direction; or you can argue, say, that if you have faith it will be manifest in salvation-qualifying deeds. What you can't do is extract guidance from scripture simply by giving it a good shake and pouring out the contents.

Scholarly exegesis can also run athwart older ecclesiastic interpretations. In the New Testament, St. Paul uses the word ἀρσενοκοῖται (arsenokoitai) twice in a list of wrongdoers: once in 1 Corinthians and once in 1 Timothy.[9] Serious scholars agree that this word picks out people who engage in some kind of sexual act. If you live in a world where Christianity is assumed to be hostile to homosexuality, you are likely to find this passage a convincing demonstration that St. Paul endorses this view; and modern translations tend to treat ἀρσενοκοῖται—derived from two roots that mean "male" (ἀρσην) and "bed" (κοίτη)—as a word for homosexuals. As is typical with scriptures, however, the scholarly tradition is divided about this, for reasons that most ordinary Christians aren't familiar with, including the fact that this word is not known in Greek before St. Paul and these two passages are not cited by the earliest Fathers of the Church on the rare occasions when they discuss sex between men.

The word ἀρσενοκοῖται echoes the Greek of passages condemning "a man lying with a man as with a woman" in the older Koine Greek rendering of Leviticus, notably one that, translated crudely but closely, reads: "And those who go to bed with *a man [in] the bed* of a woman . . ." ("A man in the bed of" translates ἄρσενος κοίτην, *arsenos koiten*.) But this is only one of the many facts that scholars must take account of in seeking a modern interpretation for this word. Among the reasons for doubting that "homosexual" is a good translation is that the idea of homosexuality—the idea of a kind of person constitutionally disposed to sexual attraction only, or mostly, toward people of his or her own gender—is simply not present in the Greek-speaking world that St. Paul inhabited. The earlier Greeks certainly had the idea that an older man could be in an erotic relationship with a younger man: Socrates famously assumes this idea in the discussions in Plato's *Symposium*. Indeed, Greeks and Romans in the classical period seem to have assumed that men might be sexually interested in attractive people of both sexes. The important distinctions focused on which of them took the "passive" and which the "active" role in sex. I am not aiming to settle this dispute.[10] My point is only that there are reasonable views on both sides. That St. Paul's words elicit a simple condemnation of homosexuality in some quarters, then, reflects the power of everyday traditions of sentiment. It is not determined by the text alone.

The concept of homosexuality has taken so firm a grip on many contemporary minds that it will seem bizarre to some to declare that there were once societies that simply didn't have the idea. It may help to make the thought more palatable to remind those skeptics that a woman who desires sex with another woman can do so for a great variety of reasons. She may or may not think of the object of her desires as a woman at all, for example, because that person is playing a man's sexual role. She may desire someone while being indifferent to her gender, or be excited because of it; she may merely be curious or want to have sex without the risk of having a child. (And, of course, the same goes, mutatis mutandis, for men.) Our idea of the homosexual picks out only one reason for same-sex sex: erotic desires directed toward people of one's own gender. Our idea further supposes that people with such sexual interests have something very important in common, and so takes a homosexual to be a kind of person. Neither of these thoughts is inevitable. In Ghana, same-sex desire for men is often conceived in negative terms, for example: in terms of not wanting to have sex with women. That way of thinking makes bisexuals uninteresting and asexuals as puzzling as gay people. The history of sexuality shows that ideas about identity and sexuality can come together in many ways.

DETERMINING SCRIPTURE

There is another issue that arises with scriptural traditions: we can disagree about which writings belong in the scriptures in the first place. The Christian Bible can serve as a case study here as well.[11] It's worth getting a sense of how a canonical Bible was extracted from the great body of written and oral traditions from which it derives.

Let's begin with the fact that, though the scriptures have been central to Christianity for a couple of thousand years, they have never been thought to be the only texts worth the attention of believers. There are other texts to consult, which may be less authoritative, including ones that some people once regarded as scriptural. More than this, the idea of a final listing of the books of *the* Bible—βιβλίος (*biblios*) in Greek just means "book"—and the idea of a settled version of the text of each book was not established in Judaism by the time of Christ.

The oldest surviving translation of Jewish sacred texts from Hebrew and Aramaic into Koine Greek is the Septuagint, which was probably produced for Ptolemy II's library at Alexandria in the third century BCE. (It's the source of the Leviticus text I just quoted.) This was the form of scripture known to Hellenistic Jews in first-century Palestine, and the main source of biblical quotations in the New Testament. It contains the Five Books of Moses (the Pentateuch) and many other books as well, and is the basis of the Catholic Bible. But what we now call the Hebrew Bible took its current form only in the second and third centuries of the Common Era, and excludes a number of books found in the Septuagint: Tobit, Judith, the two books of Maccabees, Wisdom, Ecclesiasticus, and Baruch (along with a few passages from other books, deemed to be later additions). When, after the Reformation, Protestants removed these books from their Old

Testament, it was because they were not accepted as canonical by rabbinic Judaism. But there is no reason to doubt that all the books of the Septuagint were widely regarded as scriptural at the time of Christ.

Crucially, this means that Christ himself was a Jewish teacher at a time when the idea of texts with special religious authority—what he himself presumably meant by "the Law and the Prophets," as for example in Matthew, or "the Law of Moses, the Prophets, and the Psalms," in Luke—was certainly central to Jewish life and practice but had not taken an agreed upon and definitive form. You could say that Christ's contemporaries knew of the scriptures and of the Torah (the Five Books of Moses) and the prophetic books, but did not yet have the idea of a unique Holy Book. And the early Christians certainly didn't have our Christian idea of *the* Bible, since that includes the so-called New Testament, which was composed in response to Christ's life. There were many texts that were written in the century after Christ's death and circulated in the early Christian community as it broke from other forms of Judaism. It took the church several centuries to settle which would be canonized in a New Testament— as a record of Christ's promises to all of humanity, a record of the new covenant corresponding to the Hebrew Bible, with its record of the covenant made between Yahweh and Israel.

The New Testament contains many references to the Jewish scriptures, both as a whole ("the Law and the Prophets") and by way of citation of particular passages, often, as was customary at the time, beginning with the formula "It is written." But given that Temple Judaism in the first century evidently lacked a fixed scriptural canon, we cannot take these passages to be references to what we would call the Old Testament or the Hebrew Bible. We know from Jesus's comment in Luke 24:44 and from many other sources that "the Law and the Prophets" included the Psalms, so we cannot assume that this was a reference only to what would later be called the Torah (Law) and the Neviim (Prophets). Christ himself, in the Gospels we now accept, quotes nothing from outside the Hebrew Bible; he has a special preference for the Psalms, Deuteronomy, and Isaiah, but does not cite the Song of Songs, Ruth, Lamentations, Ecclesiastes, Esther, Ezra, Nehemiah, Obadiah, Nahum, Habakkuk, or Haggai. Yet, as the Gospel of John tells us, "Now Jesus did many other signs in the presence of his disciples, which are not written in this book." So what should we take as the canon favored by the founding figure of the Christian tradition? In the New Testament taken as a whole, there are references to almost every book of the Hebrew Bible; but not from Judges, Ruth, and Esther. Should we drop those three from the Christian canon?

St. Paul at least once cites as scripture—in 1 Corinthians—a text that seems to be no longer in existence. "But as it is written, Eye hath not seen, nor ear heard, neither have entered into the heart of man, the things which God hath prepared for them that love him."[12] So it looks as though St. Paul—perhaps the first Christian—may have had in mind a different set of scriptures from any that we know.

We might look to see which Jewish scriptures were cited by the next generation of the Fathers: Clement of Rome, Ignatius of Antioch, Polycarp of Smyrna, and the authors of the *Didache* and of the *Shepherd of Hermas*—the so-called five Apostolic Fathers, who were believed to have had direct communication with some of Christ's Apostles. Scholars have noted both that they sometimes cite books of the Septuagint that are not in the final Hebrew bible and don't cite some of those books (Ruth, Ezra, Nehemiah, Lamentations, Obadiah, Micah, and Haggai) that *are*. St. Jerome, in the fourth century, was probably the first of the Fathers of the Church to favor the (by then well-established) Hebrew canon. But he was wrong if he thought that it was a canon that Christ had known or authorized.

The Fathers of the Church had to decide which of the Gospels—the accounts of the "good news" of the life of Christ—and which of the letters of the Apostles (the first generation of the followers of Christ who were the leaders of the early church) should become authoritative. They had to decide whether to include the Book of Revelation, which we know (but they may not have known) was almost certainly not written by an Apostle, in this sense. So they obviously had to be guided by some criteria, whether implicit or articulated.

The texts we have were all composed in writing after the Crucifixion. Biblical scholars now speak of three phases in the development of the canonical version of the New Testament texts. First, their recognition as scripture: divinely inspired writings that have a central part to play in guiding the life and practice of the followers of Christ. Next comes their organization into categories—Gospels, Epistles— and, finally, there is the determination of a fixed canon. But this process of forming a biblical canon began in a community of believers who were taught by the Apostles and who were able to draw on a significant body of oral tradition reporting the life and words of Jesus. Many in the early Church believed they were living in the "last days" and that Christ would soon return again, which gave less urgency to the issue of the longer-term transmission of the story of Jesus's life. When the Gospels and the Epistles were first written, they were not written *as* scriptures: their authority came from the life and words of Christ, which they reported, not from being otherwise divinely inspired. St. Paul's letters show a familiarity with the oral traditions on which the Synoptic Gospels—Matthew, Mark, and Luke—and the Acts of the Apostles clearly draw. And the canonical Gospels almost certainly began as anonymous writings, being attached to the names of Apostles (Matthew and John) and those who assisted them (Mark and Luke) only sometime after the middle of the second century. Irenaeus, in the third century, is the first of the Church Fathers to use the current names to refer to the Gospels.

All this happened long ago. But should Christians take the question of what's in and what's out to have been settled at some particular time? Modern scholars doubt for a variety of reasons that 1 Timothy, one of the two places where the word ἀρσενοκοῖται occurs, was written by St. Paul. Does that mean its inclusion in the biblical canon was based on a misunderstanding? What should a contemporary Christian, advised of this scholarly consensus, conclude?

In sum, there is plenty of reason in all this history for uncertainty about which books should be regarded as parts of *the* Book, the Bible that many Christians treat as scripture. It is unsurprising, then, that different denominations have included slightly different lists of texts. The books that Protestants, starting with Martin Luther, excluded from the Roman Catholic canon are often published with their Bibles in a section called "Apocrypha." Although they lacked scriptural authority, Luther said that they were "good and useful to read." Anglicans, in the sixth of their Thirty-Nine Articles, affirm that these books can be used "for instruction in life and manners, but not for the establishment of doctrine." By contrast, in the sixteenth century during the Counter-Reformation, the Council of Trent affirmed that for the Roman Catholic Church they were "sacred and canonical," and these so-called deuterocanonical texts retain that status for Catholics today. The details of these disputes are complex and fascinating.

INTERPOLATION AND INTERPRETATION

Christians don't merely disagree about which books are really part of the biblical canon; they can also disagree about what's *in* the books. These texts were assembled from a variety of manuscripts, copies of copies of the texts that the early Fathers of the Church like St. Jerome and St. Augustine adopted into the official list of books of the Old and New Testaments. As in all manuscript traditions, there are variants. Copyists make mistakes; people add things they think should be there or drop things they think shouldn't. Biblical scholars doubt, for example, that everything that's in 1 Corinthians was in the version St. Paul sent to Corinth. At St. George's in Kumasi, the ecumenical church I attended as a child, people sometimes discussed when women could speak in church, citing, in particular, Chapter 14:

Let your women keep silence in the churches: for it is not permitted unto them to speak; but they are commanded to be under obedience as also saith the law. And if they will learn any thing, let them ask their husbands at home: for it is a shame for women to speak in the church.

We might have been saved much trouble had we known and accepted the view of the distinguished Dominican New Testament scholar Jerome Murphy-O'Connor—a specialist on 1 Corinthians—that this passage is a "post-Pauline insertion."[13] Different people will weigh differently all these considerations (and the many others that take up the literature on the interpretation of the New Testament attitudes to gender and homosexuality). Again, all I am arguing is that what Christians decide here is bound to be affected by the attitudes and practices that surround them in their everyday lives now.[14]

Interpretation itself is a practice. Imagine that we sent the Torah and the Talmud to some utterly remote Amazonian tribe and persuaded its members to create a religion based upon its commandments. Would it look like rabbinic Judaism? That seems unlikely. What if they took to heart the parts about genocidal slaughter and passed over the parts about charity? Or simply read everything in wildly unfamiliar ways? We shouldn't be surprised whatever the outcome. It would be like sending aliens a violin and learning that they used it as a percussion instrument, or a measuring device, or a surface on which to carve love poems.

If interpretation is a practice, we should bear in mind that practice changes over time, sometimes slowly, sometimes swiftly; and that changed practice can lead to changed belief. Scriptural passages can get new readings. If they can't adapt, they're often abandoned. That passage in Psalm 137 about how blessed you'll be if you dash your overlords' babies on the rocks; the passage in 1 Peter about how slaves should submit themselves to their masters, however cruel—those we can look away from. St. Paul's powerful move was to hold on to the

Jewish scriptures while instructing the Christians to abandon large parts of them by declaring they were binding only on the Jews. In short, if scriptures were not subject to interpretation—and thus to reinterpretation—they wouldn't continue to guide people over long centuries. When it comes to their survival, their openness is not a bug but a feature.

TRADITION AND ITS ENEMIES

This feature cuts in various directions, however. Because, as we all now know, among the most vehement of the scriptural determinists are *fundamentalists*, consumed with towing others into a single version of one of the great religious traditions. These movements—whether Christian, Buddhist, Hindu, Jewish, or Muslim—all aim to defend and promulgate the One True Way, imagined often as the way things were in the earliest days when the Truth was revealed. And they wish to bring to it everyone who will listen—especially all those who claim the same religious label.

The fundamentalisms have something else in common: though they venerate old texts, they're all new—reactions to the modern world. They respond to two central aspects of that world. First, almost everyone became aware of the existence of great differences in religious belief across the world. Your creed was now one of the things that defined the differences between your kind and everyone else; and that made it important to get it right. This was, then, part of the global rise of a concern with identity. Second, the growth of mass literacy created a world in which almost everyone could look at the scriptures for themselves, and break from what they saw as the compromised or corrupt authority of traditional interpreters.

Orthodoxy in the past depended on the existence of a class of highly trained people—clerics, theologians, rabbis, Brahmins—

whose interpretations of scripture had authority for ordinary believers, not least because the laity couldn't read the texts. The authority to interpret the scriptures, the belief part, came with the right to tell people what rituals to perform, what practices to engage in, the praxis part. These experts, like all literate intellectuals, were trained in traditions, and they knew what other thinkers before them in their traditions had said. Inevitably, they read in the light of that context. When modern Christians or Muslims read a passage from the Bible or the Quran on their own, trying to decide for themselves what it means, they often do so without that context, because they lack that training. But, since everyone inevitably interprets language in the light of what they already believe, they aren't reading the text with *no* context: they are reading it with the context provided by their own experiences and beliefs. The innovative interpretations that result can further mark the differences between fundamentalists and their repudiated coreligionists.

In ways I'll return to, many who seek to characterize particular religious traditions from the outside make common cause with the fundamentalists within. They imagine that the fundamentalist represents the religion in its strongest, most concentrated form, while the more conventional forms of the religious identity reflect the attenuations of age or local custom. (Calling someone a "moderate Muslim" can suggest that this person's connection to the Muslim faith is itself moderate.) Yet whether the label that people are claiming is Islam or Buddhism or Christianity, other sincere, committed people who have also claimed that label have believed other things. Fundamentalists can insist that those others weren't *really* Muslims or Buddhists or Christians. But that would mean that most of the people who have affirmed these labels were mistaken; and the labels wouldn't have much use if they didn't apply to most of the people who have claimed them.

Once you recognize these perplexities, some of the things people regularly say about religious identities should appear in a new light. The place of women in Islam, for example, is a topic of lively discussion in communities around Britain, among both Muslims and non-Muslims. And you often hear an argument that goes like this:

> The Quran has passages that clearly treat women as inferior to men. Take the *Surah An-Nisa* (The Women) (4:11), which says that men should inherit twice the portion of women, or the *Surah Al-Baqarah* (The Cow) (2:282), which says that the evidence of two women in a dispute over a commercial contract can replace the evidence of one man, or the passage later in the *Surah An-Nisa* (4:34) that says "men are in charge of women, because Allah hath made the one of them to excel the other." These passages show that Islamic societies are bound to continue to treat men as superior to women.

Scriptural determinism of this kind, you'll have noticed, is mobilized both by outsiders to indict Islam and by insiders to defend practices they favor. Let's put aside the fact that this argument ignores lots of other relevant evidence, such as the fact that Pakistan and Bangladesh, countries where Islam is the state religion, have had women prime ministers, and have a larger percentage of women in their legislatures than the United States does. Gender inequality certainly remains the norm there, as almost everywhere else in the world. Yet the status of women in Islam can't be resolved with a handful of citations. There are a great many sources of authority to draw upon. In addition to the Quran and the hadith, there is the *fiqh* (meaning "deep understanding"), which refers to the development of Muslim jurisprudence, aiming to capture the eternal law revealed in the Quran and the Sunnah.[15] All of this seems plainly relevant.

Just as Christian feminists have pointed to the central role of women in the circle around Jesus, so some Muslims have underlined the fact that Khadijah, Muhammad's first wife, was also the first convert to Islam; that Aisha, his favorite wife, was often present when the Prophet received his revelations, and is the source of some of the important hadith. (She also led troops into battle against the fourth Caliph, because he failed to avenge the murder of his predecessor.) And the Quran stresses, in *Surah Al-Ahzab* (The Combined Forces) (33:35), that the rewards of submission to Allah are there for both women and men, in a beautiful passage that is often cited to stress the fundamental equality of men and women. So, as I say, these traditions do not speak with a single voice. To be a scriptural adept is to know which passages to read *into* and which to read *past*.

To be sure, it isn't up to an outsider like me to proclaim how these debates should play out. Muslims naturally take the lead here, though I hope they will sometimes feel that they can learn from their friends, just as (in ways I'll touch upon in the final chapter) many non-Muslims have long learned from them. Notice, too, that the scriptural arguments about women's subordination in Islam could be met with parallel arguments about Judaism and Christianity. "Wives, submit yourselves unto your own husbands, as unto the Lord," St. Paul says in Ephesians, echoing God's words to Eve in Genesis: "thy husband . . . shall rule over thee." In fact, at the beginning of the twentieth century, based on a reading of the Bible and a study of religious traditions, nobody would have predicted that, by the end of that century, there would be either women rabbis or women Anglican bishops.

And yet the first woman rabbi was ordained in Offenbach-am-Main in 1935. Her name was Regina Jonas and she died in Auschwitz. Some within Judaism, like Agudath Israel of America, an organization of Orthodox Jews, deny that women can be ordained; they might say she wasn't a real rabbi. But in the United States, where I live, there are women rabbis in each of the major branches of Judaism, including (arguably) among the Orthodox; in New York, Rabba Sara Hurwitz (along with a male rabbi) opened Yeshivat Maharat in 2009, as the first school for training Orthodox women as clergy.

The first woman Anglican priest was ordained in Hong Kong, just ten years or so after the ordination of Rabbi Jonas. Six decades later, the senior bishop of the American branch of the Anglican Church, the primate of the Episcopalian Church in the United States, was a woman. (By 2014, in England, one in five full-time Anglican clergy were women.)[16] Religious identities shift their views about gender over and over again.

That's a global truth. Some Buddhists don't think female monastics ever outrank a male, but Buddhism has traditions of holy women going back to its beginnings. In the Buddhist *Vimalakirti Sutra*, some two millennia old, a goddess changes Shariputra, one of the Buddha's original male disciples, into a goddess. Then she says to him:

Shariputra, who is not a woman, appears in a woman's body. And the same is true of all women—though they appear in women's bodies, they are not women. Therefore the Buddha teaches that all phenomena are neither male nor female.[17]

The same St. Paul who said women should cover their heads in church, and men shouldn't, told the Galatians: "there is neither male nor female: for ye are all one in Christ Jesus."

Unless you think Islam is completely unlike every other religious tradition, you should expect the meaning of Muslim identity to develop in ongoing debates among the faithful. There's simply no reason to credit the determinist claim that, because one interpretation of some Muslim text or tradition has been central at some point in religious history, those who follow Islam are condemned to stick with that view. The story of sacred texts has always been the story of their readers: of shifting and often clashing interpretations. We can understand why insiders sometimes want to deny this. They want theirs to be the whole everlasting truth. But objective observers can see that religion, like everything else that is important in human life, evolves. And some of those objective observers are within these traditions, and celebrate these developments as a sign of a deepening understanding of their faith.

THE TEXT IN TIME

The combination of historical and textual scholarship is one way that interpretations come to shift, in part because in deciding what to make of a text, it often makes sense to consult context. When St. Paul says women should keep their heads covered, it's reasonable to wonder what the customs of dress were in Corinth in his day. If it turns out that no respectable woman in that Roman city would have gone around with her head uncovered, you could conclude, as my mother did, that you should dress respectably by local standards when you are in church. That meant the standards of Kumasi, where she went to church, not those of Filkins, the village where she grew up, let alone those of first-century Corinth. St. George's, my mother's church in Kumasi, was a simple, white, single-room concrete building, its roof made of corrugated iron sheets, with an altar on a slightly raised platform at one end, and above it, on the wall, a large simple wooden cross. St. Peter's, her church as she grew up, was a mid-Victorian Gothic building, with stained-glass windows designed by William Morris. (The poet Sir John Betjeman, a connoisseur of English church architecture, described it as "simple and subtle in local stone.") One can barely imagine two buildings more different. And the people in them on a Sunday could not have been more differently dressed either. In England, sober-suited men, and women dressed in quiet tweeds, hats tilted stylishly; in Ghana, brightly colored clothing, men in their Asante *ntoma*, the toga, or wearing crisp white shirts; women with silk headscarves, elaborately folded. Surely, St. Paul would have understood that the dress of a modest Christian wife was one thing in one place, another in the other.

Edicts can also be dependent for their force on institutional structures that do not survive. That's why, although the Torah prescribes stoning for adulterers, no reputable modern Jewish or Christian authority would defend the imposition of that penalty. In the Jewish case, the highest Jewish court, the Sanhedrin, which sat in the Temple in Jerusalem, stopped issuing capital sentences altogether in the first century CE. There were rabbis who opposed capital punishment for various reasons, but, in any case, the Roman overlords retained to themselves the right to execute people when they took over Palestine. Then, with the destruction of the Temple in 70 CE, the Sanhedrin ceased to exist altogether. Since Jewish law required the Sanhedrin as the highest court of appeal for capital sentences, no Sanhedrin, no stoning to death. Jewish law, like all living law, was an evolving tradition. Given the vicissitudes of Jewish experience, it had to be.

For Christians, the issue is, in some ways, more interesting. As anyone raised with the New Testament will know, there is a story in St. John's Gospel in which Jesus, when asked if it was permissible to stone a woman "taken in adultery," told the Pharisees that one of them who was without sin should cast the first stone. When none of them was willing to condemn her, Jesus said he wouldn't condemn her either. And then he told her to "go, and sin no more."

An episode like this in the life of an exemplary figure does not carry its meaning, so to speak, on its face. Nowhere in this account, for example, does Christ actually reject the Mosaic Law. True, he lays a condition on its implementation that nobody but him could meet. And then he, the only person without sin available, forgives this capital offense. It's natural to think that, like some of the other rabbis in first-century Palestine, he doesn't have much sympathy with capital punishment, at least for adultery. But that's not what he literally says. One might make a similar speculation about Muhammad's attitude to adultery, since the Quran requires four witnesses to convict a woman of adultery (and penalizes anyone who makes an accusation without producing them). Given the nature of the offense, this is a very high bar. Later interpreters have placed Christ's episode with the woman taken in adultery in the context of a larger story, developed in the writings of St. Paul, according to which some parts of the complex set of laws laid out in the Torah were not binding on those Gentiles who became followers of Christ. Jewish tradition anticipated that when the final Savior, the Messiah, came, he would establish new laws. Christ himself says, in the Sermon on the Mount, that he has come to "fulfill the Law," not to destroy it. And yet St. Paul, the Apostle to the Gentiles, was clear that in order to follow Christ, non-Jewish men did not have to be circumcised, which was one of the clearest demands of the Torah.

Maimonides, writing in the twelfth century, identified 248 positive and 365 negative commandments, or *mitzvot*, in Jewish law. Ritual laws (holding, say, that men were not supposed to cut the hair on the side of their heads, or shave their beards with a razor) were interspersed among what we would think of as moral commands: in favor of charity, against adultery, incest, and murder. St. Paul's understanding of what it meant to fulfill the law jettisoned not just the requirement of circumcision but the prohibition of pork; on the other hand, he also thought that the proscriptions of adultery, incest, and murder were binding on everyone, and, again, Christians have followed him in this. Among the commandments in the Torah are rules governing the performance of specific roles: as a judge, a priest, or a king. So a question arises as to whether the commandment that one should execute those who engage in adultery—a commandment presumably addressed to those courts and judges—is like the requirement of male circumcision, which is no longer binding, or like the prohibition of murder, which clearly is.

A summary of all the discussions of this single question over the 2,000 years of Christian history would be an encyclopedic enterprise. I want simply to emphasize what scriptural determinism denies—the sheer complexity of the task of seriously interpreting what Jesus says.

METAFUNDAMENTALISM

Appeals to history, to be sure, are not arguments against fundamentalism. The fundamentalist is concerned with what accords with some ultimate, sacred truth, as vouchsafed to an ancestral scribe or prophet, and not with traditions of human errancy. Yet, as we've seen, the same ahistoricism is shared by *critics* of fundamentalism who equate a religious identity with some fixed set of beliefs or some reading of its scripture. They succumb to what might be called the source-code fallacy: the idea that the true nature of a religion lies with its deepest, most foundational texts, abstracted away from the real-world range of its actual adherents; that access to these codes can reveal that religion's essence.

All of us are conscious today of interpretations of Islam that are wielded in support of violence against Muslims and non-Muslims, that incite terror and murder and destruction. You can, indeed, find sources in Muslim tradition that sustain these ideas; you can find such sources in all the great religious traditions. Yet the notion that because some Muslim texts speak of warfare Muslims must be engaged in endless bloodshed is no more sensible than the same claim made for any other religious tradition.

At St. George's, that white concrete church in Kumasi, one of our favorite hymns ran:

Onward Christian soldiers,
Marching as to war
With the Cross of Jesus,
Going on before.

It has a great tune, by Sir Arthur Sullivan, of Gilbert and Sullivan fame. Taken on its own, this hymn—a favorite among Salvation

Army marching bands—could lead you to a pretty violent version of Christianity. And it's not the only Christian text that could do so. Since the time of the Emperor Constantine, in the fourth century, the cross has been carried into battle by Christian armies, along with the ancient Latin slogan *in hoc signo vinces*, "in this sign you conquer." On the other hand, in that passage I quoted from Isaiah, which many Christians hear every Christmas in the Festival of Nine Lessons and Carols, the Messiah is referred to as "The Prince of Peace." Muslims, like Christians, have choices to make in interpreting their traditions. To deny this is to fall into the sort of essentialism I have been urging us to abandon.

Essentialism of this sort will not help the Muslims of Europe or their non-Muslim neighbors as they seek together to find successful forms of cohabitation. Western European Muslims—like the Muslims of North America—are living through a modern experiment, unknown to most of the intellectuals whose reflections shaped Islamic ideas about politics, in which Muslims have chosen not just to travel for trade or diplomacy but to settle permanently in non-Muslim lands. And questions of gender, in this new setting, will be only a part of the challenge. In meeting it, the recognition that identity survives through change—indeed, that it survives only through change—will be a useful touchstone for us all. Religious identities, like all identities, as we shall see in the next chapters, live in history.

ANCESTOR WORSHIP

Not long ago, in a Ghanaian village far from where I now live in New York, I found myself in the company of various local chiefs doing as Asantes do: pouring libations to our ancestors. Since long before I was born, the custom has been for serious offering to be made in schnapps, one of the many valuable goods traded with Europe over the last few centuries. (Kaiser Schnapps is particularly favored in Asante: its advertisements call it the "Schnapps for Kings.") So, shoulders bared out of respect for the ancestors, I was pouring Kaiser Schnapps on the family shrines. One offering went to the founder of my father's lineage (and of the village), the great warrior Akroma-Ampim. *Nana Akroma-Ampim, bɛgye nsa nom*—Grandfather Akroma-Ampim, come take this alcohol to drink, I said. Another was to my own father: *Papa Joe, bɛgye nsa nom.*

Among the Asante, your ancestors are spirits who can help or hinder you, and you supply them with food and drink out of prudence as well as the fullness of your heart. Doing so is part of daily life, because daily life is where you interact with spiritual beings. Nobody is warned against faltering in their faith. Here, you feel that an obsession with individual faith is a sign of religious modernity, a *private* interrogation that's alien from older worship practices. Indeed, when I'm among Ghanaians pouring libations, what strikes me is how *unanxious* it all is.

For many in Asante, religion—what anthropologists often call "traditional religion"—is not merely sacrament; it is government. Among the spirits, you've got the equivalent of your local assemblyman, your town mayor—the locals whom you expect to take your calls—and yes, overlords elsewhere and higher up, whose engagement with your doings is more diffuse. You wait in line, as in the department of motor vehicles. There are forms to process, exchanges to be proffered, taxes to be paid, mainly in the form of libations, salutations, and sacrifices. Sometimes your requests get held up, or never acted upon. (As I say, it's like government.)

And these practices are taken by most people—Asante Catholic bishops and imams included!—to be perfectly consistent with having other confessional allegiances, with being Muslim or Christian. That was certainly true of my own father. He was, like *his* father, an elder of the Wesley Methodist Cathedral in Kumasi. But his Methodism had to live with the fact that he was also an Asante. And so, when my father opened a bottle of spirits, he poured out the first drops in an offering to his ancestors, and asked them to watch over the family, as an Italian Catholic might call on Mary, Mother of God, or an Indian Muslim might call on a Sufi saint at his shrine. The missionaries who converted my grandfather might have complained that this was a reversion to idolatry; he and my father would have thought that complaint absurd. Philo of Alexandria, expounding Exodus, had some well-judged counsel for them: to be faithful to your god, he said, you need not revile the gods of others.[18] And so there I was, in my father's ancestral village, pouring those libations—a practice embedded within a spirit of community and fellowship.

Here's one thing we can agree with the fundamentalists about, then: Our ancestors *are* powerful, though not in the ways the fundamentalists imagine. For none of us creates the world we inhabit from scratch; none of us crafts our values and commitments save in dialogue with the past. Dialogue is not determinism, however. Once you think of creedal identities in terms of mutable practices and communities rather than sets of immutable beliefs, religion becomes more verb than noun: the identity is revealed as an activity, not a thing. And it's the nature of activities to bring change.

Our ancestors grip us in ways we scarcely realize. But as I poured the schnapps on the ancient family altars, I found myself reflecting that in the ethical realm—whether civic or religious—we have to recognize that one day we, too, shall be ancestors. We do not merely follow traditions; we create them.

THREE

COUNTRY

My God, the Breton mariner prays as he sets sail, *protect me: my boat is so small and your ocean so vast!* And this prayer expresses the condition of each one of you, unless you find a means of indefinitely multiplying your forces, your powers of action.

This means was provided for you by God when he gave you a fatherland. . . .

Giuseppe Mazzini, *Doveri dell'uomo*
(1860)

THE BOUNDARIES OF IDENTITY

Aron Ettore Schmitz was born in the city of Trieste at the end of 1861. His mother and father were Jews, of Italian and German origin, respectively. But Trieste was a free imperial city, the main trading port of the Austrian Empire, brought to greatness in the nineteenth century as it connected the empire to Asia. ("'The third entrance to the Suez Canal,' they used to call it," Jan Morris, the English travel writer, tells us.)[1] Young Ettore was, therefore, a citizen of the empire, which was rebaptized as the Austro-Hungarian Empire when he was six. Indeed, whatever the words "German" and "Italian" meant when he was born, they didn't mean you were a citizen of Germany or of Italy. When, in 1874, Ettore arrived at a new school near Würzburg, in Bavaria, he was visiting a Germany that was younger than he was. The country had been created, a mere three years earlier, through the unification, under the Prussian monarch, of more than two dozen federated kingdoms, duchies, and principalities with three cities of the ancient Hanseatic League. A month or so later, they would be joined by Alsace-Lorraine, ceded to Germany by France at the end of the Franco-Prussian War.

As for Italy? Ettore and Italy were practically born twins. The modern Italian state was created in the year of his birth, when Victor Emmanuel, King of Piedmont-Sardinia, was proclaimed King of Italy, uniting Piedmont-Sardinia with the Venetian territories of the Austrian Empire, the Papal States, and the Kingdom of the Two Sicilies. So, like his father's German-ness, his mother's Italianness was more a matter of language or culture than of citizenship. Only in his late fifties, at the end of the First World War, did Trieste become what it is today, an Italian city. So Ettore Schmitz—Jewish by upbringing, a Catholic as a courtesy to his wife—had claims to being German and to being Italian, and never felt other than Triestine, whatever that meant exactly.[2] Born a subject of the Austrian Emperor, he died a subject of the King of Italy. And his life poses sharply the question how you decide what country, if any, is yours.

Schmitz lived in an era when nation-states were only gradually becoming the dominant form of political organization around the world. In his youth, when Europeans used labels like "German" and "Italian," they were not usually thinking about political citizenship. They were thinking, as Schmitz would have, about individuals with a language, culture, and traditions in common. Like him, you could be German or Italian, in this sense, without the right to a German or Italian passport. In 1914, you'd have found Germans, like his father, in communities not only in Germany, Austria, Hungary, and Bohemia, but also in Switzerland, Russia, Africa, the Americas, and Australasia. (There was even a German colony in Qingdao in China; and if you choose Tsingtao beer at a Chinese restaurant today, you are enjoying a German tradition!) Jewish communities were on every habitable continent. Slavs were divided between the Austro-Hungarian, Ottoman, and Russian empires and were found in small pockets elsewhere. There were Arabs all over the Middle East and North Africa, of course, and not just in Arabia; but there were also Lebanese and Syrian communities in West Africa and Brazil. And all of these groups could tell you who they were without pledging fealty to a government that governed them specifically.

Starting in the nineteenth century and continuing in the twentieth, many peoples who had never controlled a state were engulfed by political movements that sought an alignment of their peoplehood with political arrangements: they wanted nation-states to express their sense that they already had something important in common.

So we need a name for these groups that doesn't imply they *already* have a shared political citizenship, and I'm going to continue to call them peoples. A people, as I said in the previous chapter, is a group of human beings united by a shared ancestry, real or imagined, whether or not they share a state.

In 1830, the great German philosopher Georg Wilhelm Friedrich Hegel wrote:

> In the existence of a *people* the substantial purpose is to be a state and to maintain itself as such; a people without state-formation (a *nation* as such) has no real history. . . .[3]

Hegel thought that as world history proceeded, all the peoples that mattered would gradually become the masters of states: over the next century that thought took hold around the world.

Today, in what we like to think of as a postimperial age, no political tenet commands more audible assent than that of national sovereignty. "We" aren't to be ruled by others, captive to a foreign occupation; "we" must be allowed to rule ourselves. This simple ideal is baked into the concept of the nation itself. It helped to propel the collapse of empires and the era of decolonization. Maps were redrawn to advance the cause; even in our own time, borders have given way to it. It remains a vaunted principle of our political order. And yet this ideal has an incoherence at its heart. That is the next of the great mistakes about identity that I want to explore.

NATIONS

To begin to understand this, ask yourself why, if everyone agrees that "we" are entitled to rule ourselves, it is often so hard to agree about who "we" are. The nationalist says, "We are a people, we share an ancestry." But so does a family, to take the idea at its narrowest; and the whole species, at its widest, shares its ancestry, too. In seeking nations, where should we draw the line? The people of Asante in Ghana, where I grew up, are supposed to share ancestry; but so is the wider world of Akan peoples to which we also belong. There are not just Asante, but Abron, Ahafo, Akwapim, Akyem, Baule, Fante, Kwahu, Nzema, and a bunch more. So if you were going for a nation-state, perhaps Akan would make more sense than Asante: bigger may be better in modern nations, and there are twice as many Akan as Asante, their homes spread through southern Ghana and Ivory Coast. But, following that thought, why not go for something even bigger, as Pan-Africanists argued, seeking to create a megastate of people of African descent? Which should it be? There are no natural boundaries. Once you move beyond the village world of the face-to-face, a people is always going to be a community of strangers. That is a first quandary—one of scale.

A second is that, though we often speak of someone as belonging to one nation—Schmitz's mother, I said, was Italian—all of us in fact belong to more than one group with shared ancestry. The incest taboo guarantees that most people are the result of a union of two families, and many people—like Ettore Schmitz, like me—have parents from two peoples. So what, beyond a putative shared ancestry, makes a nation yours? How do you pick among the many groups of shared ancestry to which you belong?

It's worth remembering that we all have a great diversity of ways in which we could carve out our ancestries. I mentioned in the introduction that my mother's grandfather traced his family back to the early thirteenth century, to the time of King John. The genealogist he employed was following a single line of men. But if you are open to exploring your maternal ancestors (as my Asante forebears do) or to following men and women indifferently back through the generations, you have a vast range of families to pick from.

Genealogical research was harder in the early twentieth century, before all those records went on the web. And it might have amused my great-grandfather to know, as I do, that he descended—by a more circuitous route—from Henry II, or that others of his ancestors signed the Magna Carta. But this is not very surprising. When you go that far back, we all have family trees with many more branches than there were then people on the planet. As a result, many of those branches are occupied by the same people: or, to put it another way, if you have any recent English ancestors, you are likely to be multiply descended from many thirteenth-century English men and women. The English family historian Andrew Millard has argued that "a modern English person with predominantly English ancestry" almost certainly descends from Edward III, who reigned for more than half a century, beginning in 1327. Whether you agree with the details of his argument or not, the chances are certainly very high. (Since Henry II was an ancestor of Edward III, the same applies to him.)[4] You are almost certain to have ancestors then who were not English, too; for people have been coming and going into the British Isles all along. Shakespeare's John of Gaunt thought that "the silver sea" that lapped the island's shores,

> serves it in the office of a wall,
> Or as a moat defensive to a house
> Against the envy of less happier lands.

But the country often let down its drawbridge. Anglo-Normans maintained connections with their cousins in France; Polish merchants settled in England in the sixteenth century; in the next century Dutch Jews were admitted with the acquiescence of Cromwell during the Protectorate; tens of thousands of Huguenots came at the turn of the eighteenth century. And English aristocrats, including the royals, continued to get spouses from abroad. If we go back farther, we know that the Romans who, in the first century BCE, settled in Britain from all over the empire, including Egypt, have left their genetic traces, too; as did the Norsemen from Scandinavia who ruled the Danelaw, which meant much of the North and East of England, in the ninth century, while Alfred the Great held out in Wessex in the South and West. Traffic passed, as well, in the other direction: among your English ancestors will be some whose other descendants ended up in other places on the planet . . . or who were sailors who left children in one of hundreds of ports around the world. These are some of the facts that make it hard to answer that question, "How to pick among the many groups of shared ancestry to which you belong?"

This question has, I suggest, only one serious answer: a nation is a group of people who think of themselves as sharing ancestry and also *care* about the fact that they have that supposed ancestry in common. To be a nation, it is not enough to meet an objective condition of common descent; you have to meet a subjective condition, a condition that lies in the hearts and minds of its members. (And, in practice, the condition of common descent doesn't have to be all that objective; the purported common descent of many groups is imaginary.) Hegel thought that the *point* of caring was that you should take your shared national identity and create a state, if you didn't have one already. But human beings can care about their shared ancestry—as Schmitz and his father surely cared about being Jewish—without yet wanting to live under a government that was solely theirs. Zionism is only one possible response to being Jewish. That's why there are nationalities without nation-states.

I've insisted that there are no natural boundaries to the peoplehood you might come to care about. You could always draw the boundaries tighter, making your nation more and more like a literal family: and then you might find yourself with a nation that has a great deal in common. Or you could draw them more loosely, and end up with a group that will probably be more multifarious. More important, though, how much ancestry you share and how much you have in common are different questions; and once you get to groups above a certain size, it's very unlikely that shared ancestry will guarantee shared character. It is said that the Celts of Brittany, Cornwall, Ireland, Scotland, Wales, and the Isle of Man have a shared ancestry: to become a nation, though, enough of them would have to care enough about that fact to want to act together as a people. Right now they don't. They're not a nation.

And so, if you want to build states around nations, you're going to have to do more than simply summon an existing people and make a constitution. You're going to have to *make* a nation: you will take a population most of whom wish, for some reason, to live under a shared government, and then, after wresting them from whatever states they currently live in, you will need to build in them the shared sentiments that will make it possible for them to live productively together.

MOVING BOUNDARIES

Deciding which nation is yours is further complicated when political boundaries keep shifting. Schmitz's life epitomizes, in a somewhat exaggerated form, the experience of millions of people in the twentieth century: he was a citizen of one country who became a citizen of another without leaving home.

The turn of the twentieth century was an age of empires. In the Scramble for Africa, between the Berlin Conference of 1884–85 and the First World War, almost all of Africa was colonized by European states. Asante, where I grew up, became a British protectorate in 1902. In 1900 most of Central and Eastern Europe was part of the Russian, Austro-Hungarian, or Ottoman empires. Then, after the First World War, Albania, Austria, Bulgaria, the Baltic States, Czechoslovakia, Hungary, Poland, and Romania were freed from imperial rule; independent nation-states were ushered blinking into the light. After the Second World War, millions of German speakers from Czechoslovakia were deported to East and West Germany and the Iron Curtain reshaped the continental map once more.

It wasn't just Europe and Africa that saw shifting boundaries. With the partition of British India, in 1947, enormous populations crossed the new borders between India and Pakistan: Hindus and Sikhs into India, Muslims into Pakistan (itself split into two by more than a thousand miles of India). In many parts of the subcontinent there were brutal attacks—mass rapes, beatings, arson, and murder—by Muslims on Hindus and Hindus on Muslims. Millions of people crossed the borders in Punjab, in the west, and Bengal in the east, which were divided between India and Pakistan. Six and a half million Muslims moved into West Pakistan, nearly 5 million Hindus moved in the opposite direction into India. Perhaps three-quarters of a million Muslims moved into East Pakistan, and more than 2.5 million Hindus moved from there into India. This was the largest mass migration in human history, involving a total of nearly 15 million people. Nevertheless, between 30 million and 40 million Muslims remained in India, which will soon have the largest Muslim population of any country in the world.

For some South Asians, the new borderland was a scar. Several years after Partition, the Indo-Pakistani writer Saadat Hasan Manto wrote a story, in Urdu, titled "Toba Tek Singh," and it told of a decision of the Indian and Pakistani governments to exchange members of its lunatic asylums, as they had exchanged prisoners. A Sikh inmate of a Lahore asylum is sent to India, where one guard tells him that his hometown is now in Pakistan, while another tells him that it is, or soon will be, in India. He decides to stay between the barbed wire fences of the two nations, "on a piece of land that had no name." Manto's point, of course, is about what he saw as the larger lunacy of the borders.[5]

Which isn't to say that earlier borderlines, such as those inscribed by the Berlin Conference, had any greater claim to reason. As it happened, the South Asian partition was the first of many redrawings of boundaries after the Second World War.[6] With the final end of Europe's colonial empires, dozens of independent states in Africa and Asia appeared on the world stage. In 1945 on the African continent, only Egypt, Ethiopia, and South Africa were independent, South-West Africa was administered from Pretoria as a mandate territory, and the rest of the continent was governed from Paris, London, Lisbon, or Madrid. The first of Britain's African colonies to achieve independence was Ghana (and few remember that it was the union of the Gold Coast with the British-administered part of the former German colony of Togo; that's why there are so many Ewes in Ghana).[7] Elsewhere on the continent, the process was slower, and sometimes bloodier, but it was unstoppable. There are fifty-five independent states in the African Union.

After the fall of the Soviet Union, another fourteen independent states emerged, in the Baltics, Eastern Europe, the Caucasus, and Central Asia. (That's not counting Russia.) In the countryside around Ettore's Trieste, most people spoke Slovenian, a language whose written history goes back a millennium. But the first time that the majority of its speakers were gathered together into a single country was in 1991, when Slovenia emerged as Italy's eastern neighbor amid the chaotic end of Yugoslavia. Today, Europe includes six other countries that had once been Yugoslavian. You peer at this gleaming canvas of countries . . . and you can see that the paint is still wet.

WHAT'S NEW?

Being a people is not just a matter of how you think of *yourselves*. What *others* outside the group think is important, too. Identity, as we learned in the first chapter, is negotiated between insiders and outsiders. And throughout the twentieth century your fate could be determined by the decisions that other people made as to which people you belonged to. Many of the genocides of the twentieth century—against Turkey's Armenians, Europe's Jews, and Rwanda's Tutsis—were perpetrated in the name of one people against another with the aim of securing a homogenous nation. But they were only the extreme end of a spectrum that included mass expulsions, forced assimilation, and minority oppression.

I mentioned earlier two difficulties for making a nation. First, how wide do you go? Asante or Akan or something bigger still? Second, how do you deal with the fact that we all belong (at least potentially) to many peoples? A third now looms. For living side by side with Akan people are people of other ancestries. There are Guan people, for example, whose ancestors migrated to Ghana perhaps a millennium ago. The logic of shared ancestry offers only three possible answers: annihilate them, expel them (along with all the others of separate ancestry), or assimilate them, inventing a story of common ancestry to cover up the problem. All of these "solutions" have been tried in the last couple of hundred years. None of them would be necessary if we were not trying to match states to nations.

The thinkers who developed nationalism borrowed a set of ideas about what it meant for a people to be a nation that developed in eighteenth- and nineteenth-century Europe. They used these ideas to define their own nations, but also to identify others. And, in a period of increasingly global cultural interconnection, these ideas then spread across Europe and eventually across the world.

It may seem surprising to insist that nationalism is a recent invention. Its global *diffusion* may be a modern phenomenon, but you might think that you hear the strains of nationalism already in Shakespeare's history plays. Henry V addresses his soldiers as "you noblest English, / Whose blood is fet from"—that is, comes from—"fathers of war-proof!" Isn't that just nationalism? What's so new about it?

Indeed, with these words ringing in our ears, we can hear echoes of Virgil's *Aeneid,* whose first sentence ends with Aeneas bringing "the gods to Latium, from whom come the Latins, the Alban fathers and the high walls of Rome"; or Pericles' boast, as articulated by Thucydides, that Athens was "the school of Hellas."[8] Something—the gods of Latium, English blood, Athenian civilization—bound each of these earlier peoples together. And these stories generally celebrated their respective peoples as a pretty terrific lot, an in-group well worth belonging to. As I pointed out at the start, clannishness is a basic feature of our human psychology.

Let me make a few simple points, then, about what is and isn't new here. Human beings have long told stories about heroes leading their people in great deeds of derring-do. That's a feature of Shakespeare's history plays, or the tales of Asante rulers on which I grew up . . . or, for that matter, the *Iliad* or the *Aeneid* or the *Mahābhārata* or the *Spring and Autumn Analects*, to mention only classics in Greek, Latin, Sanskrit, and Chinese. Every child in the city where I grew up was nourished on tales of our first king, Osei Tutu, and Okomfo Anokye, the brilliant priest who helped him make the nation; we knew that Yaa Asantewaa, Queen Mother of Ejisu, had led the last of the Asante wars against the British. We knew their stories, because their deeds were ours, they belonged to all of us. The Old Testament is filled with the names of peoples: Assyrians, Babylonians, Canaanites, Chaldeans, Cushites, Edomites, Medes, Persians, Philistines, Syrians, and so on. These peoples are collective agents. They do things together. The Assyrians attack Israel; the Asante resist the British; the Romans conquer the Greeks . . . and then, as Horace famously pointed out, Greek culture captured Rome.[9]

But something new really did enter the way of thinking about peoples toward the end of the eighteenth century in much of Europe. In reaction against the rationalism and restraint of the Enlightenment, Romanticism produced a great upwelling of new feelings and ideas, especially in the expanding middle classes. Among the many marks of the movement were a miscellany of attitudes: a new enthusiasm for the emotions, an appreciation of nature in the face of the encroachments of industry, a passion for the democratic spirit of the French Revolution, and a paradoxical celebration both of folk traditions, like Grimm's fairy tales, and of modern heroes. Romantics were entranced by the military exploits of Napoleon and the creative genius of men like Beethoven, Byron, and Goethe; but they also celebrated the songs and stories of ordinary men and women.

In Scotland—Caledonia, as the Romans had called it—toward Europe's western rim, Robert Burns, the Bard of Ayrshire, who lived in the latter half of the eighteenth century, embodied many of these attitudes: collecting and adapting the folk songs of ordinary people, composing in the language of every day, expressing extravagant romantic feelings in his love poetry, communing with the natural world. His love was "like a red, red, rose . . . newly sprung in June"; he empathized with a cowering mouse; but he also insisted that

There's themes enow in Caledonian story,
Would shew the Tragic Muse in a' her glory.[10]

A poet belonged, above all, to his nation.

NATIONAL SPIRITS

Nationalism grew with Romanticism, then, and so one of its central themes was a new Romantic sense of what made a people a people. The understanding of national character was transformed through a celebration of something spiritual, the soul or spirit of the folk: the *Volksgeist*, to use the term that captured the idea as it developed in German philosophy. Hegel seems to have been the first philosopher to use this word, but the idea of a national spirit is already there in the writings of the great German Romantic philosopher Johann Gottfried Herder.

In the literary and philosophical movement that began European Romanticism, which was known, because of its rapidly shifting sentiments, as the Storm and Stress *(Sturm und Drang)*, Herder explored the idea that the German people were held together by a spirit embodied, above all else, in German language and literature, just as Scotland, for Robbie Burns, spoke through its verse. At the start of the nineteenth century, Sir Walter Scott collected the folk songs of Scotland in his *Minstrelsy of the Scottish Border,* aiming, he said, to "contribute somewhat to the history of my native country." And as print media and literacy spread across great territories, more and more ordinary people could begin to conceive of themselves as sharing in the life of a vast community of fellow nationals . . . in part by reading people like Burns and Scott. And the essential idea gained urgency as the nineteenth century wore on. The Genoese revolutionary patriot, Giuseppe Mazzini, ardent republican and founder of the secret society Young Italy, inspired many with his call for "awakening the soul of Italy."

In Schmitz's Trieste, though, many people might have favored keeping the Italian soul asleep. This city was composed, like the empire, of a heterogeneous assemblage of peoples. Most of them spoke either German or Triestino, the local dialect of Italian, but, as I've already mentioned, in the areas around the city many actually spoke Slovenian.[11] Italian and Slavic nationalism had to contest with educated Germans who defended the cosmopolitanism of a multinational Austro-Hungarian empire. At a dinner in honor of Richard Cobden, the English Liberal statesman, in 1847, a Herr von Bruck shouted aloud, "We are Triestines; we are cosmopolites; we . . . have nothing to do with Italian and German nationalities."[12]

Yet Ettore Schmitz, despite his German father, Teutonic education, and Austrian citizenship, wasn't deaf to Mazzini's call to awaken the soul of Italy. Lady Isabel Burton, whose husband was the British consul in Trieste in the 1870s and '80s, reported that most of Trieste's Jews sided with what she called the "Italianissimi"—the most Italian of the Italians.¹³ Schmitz followed suit. When he began his literary career, he decided to write, effortfully, in standard Italian. Though not precisely *as* an Italian. For he published under the name Italo Svevo. It means "Italian Swabian." Since Swabia is a region of southern Germany, this is a not-so-subtle reference to his double heritage.

We probably wouldn't know much about Italo Svevo if it weren't for an Irishman who lived in Trieste, from 1904 to 1920, and who tutored Svevo in English. His name was James Joyce, and he had his own very complicated relationship with nationalism. Joyce read the manuscript of his long short story "The Dead" to Svevo and his wife, Livia, and was rewarded not only with praise but also with a bouquet of flowers from Livia's garden.¹⁴ In the story, Miss Ivors, the Irish nationalist, tells Gabriel, the protagonist—who says he wants to travel to "France or Belgium or perhaps Germany"—that he needs to visit his "own land," to get to know his "own country." Nationalist themes were everywhere in the literature of the age.

Svevo was one of the first great enthusiasts for Joyce's writing, and Joyce returned the favor. Years later he read Svevo's self-published book *La coscienza di Zeno* and admired it so much that he arranged for its translation and publication in Paris, where he was then living. No one had noticed the Italian publication very much, even in Italy; Svevo's written Italian, shaped as it was by Triestino, was, critics have said, imperfect. (Think of this as like an Englishman complaining about Robert Burns's English!) The French translation championed by Joyce was widely praised and *Zeno's Conscience*, as the book is usually known in English, is still regarded, with justice, as one of the great novels of European modernism.

Svevo is an emblem of the complex national and cultural identities of modern life. But his life as a cosmopolitan Jew, living in a modern city, made him ideal for one other purpose: he is a critical model for Leopold Bloom, the protagonist of *Ulysses,* Joyce's masterpiece, which follows a day in the life of a nonobservant Dublin Jew surrounded by Catholics. Bloom is introduced as a man of strong appetites: Joyce punningly tells us, when we first meet him, that he "ate with relish the inner organs of beasts and fowls." But he is, above all, like Svevo, a man who wanders his own city, soaking up its sights, smells, and sounds.

Umberto Saba, another Jewish-Catholic writer from Trieste, once wrote that "Svevo could have written well in German; he preferred to write badly in Italian."[15] How had Italo Svevo picked among his potential allegiances in creating a literary identity? He felt no real alignment with Austria, and had little enthusiasm about the idea of military service for the emperor's causes. Young Ettore had had a traditional circumcision and his father was a prominent member of his synagogue; before attending his Bavarian boarding school, he had attended a Jewish school and learned some Hebrew. But, in ways he shared with Kafka, his Jewishness mattered more to him as a matter of culture, even of cultural dislocation, than of faith. Despite his courtesy conversion to Catholicism, he was, in fact, an atheist all his adult life. As an assimilated Jew, in any case, he wouldn't have considered writing in Hebrew or Yiddish—as other European Jewish writers of his day, like Sholem Aleichem or Sholem Asch, were beginning to do—because, first of all, these were languages of which he had no real command. Trieste was on the Adriatic, even if it was also part of Mitteleuropa.[16]

Svevo's name, of course, was meant to convey both his German debts and his Italian loyalties; but the yearning for *italianità* he felt was common in Trieste. You can see this background in a nice moment in *Zeno's Conscience* that reveals the interplay of German, Italian, and local Triestino identities. Zeno is in love with Ada, who is herself in love with an attractive young man named Guido Speier. When Ada introduces them, Zeno smiles a forced smile. Then, he says,

> My smile became more spontaneous because I was immediately offered the opportunity of saying something disagreeable to him: "You are German?"

He replied politely, admitting that because of his name, one might believe he was. But family documents proved they had been Italian for several centuries. He spoke Tuscan fluently, while Ada and I were condemned to our horrid dialect.[17]

Our Italian Swabian enjoys these moments of self-deprecation, but, almost despite himself, he conveys the allure of Trieste itself, in all its multiplicity. Although he once referred to Trieste as a *crogiolo assimilatore*—an assimilating crucible, or melting pot—Svevo knew how much remained unmelted. His Zeno is, above all, a walker in the city, a boulevardier and rambler, moving from one neighborhood to another. He is also a man always struggling with his own irresolution, always smoking his "last cigarette," always betraying his ideals, and forever scrutinizing his own prejudices and preferences like a quizzical ethnographer. He wants to confront uncomfortable truths—to side with reality, however much it stings.

And the reality of linguistic and cultural variation within a community, Svevo reminds us, can be in tension with the romantic nationalist vision of a community united by language and culture. Indeed, this tension is the rule, rather than the exception.

TENSIONS

Take Scotland again, Robert Burns's homeland. For hundreds of years it has been a country of more than one language (Gaelic, Lallans or Broad Scots, and English) and more than one religion (the Church of Scotland, Anglicanism, Catholicism) with regional differences between the cultures of the Highlands and the Lowlands, the Islands and the mainland, country and city, even Edinburgh and Glasgow. What the Scots mostly have in common is more than a millennium of institutional connection to the crown of Scotland: Scott's border minstrelsy and Burns's "braid lallans" verse have little in common with Gaelic folk song. Many of the things that are identified with Scots culture aren't widely shared. Fewer than 60,000 Scots speak Gaelic today; it hasn't been the mother tongue of a majority of the people of Scotland in five hundred years. People speak of Scotland as the land of the Protestant Kirk (the Church of Scotland), but Catholics outnumber adherents of the Kirk in Glasgow, Scotland's largest city. And, like most of Europe, Scotland has a long-established Jewish presence and a growing Muslim population.

Nor does Scottishness belong just to the territory of Scotland. The Scots played a huge role in creating and managing the British Empire. If you travel north and west from Glasgow and take the boat from Oban to the tiny isle of Colonsay, with its landscape of rock and peat, and a miraculous rhododendron garden made possible by the warm waters of the northern Gulf Stream, you will find the home of Lord Strathcona and Mount Royal. Strathcona is another name for Glen Coe. But Mount Royal is Montreal, in Quebec; and the first Lord Strathcona, Donald Smith, was a governor-general of Canada, who descended from a family of farmers in Knockando, east of Inverness. Burns Night is celebrated in Scottish communities around the world. The graduation ceremonies at New York University, where I teach, are led off by a band of bagpipers.

These complexities are not, let me insist, ways in which Scotland differs from much of the rest of Europe. England has been both Protestant and Catholic more or less since the distinction was invented. When I first went to university in England, there was a young man across the hall, a medical student like me, who came from Newcastle. Something called English was a mother tongue for both of us. But for the first few weeks of term I could understand little of what he said. I had to learn his accent. (He understood mine, no doubt, because I sounded like the radio!) The tales that Yorkshiremen tell so ably are different from the folk traditions of the West Country; and so are their idioms. England's multiculturalism did not start with the arrival of West Indians in the 1950s.

Internal complexities of this sort are common throughout the world. Eugen Weber, the Romanian-born, British-educated American historian of Europe, taught a generation of students of French history that, as late as 1893, roughly a quarter of the 30 million citizens of metropolitan France had not mastered the French language.[18] Italy, as we saw, was created by the Savoyard monarchs in the mid-nineteenth century, but it contained a great variety of mutually unintelligible dialects. Even now it recognizes twenty regional dialects, to say nothing of Amharic or of the Arabic of a growing number of refugees. It is conventional to describe the version of the language taught in schools and printed in most newspapers as *"lingua toscana in bocca romana"*—the Tuscan tongue in a Roman mouth.

If the states of Western Europe where the Herderian ideology developed do not fit the mold of the monoethnic nation-state, it is rare to find anything like it anywhere else. India and China and Indonesia are wildly diverse in their ethnicities, whether or not they fully acknowledge it. The countries of the Americas, including the United States, all *do* acknowledge their origins in a multiplicity of peoples. There are no doubt candidates for Herderian states: in Japan, 99 percent of the population identifies as Japanese.[19] But their script originates from Chinese; their second-largest religion, Buddhism, is from India; and ethnologue.com lists fifteen Japanese languages, including Japanese sign language. As a rule, people do not live in monocultural, monoreligious, monolingual nation-states, and they never have.

Given these realities, how have we dealt with the fact that self-determination—which could disrupt any imaginable political order—remains a sacrosanct ideal? Well, with caution and inconsistency. Consider the last of the countries recognized in Europe issuing from Yugoslavia's collapse. The U.N. recognizes the "territorial integrity" of existing states while also endorsing the principle of self-determination. Weighing the two at the request of the U.N. General Assembly, the International Court of Justice declared, in a 2010 advisory opinion, that Kosovo's unilateral declaration of independence was consistent with international law. Britain's U.N. representative agreed: territorial integrity, he said, was "qualified by the principle of self-determination." In that spirit, more than a hundred countries recognized Kosovo as a sovereign nation. The Serbs, naturally, objected, maintaining that Kosovo was the "cradle" of their national identity. And nobody spoke louder in defense of their "territorial integrity" than Vladimir Putin.

Several years later came the matter of Crimea and the 2014 Crimean status referendum. Under the watchful gaze of the Russian army, the people of the Crimean Peninsula were asked if they wanted to join the Russian Federation. When the somewhat implausible results were announced—96.7 percent in favor of joining the federation, with an 83 percent turnout in a region where elections typically gathered half that percentage of eligible voters—the world community was divided as to whether to accept the outcome. Like cricket teams switching sides at the end of an inning, the advocates of self-determination became defenders of territorial integrity, while the great defender of territorial integrity, the Russian Bear, became a snarling advocate for self-determination. The U.N. General Assembly voted to condemn the referendum by 100 to 11, with 58 countries abstaining.

Notice, however, that nobody directly quarreled with the premise that a people is entitled to withdraw from a polity and form its own state. Instead, Western diplomats questioned the procedural and the empirical validity of the Crimean referendum. But they could also invoke self-rule *against* self-rule. The argument was that all the Ukrainian people, not merely those who lived in Crimea, should have been consulted. Indeed, was there really a Crimean people to consult? It's a time-honored strategy, since what a "people" wants is always going to depend on where you draw the lines. One of Abraham Lincoln's arguments against Southern secession is the same as China's argument against Tibetan independence and Spain's against Catalan independence: namely, that the people, that is, the majority of the citizens of the whole country, do not favor it.

My point is not that all these cases are the same. It is rather that the ideal of national sovereignty remains a profound source of legitimacy, however obscure and unstable our definition of a people. We face here the incoherence I promised to identify at the start of this chapter: Yes, "we" have the right to self-determination, but this idea can guide us only once we've decided who "we" are. That question, as I've been suggesting, almost never has a single possible answer.

A MODERN CITY-STATE

There are always choices to be made in shaping national identity, then. And the romantic nationalist story that dominated the period from the Napoleonic wars to the middle of the twentieth century is not the only possibility. Trieste, the one place in which Svevo felt an abiding sense of *patria*, was officially a free territory, a city-state, for several years following World War II, and spokesmen for today's Free Territory of Trieste movement emphasize its culturally plural nature (as they insist on the ongoing validity of a 1947 agreement that recognized Trieste's independence by putting it under the direct control of the U.N. Security Council). "This Territory is the crossroad of Latin, Slavic and Germanic cultures, intrinsically multicultural and multilingual," an organization set up to advocate for independence boasts. "Diversity means richness."[20] Some Triestini, it seems, are still cosmopolites. To be sure, the Duchy of Grand Fenwick—conjured up in *The Mouse That Roared*—will probably establish its independent sovereignty before Trieste does; and yet, on the other side of the world, there's a thriving city-state, born in the mid-1960s, that defines itself, in part, through its ethnic heterogeneity.

That would be Singapore, and it's an instructive example of a national identity that makes much of the plurality of its origins and the complexity of the question, "Who are we?" The Lion City (*singa* is Malay for "lion," *pura* is Sanskrit for "city") had been a British possession since the early nineteenth century, and a Japanese conquest during World War II; but its postcolonial existence began in 1963, as part of the new Federation of Malaysia, which represented the union of the Federation of Malaya with three ex-British colonies: North Borneo, Sarawak, and Singapore. Two years later, Singapore was expelled. There were many reasons why the union didn't work. But the simplest story starts with the fact that the people of Singapore were predominantly of Chinese ancestry, while the rest of the federation was about two-thirds Malay. Independent Malaysia sought to be governed by Malays.

Singapore, by contrast, had to arrive at a very different self-conception. In the summer of 1964, race riots scourged the island, beginning, it was claimed, with an attack by Chinese on a procession of some 20,000 Malays celebrating the birthday of the Prophet Muhammad, and ending with widespread communal violence. The result was something like a national trauma that has shaped Singapore's domestic policies to this day.

The island's linguistic and demographic inheritances were certainly never straightforward. By the end of the colonial period, many Chinese families in the city had adopted English as their home language because it was the lingua franca of government and business. At the start of the twentieth century, though, most families spoke some form of Chinese at home, using not Mandarin but dialects of other languages not mutually intelligible with Mandarin. The commonest was a form of Hokkien, spoken by two-fifths of the population, because many Singapore Chinese came from Fujian Province, in southeast China, where a variety of Hokkien dialects are spoken. Singapore Chinese also spoke Teochew, Cantonese, Hakka, Hainanese, and Shanghainese.

There were people, too, of mixed Chinese and Malay ancestry, whose families were the result of marriages between Chinese men, who migrated to the Malayan peninsula between the fifteenth and the seventeenth centuries, and local Malay women. They spoke a Malayan creole called Baba Malay, which had many Hokkien loanwords.[21] In the early years of the twentieth century, however, prominent Singaporeans of Chinese ancestry developed a system of schools that taught Mandarin and pushed for its use in the community of Chinese ancestry, so knowledge of Mandarin increased through the twentieth century. Mandarin here, as in the Chinese mainland, became the prestige language for many. At the turn of this millennium, four out of five people living in Singapore were citizens or had the right of permanent residence, and about three-quarters of these residents (and a majority of the nonresidents) identified as Chinese.

A second large group of Singaporeans are of Malay ancestry, Singapore being an island of the Malay Archipelago. About 15 percent of the citizens of Singapore identify as Malay, although, having arrived from many parts of the Malay world, their ancestral dialects and languages are quite diverse.

A third group of Singaporeans derive their ancestry from India, mostly from the South where Tamil is spoken; others came from elsewhere in the subcontinent, speaking other home languages. In all, about 7.5 percent of Singaporean citizens identify as Indian. And, as in all modern societies, there are also Singaporean citizens and permanent residents whose ancestors came from other parts of the world.

At Singaporean independence, the ruling party responded to all this ethnic and linguistic complexity with what might seem to be a radical simplification. All citizens were classified, for government purposes, as one of four "racial" groups: Chinese, Malay, Indian, or Other, using what came to be called the CMIO system. Choosing a language associated with any of the major groups as the language of government (especially if it had been Chinese) would have significantly disadvantaged the other two major groups. So the government made the same decision that had been made in many other parts of the former British and French empires, with the aim of avoiding ethnic conflict: they chose to stick with the colonial language. They also argued that being Anglophone would strengthen the nation's capacity for effective participation in global trade, the lifeblood of a port city.

At the same time, the government adopted the following complex of policies. Though English became the *official* language of government, Malay was the *national* language, recognizing the status of Malays as the indigenous people of the region. The national anthem is in Malay, as are the parade commands of the Singaporean armed forces. All citizens would learn English in school. If you were Chinese or Indian, you would also learn Mandarin or Tamil, respectively. If you were Malay, you would study Malay. Everyone had to be at least bilingual; but your second language was to be determined by your ethnic origin.

WHOSE LANGUAGE? WHICH RELIGION?

You might think that building a Singaporean identity would require the playing down of ethnic and linguistic differences. Malaysia next door had an ethnic conception of the state; it was a country in which Malays (who were legally required to be Muslim) held, as the Constitution puts it, a "special position."[22] By contrast, Lee Kuan Yew, Singapore's first leader, insisted on a multiracial, multireligious, multicultural model to provide a cohesive identity for the new nation. (Governmental efficiency and noncorruption were supposed to be— and were—additional sources of legitimacy in a region where they could not be assumed.) As modern state-builders, Singapore's leaders knew the language of identity, knew that it was essential to establish some normative significance for the shared label "Singaporean." Since Singaporeans did not yet think of themselves as a single people, the romantic model built on a preexisting *Volksgeist* was a nonstarter. The country was not one people—at least not yet. But it could be a union of peoples. All that was required was a set of forward-looking commitments.

What developed was a system in which each group participated in the common national life, but was also sustained in its narrower communal life by the recognition of "mother tongues" for each of the major "racial" groups. The state set out to make sure that C, M, I, and O did not segregate themselves too much geographically: it built large amounts of public housing, and allocated it so that every large settlement had people of all the official racial groups, living side by side.

But there was more than gentle suasion at work here. Anyone who commented publicly in a negative way on the habits of their neighbors risked official penalties for sedition; for, under Singapore's "Sedition Act," it is a crime to "promote feelings of ill-will and hostility between different races or classes of the population of Singapore."²³ That's a potent prohibition; after all, given our clannishness, commentary on differences always carries some risk of creating ill will. In 2012, for example, a senior member of the staff of the National Trades Union Congress (NTUC), who was a permanent resident of Chinese ancestry, was fired for complaining about a Malay wedding held in the public space—the "void deck," as they call it in Singapore—of her apartment building. Her profanity-laced Facebook posts suggested that Malays were cheap (if they paid "for a real wedding," she groused, "maybe then the divorce rate won't be so high") and inconsiderate. "How can society allow ppl to get married for 50 bucks?" she went on.

These are not, plainly, the sentiments of someone who has a fair and balanced view of Malays: not least because the divorce rate for Muslims in Singapore—and most Malays are Muslim—is lower than average and has actually gone down recently. So it's not surprising that her posts, which were widely circulated, prompted outrage; or that complaints to her employer cost the woman her job the next day. But things could have gone much worse for her. Three years earlier, a Christian evangelical couple in Singapore was charged with violating the Sedition Act (and the Undesirable Publications Act) when they mailed out tracts that criticized Islam and Catholicism, denigrating them as false religions; the two were sentenced to sixteen weeks in prison. In the wake of the NTUC official's bad-tempered Facebook posts, the secretary of an Inter-Racial and Religious Confidence Circle filed a complaint with the police, who visited the offending party and issued a warning; taking the hint, she moved back to Australia, where she was born.[24] This is a high price to pay for an irritable posting on the web, but the intensity of the response reflects Singaporean sensitivities. The police don't have to scan Singaporean social media for moments of racial prejudice: citizens who support the nation's policies report them eagerly to the authorities. And so, as you'd expect, sometimes remarks about other groups that seem less obviously bigoted can also land you in trouble.

The one-race-one-mother-tongue policy has also had some unfortunate consequences. Hokkien-speaking grandparents can lack a common language with their Mandarin-trained grandchildren; naturalized Hindi-speaking Indians have to deal with Tamil-speaking children; and then there are children whose parents are Chinese and Indian. Meanwhile, the one distinctively Singaporean language—the English-Malay-Chinese-Tamil creole called "Singlish"—has been subject to official disapproval. In short, it's not the language you or your ancestors actually spoke but the identity the state has settled on for you that determines which language is "yours." No one should deny that the CMIO system reflected existing ideas about ethnic identity in Singapore: if it hadn't, it would not have worked at all. But it entailed a radical simplification of a very complex ethnolinguistic reality.

I have mentioned, so far, only the diverse origins and languages of Singaporeans. I could equally have stressed religion. Many Malays in Singapore, and some Indians, are Muslim; about one in seven of the official residents. The magnificent Sultan Mosque on North Bridge Road is nearly a century old, built to replace an earlier mosque—itself a century old—that had grown too small for the Sunnis of Singapore. There are colorful Hindu temples, devoted to Ganesha and Shiva and Vishnu, among other gods of the Hindu pantheon, serving the one in twenty residents who are Hindu. About a third of Singaporeans are Buddhist, and the Buddha Tooth Relic Temple, on South Bridge Road in Chinatown, rises to its magnificent red roofs in the Tang style developed in the later part of the first millennium CE, even though it was completed only in 2007. You can find Catholic and Protestant and Eastern Orthodox churches, and Presbyterian, Anglican, and Methodist schools, serving the almost one in five Singaporeans who are Christian. One in ten Singaporeans officially adheres to Taoism, and the Thian Hock Keng Temple goes back to the early nineteenth century. But Buddhism and Taoism intertwine; and many Chinese families have ancestral shrines at home, and perform rituals honoring their ancestors, whatever their public religious affiliation. Did I mention the two Jewish synagogues that have been designated as national monuments?

THE MEDUSA SYNDROME

A Chinese-majority island surrounded by an ocean of Malays; a country with a Muslim minority surrounded by Malaysia and Indonesia, one a constitutionally Islamic state, the other officially secular, but with the world's largest Muslim population; a population of under 6 million, whose large neighbors number more than 30 million and more than 260 million people, respectively. In these circumstances, I suppose it is not surprising that Singapore's laws clamp down on discussion of racial and religious tensions. The impulse to keep things tidy in the sphere of race and language and religion spills over into taking littering with great seriousness and severely limiting political criticism of the government.

Singapore's extraordinary efforts to avoid internal cleavages, through a national project of respectful accommodation of racial and religious differences, embody the promise and perils of what the Canadian philosopher Charles Taylor has called the "politics of recognition." In that model, various identities receive public acknowledgment from the state. Promise and perils: to recognize is to respect, but it is also, to return to one of my themes, to essentialize.

When the state gazes at us—with its identity cards, educational stipulations, and other instruments of recognition—it invariably fixes and rigidifies a phenomenon that is neither fixed nor rigid. I have called this the Medusa Syndrome: what the state gazes upon, it tends to turn to stone.[25] It sculpts what it purports merely to acknowledge. The strategy, as we've learned, is inadequate to the real-world complexities, to compound identities that grow as pleated as an accordion, with all its folds and fissures. But it may be the only strategy that such a nation-state has. In later years, Lee Kuan Yew's speeches became less focused on values and aspirations and more on policy, precisely because the Singaporean identity had been to some degree stabilized. If the state he created was watchful and intrusive by the standards of a European liberal democracy, it had also convinced most of its citizens that they were engaged together in a meaningful national project. Someone I know once put it like this: the people of Singapore felt watched but also seen. The death of Lee Kuan Yew in 2015 produced a vast and genuine outpouring of grief in Singapore. There was a week of national mourning with flags at half-mast. Nearly 450,000 people paraded past his coffin in Parliament over three days and nights, with public transportation running twenty-four hours a day to enable their visits. But the state-imposed silence about intergroup difficulties remains. Someone is still always watching; younger Singaporeans may no longer be quite so glad to be seen.

To set out to govern identities is to set out to govern the ungovernable. Whatever you do, ordinary people will ignore the boundaries you set. In the first decade of this millennium, interracial marriage rates roughly doubled in Singapore.[26] Now a quarter of new marriages cross the boundaries between C, M, I, and O. I am not suggesting that the government of Singapore should ignore the ethnic and religious identities of its citizens. But it will have to acknowledge that it's no longer just the society that's multiracial: more and more of its citizens are, too.

ESCAPING EMPIRE

Earlier, I described nation states emerging from an age of empire. In the decades after Singapore came into being, many theorists of globalization predicted that the process would reverse itself: the nation-state, we were told, would be demoted to middle management, a mere node in a vast transnational flux of capital and labor, of banking treaties and trade pacts, of the supranational security arrangements required for transnational adversaries, from drug cartels to terrorists. The national age was to be edged aside by the "network age."

What's everywhere in evidence today, instead, are the forces of resistance to this sort of globalization. Boris Johnson, first London's mayor, then Britain's foreign secretary, tapped into them when he said in 2016 that Brexit was "about the right of the people of this country to settle their own destiny." But which people was he talking about? Not the Scottish people, who voted overwhelmingly against taking Britain out of Europe; two years earlier, in fact, more than 40 percent of them favored taking themselves out of Britain.

Not the Londoners, who also voted overwhelmingly to remain. Who are "we"?

If there was a chauvinist, Little Englander strain in Brexit nationalism, you'll find more overt hard nationalism elsewhere. In India, the ruling party, the BJP (Bharatiya Janata Party), built a following by claiming that only Hindutva (Hinduness), a putative unity of language, religion, and culture, can bring the nation together. Citing those arguments that Hinduism might be a nineteenth-century British invention would be a bad idea at a BJP rally. In Austria, the Freedom Party, which won more than a quarter of the vote in the 2017 legislative elections, announces that the Austrian homeland—the *Heimat*—is held together by a German heritage. In Hungary, Poland, and elsewhere, ruling parties have made similar avowals; they defend "Christian values" against Middle Eastern migrants, denounce the "eurocrats," and extol the purity of national heritage. In *their* political imagination, the network is down. And in asserting these nationalisms, they deny ethnic and religious minorities like the Roma or Muslims an equal place within the nation. As the political theorist Jan-Werner Mueller notes, populists claim to represent 100 percent of the people, by dismissing their opponents as inauthentic betrayers of the people or else as foreigners, not part of the people at all.[27]

These vectors of reaction have their precursors. You won't be surprised to hear that Ettore Schmitz, given his penetrating realism, was little moved by such preachments of purity. Late in his life, the Italian state started to pressure new nationals like him to adopt Italian surnames. Schmitz volunteered to change his name to his pen name, Italo Svevo. They said no: the new Italian name had to be a dictionary translation of the old name. Schmitz walked away. "I've got two names already; why do I need a third?" he grumbled. His enthusiasm for Italianness had its limits. But once we reject the notion that some natural unity gives countries their shape, we're left with a puzzle. What *does* hold countries together?

INVENTING NATIONS

Singapore tried one very top-down solution. Ghana—a country only seven years older—tried another one, characteristically more relaxed and organic. My father, an anticolonial firebrand and a leader in Ghana's independence struggle, once published a newspaper article headlined, "Is Ghana Worth Dying For?" This was, for him, a question only worth asking rhetorically: his answer, of course, was yes. And it wasn't an abstract issue for him. When Jerry Rawlings came to power in a coup in 1979, my father was swept up in the mass arrests that followed. He ended up sharing a cell with a friend of his, General Akwasi Afrifa, who had led the first Ghanaian coup, in 1966, which had removed President Nkrumah from power. One morning Afrifa was taken out and shot. My father survived only because he persuaded a group of angry soldiers that everything he had done had been in the service of Ghana. Perhaps he was helped by his experience as an advocate in the courts. Still, it was a close thing.

Yet what, exactly, would my patriotic father have been dying *for*? As in Singapore, the nation's identity is very complex. Singapore has its CMIO system and all those religions. From Ghana, that variety looks modest. More than half the population is Christian, more than a quarter, Muslim, and many people (including those who consider themselves Christian or Muslim) still follow one of the many indigenous religious traditions. But we have people of almost every faith: there's a huge new Mormon Temple in the capital, Accra, and, less than ten miles northwest, there's one of the largest Nichiren Shoshu Buddhist temples outside of Japan. The only religious rarity is atheism. As for linguistic diversity: Ghana has 9 government-supported languages, but 23 of the country's languages are spoken by more than 50,000 people and there are 80 or so languages altogether. More than 17 million of Ghana's 28 million people speak Twi, the most common indigenous language, with its three major dialects; nearly 4 million have some form of Ewe as their mother tongue; but the most widely spoken language is English, the language of government. It is the language of Ghana but not, one might say, of any of the peoples of Ghana.

Sticking with a colonial language for the purposes of government, as I said, has been a common policy in former French and British colonies. The East African countries of Kenya, Uganda, and Tanzania also use Swahili, a language that had long spread throughout the region as a lingua franca for trade; Swahili works because, though it is the mother tongue of a few million people, most of the 50 to 100 million people who speak it do not associate it with their ethnicity. It is not seen, therefore, as granting a privilege to one ethnic group. By contrast, Twi, even though it's the most widely spoken mother tongue in Ghana, would have been hard to accept as the national language, since, for many Ghanaians it was the language of the Asante Empire, which had been their imperial overlord before the British.

Because of this diversity and diffusion, Ghanaians (like Singaporeans) are perfectly aware that they are not a Herderian people, with one history and culture, a single unifying *Volksgeist*. But that doesn't stop anyone from thinking of themselves as Ghanaian at elections, or when they are following the Olympics or the World Cup, or when they travel or take up residence abroad. (Ghanaians live all over the map: there are hundreds of thousands in Nigeria, close to a hundred thousand in the United States and the United Kingdom, and thousands in the Netherlands, South Africa, and a host of other countries.) You do not have to be Asante to be proud of former U.N. Secretary-General Kofi Annan, or Fante to take pride in the novels of Ama Ata Aidoo. Kente, the silk fabric originally woven in Bonwire, near Kumasi, is now worn proudly by Ghanaians around the world. And so Ghanaians are slowly becoming a people, drawn together over a few decades, as the Scots have been over cen-

turies, by living together under a single government. It's this process that matters.

For my father, then, national consciousness wasn't a mineral to
be excavated, like bauxite; it was a fabric to be woven, like—well, like
kente. He would have agreed with Svevo's observation that "inventing is a creation, not a lie."[28] National identity doesn't require that
we all be already the same. Still, for the purposes of government,
citizens need to have languages in common. In developing national
education, a state has to decide which dialects of which languages
should be taught. It would be nice if the history taught explained why
this people was gathered in *this* state; and a government, concerned
to get citizens acting and feeling together, would like a story that
connects them. With a diverse population, filigreed with potentially
divisive local histories and traditions, it might be necessary to glide
over conflictual claims on the truth. Ernest Renan, the conservative
French historian and patriot, declared, in 1882, "Forgetting and, I
would even say, historical error, is an essential element in the creation of a nation."[29]

Recognize that nations are invented and you'll see they're always
being *re*invented. Once, to be English, you had to imagine your ancestors were recorded a millennium ago in the Domesday Book. Now a
Rohit or a Pavel or a Muhammad or a Kwame can be English. Once
the Anglican Church defined Englishness; now an array of creeds
can be embodied in the teams who play for England in a cricket test
match. Today, a brown-skinned Scot, whose grandfather came from
Mumbai, can take pride in the Scottish Enlightenment or thrill to the
tale of Bannockburn.

But, as Renan also argued, what really matters in making a nation,
beyond these shared stories, is "the clearly expressed desire to continue a common life." That's why he said that a nation's existence "is,
if you will pardon the metaphor, a daily plebiscite."[30] What makes
"us" a people, ultimately, is a commitment to governing a common
life *together.*

DEMOCRATIC DIFFICULTIES

The challenge this poses for liberal democracies is formidable. Liberal states depend upon a civic creed that's both potent and lean—potent enough to give significance to citizenship, lean enough to be shared by people with different religious and ethnic affiliations. The Romantic state could pride itself on being the emanation of one *Volk* and its primordial consciousness; the liberal state has to get by with a good deal less mystical mumbo-jumbo. The Romantic state could boldly identify itself with the General Will; liberal states must content themselves with a general willingness. The Romantic state rallies its citizens with a stirring cry: "One people!" The liberal state's true anthem is: "We can work it out."

And often enough, we can. People have long known in America what many in Europe have come to grasp—that we can hang together without a common religion or even delusions of common ancestry. In the second decade of the twenty-first century, various independence movements gained traction in Europe, from Caledonia to Catalonia. Neither the logic of territorial integrity nor that of national sovereignty can resolve such matters. But let the arguments not be made in terms of some ancient spirit of the Folk; the truth of every modern nation is that political unity is never underwritten by some preexisting national commonality. What binds citizens together is a commitment, through Renan's daily plebiscite, to sharing the life of a modern state, united by its institutions, procedures, and precepts.

My father, who subtitled his memoir *The Autobiography of an African Patriot*, used to celebrate Burns Night. Even after an evening of knocking back the whiskey, though, he wasn't deluded into thinking he was a Scot. He just admired the poet's principles, alongside his poetry. Because when Burns had Robert the Bruce ask for his followers' allegiance, he wisely did it not in the name of a Scottish identity but in the name of Freedom.

Wha for Scotland's king and law
Freedom's sword will strongly draw,
Freeman stand, or freeman fa',
Let him follow me![31]

However ardently he felt the romance of the national spirit, Burns realized that Scotland was not a fate but a project.

As a spumy wave of right-wing nationalism surges across Europe once more, we are bound to think about how fragile pluralism can seem. Few had a more acute sense of this than Italo Svevo, a man who, during the First World War, was regularly summoned for inter- rogations by the Austrian authorities, and who found himself chafing no less under later policies of Italianization.[32] Like Zeno, his greatest creation, Svevo was never happier than when walking among Trieste's diverse neighborhoods; an inveterate ironist, he thrived on being sort-of Jewish, sort-of German, and, in the end, only sort-of Italian. For Svevo, who was at heart a man without country or cause, life was a dance with ambiguities. And when fascism convulsed Europe after his death, his kin were dashed against forces that detested ambiguity and venerated certainty—his Catholic wife, Livia, forced to register as a Jew, his grandsons shot as partisans or starved in camps.

And yet, in the canons of our culture, Italo Svevo is still with us. The tolerant, pluralist, self-questioning, and cosmopolitan modernity he embodied is, to be sure, under attack. The confessors of ambiva- lence will always seem at a disadvantage amid the fervent partisans of nativism. But to come to terms with Svevo's complex allegiances is to understand that we don't have to accept the forced choice between globalism and patriotism. The unities we create fare better when we face the convoluted reality of our differences.

FOUR

COLOR

Some view our sable race with scornful eye,
    "Their colour is a diabolic die."
Remember, Christians, Negros, black as Cain,
May be refin'd, and join th' angelic train.

> Phillis Wheatley, "On Being Brought
> from Africa to America"
>
> (1773)

THE EXPERIMENT

In 1707, a boy no more than five years old left Axim, on the African Gold Coast, for Amsterdam, aboard a ship belonging to the Dutch West India Company. In those days, the trip to Europe took many weeks, but his arrival in the Dutch port was not the end of his long journey. He then had to travel another few hundred miles to Wolfenbüttel, the home of Anton Ulrich, Duke of Brunswick-Wolfenbüttel. Anton Ulrich was a major patron of the European Enlightenment. His librarian was Gottfried Leibniz, one of the leading philosophers, mathematicians, and inventors of his era, and cocreator, with Isaac Newton, of calculus; and the ducal library in Wolfenbüttel housed one of the most magnificent book collections in the world.

The child had apparently been offered as a "gift" to the duke, who, in turn, handed the boy on to his son, August Wilhelm; and we first hear of him as a member of August Wilhelm's household. From his baptism until 1735, the boy continued to receive the patronage of the dukes of Brunswick-Wolfenbüttel, as Anton Ulrich was succeeded by August Wilhelm, and August Wilhelm was succeeded by his brother, Ludwig Rudolf, in turn. And, as a child, he would no doubt have met Leibniz, who lived, as he did, under their patronage.

We don't know what the African boy's status was: Had he been enslaved? Was he sent by missionaries for a Christian education? What we do know is that Anton Ulrich took a special interest in him, arranging for his education, and giving him, at his baptism, both his own Christian name and his son's middle name: so the young man came to be known as Anton Wilhelm. The dukes had apparently taken the occasion of the gift of an African child to conduct one of those famous Enlightenment experiments, aiming to explore whether an African could absorb and contribute to modern scholarship. The ducal family might have been aware of a similar experiment, which began a few years earlier, when Tsar Peter the Great of Russia took an African slave as his godson, naming him Hannibal. He went on to be a successful Russian general, and was the great-grandfather of Alexander Pushkin, the founder of modern Russian literature. (Pushkin began, but never finished, a novel called "The Moor of Peter the Great.")

We're not sure when Anton Wilhelm started using his Nzema name, Amo. At his confirmation, the church records in Wolfenbüttel call him Anton Wilhelm Rudolph Mohre; *Mohr* (Moor) being one of the ways Germans then referred to Africans. But in later life he often called himself Anton Wilhelm Amo Afer, using the word for African in Latin, which was the language of European scholarship. So he wanted to be known as Amo the African.

The experiment with the young African has to be accounted a success. Our knowledge of his early education is sketchy, but Amo, as the duke's godson, perhaps began his schooling at the Wolfenbüttel Ritter-Akademie, alongside the children of the local aristocracy (*Ritter* is the German word for a knight). We do know he went on to the nearby university at Helmstedt, founded more than a century earlier by one of the duke's predecessors. Amo must have flourished there, because he earned the right to go on, in 1727, to study law at the University of Halle, then (as now) one of Germany's leading centers of teaching and research.

Halle took Amo out of the duke's domain into the state of Brandenburg, which was then ruled by the Prussian king. He was awarded a master's degree for his legal thesis at Halle—which dealt, aptly enough, with the European law of slavery—and then went on to study at the University of Wittenberg (where a young Martin Luther had taught theology), becoming the first black African to earn a European doctoral degree in philosophy. Here, he was in the domain of the Elector of Saxony, who was soon to become King of Poland, as well. Along the way, Amo added knowledge of medicine and astronomy to his philosophical and legal training. When the Elector of Saxony came to visit in 1733, Amo was chosen to lead the students' procession in his honor. His Wittenberg thesis, which was published in 1734 under the title, *On the Apatheia of the Human Mind*, makes important criticisms of Descartes's views of sensation.

Amo, who came to know Dutch, French, Latin, Greek, Hebrew, and, perhaps, English, as well as German, went on to teach at Halle and Jena, publishing, in 1738, a book entitled *The Art of Sober and Accurate Philosophizing*, which discussed issues in almost every area of the subject. He won eminent admirers. The great physicist and philosopher Martin Gotthelf Loescher, who examined his thesis at the University of Wittenberg, spoke of the Gold Coast as "the mother . . . of the most auspicious minds," and added:

> Among these auspicious minds, your genius stands out particularly, most noble and most distinguished Sir, seeing that you have excellently demonstrated felicity and superiority of genius, solidity and refinement of learning and teaching, in countless examples before now, and even in this our University, with great honor in all worthy things, and now also in your present dissertation.[1]

I have said that Amo's education was an experiment. But we need to be careful in deciding what hypothesis it was designed to explore. Amo, as we saw, was referred to as a Moor in his baptismal records and called himself, later, *Afer*, the African. When he wrote about the law of slavery, he titled his work *De jure maurorum* (On the Law of the Moors). The great contemporaneous encyclopedia the *Zedler*, in its definition of the word "Moor," treats it as equivalent to Ethiopian or Abyssinian, but continues, "this name is also given to all blacks, like the Negroes, and other African peoples of this color."[2] "*Afer*," in classical Latin, referred to a people—the Afri—who lived around ancient Carthage. But gradually it came to mean a person from Rome's African colonies, and, finally, anyone from the whole continent. Still, it is clear that Amo's black skin linked him in the minds of his German contemporaries not just with all black people but also with other inhabitants of the African continent. These are not, however, as they knew as well as we do, the same thing.

When Johann Gottfried Kraus, the Rector of Wittenberg, complimented Dr. Amo on his successful defense of his dissertation, he began by talking about his African background, mentioning some of the most famous African writers from Antiquity, including the Roman playwright Terence—who, like Amo, had given himself the last name Afer—and Tertullian and St. Augustine, along with other Fathers of the Church born in North Africa. He mentioned the Moors who conquered Spain from Africa. All of these people, as Kraus surely knew, were of Berber or Phoenician or Roman ancestry. None of them would have had dark skin or tightly curled black hair like Amo's. When Luther lived in Wittenberg, his home was an Augustinian monastery, but no picture he would have seen of St. Augustine would have depicted him as black.

So, if the dukes who supported him were interested in whether an African could be a brilliant intellectual, they already knew the answer: people such as Terence, Tertullian, and St. Augustine had long ago proved that they could. Presumably, they were interested in a question not about Africans but about black people, about Negroes. Yet what would you learn from a single experiment with one black man? Did Anton Ulrich and his friends conclude that any black child, taken at random and given Amo's education, would have ended up as a professor of philosophy? And if Amo had not passed the exams, would they have concluded that this showed something about every black person?

THE RISE OF RACE

Three hundred years later, we are bound to see his story through the prism of the modern idea of race. This was not so in Amo's day. Then, everyone agreed there were what I earlier called "peoples," groups of human beings defined by shared ancestry, real or imagined, as there had been since the beginnings of recorded history. But the idea that each people shared a common, inherited biological nature was not yet the consensus among European thinkers. For one thing, most of them still believed in the truth of the biblical story of creation, and that meant that every living person was a descendant of Adam and Eve, and each was also a descendant of one of the sons of Noah, whose family was the only one to survive the Biblical Flood. For another, the idea of distinguishing between the biological and the nonbiological features of human beings was still in the intellectual future. When Leibniz wrote about what distinguished one people from another, he thought what mattered was language. (Indeed, he spent much of his life trying to persuade people to send him information about the languages of various peoples in Europe and Asia, for exactly this reason.) And if you read contemporaneous accounts of what distinguishes the various peoples of the world in the writings of European travelers and the thinkers who read them, the great debates were about the role of climate and geography in shaping color and customs, not about inherited physical characteristics.

This shouldn't be very surprising. The very word "biology" was invented only around 1800 (in Germany, as it happens). Until then, the discussion of the nature of living things took place under the heading of Natural History. And it's only with the Swedish naturalist Carl Linnaeus, Amo's contemporary, that scholars began to think of human beings as part of nature in a way that meant that we could be classified, like other animals and plants, by genus and species. Linnaeus, the father of modern taxonomy, was the person who first classified us as *Homo sapiens*, and who placed us alongside monkeys and apes in the natural order. As he wrote to a colleague, "But I seek from you and the whole world the difference of kind between men and monkeys that follows from the principles of Natural History. Very certainly, I know of none."[3]

Beginning in the years that Amo was in Europe, a contest developed between the older biblical understanding of the nature of humanity and this newer one that grew with the increasing prestige of the scientific study of humankind. In Amo's day, almost everyone would have agreed that, since all human beings had to be descended from the sons of Noah, the different kinds of people might be different because they descended from Shem or Ham or Japheth. The basic division of humankind suggested by this typology was threefold: first, the Semites, like the Hebrews and the Arabs and the Assyrians; second, the darker-skinned people of Africa, including Egyptians and Ethiopians; and, third, the lighter-skinned people of Europe and Asia, like the Greeks, the Medes, and the Persians. That gives you three races: Semites, Blacks, and Whites.[4]

But the travels of European scientists and explorers led to increasing knowledge of the diversity of types among modern human beings, and a greater familiarity, too, with other primates. And it became increasingly difficult to fit every kind of human being into this framework. To begin with, there was the absence of East Asians—like the Chinese and the Japanese—or of Amerindians from the biblical account. Some thinkers even began to wonder if all the people in the world were really descendants of Adam. Over the course of the nineteenth century, out of a noisy debate, three ideas increasingly took hold, ideas that made it harder to accommodate the earlier, biblical picture.

THE RACIAL TRIAD

The first was that you could explain many of the characteristics of individual human beings as a product of their race. People might be assigned to the Negro race on the basis of their skin color and hair, their thicker lips and broader noses. But these visible differences, though important for classification, were only the beginnings of a catalogue of deeper differences. (You'll hear echoes here of the essentialisms I explored in my first chapter.) Arthur de Gobineau, a French count who, in the mid-nineteenth century, published the mammoth *Essay on the Inequality of the Human Races*, sought to expose the differences in aptitudes and appetites that underlay such morphological differences, distinguishing not only among black, yellow, and white, but, within the white race, the distinctly favored "Aryan family." For him, race was a motive force of history. Other theorists produced racial cartographies that varied in detail, but the essential idea—that much that mattered about people was shaped by their race—was broadly accepted.

We might call this idea the racial fixation. And by the last half of the nineteenth century in the world of the North Atlantic, the racial fixation was everywhere. It wasn't just found among medical scientists like Josiah Nott, whose *Types of Mankind,* written with the Egyptologist George Gliddon, became the bible of racial hierarchy for planters in the American South. Literary critics like Matthew Arnold in England, or Hippolyte Taine in France, would explain the work of poets and novelists by speaking of the innate character of the race to which they belonged. "Science has now made visible to everybody the great and pregnant elements of difference which lie in race," Arnold writes in the 1860s. Physiologists can contribute to

understanding the nature of races by cataloguing the physical differences between them, he says, but the literary critic must consider the
"data . . . afforded by our literature, genius, and spiritual production
generally."[5] For each race has a specific genius, a spirit that shows
up in its literature. Here is what he thinks the "data" show about the
Celtic race, for example, which includes, as I mentioned earlier, the
people of Wales and Ireland and Scotland and parts of France: "The
Celtic genius [has] sentiment as its main basis, with love of beauty,
charm, and spirituality for its excellence, ineffectualness and self-
will for its defect."[6] And the "data" here include what the critic sees
in their poetic traditions.

Taine, writing again about literature a decade later, says:

A race, like the Old Aryans, scattered from the Ganges as far as
the Hebrides, settled in every clime, and every stage of civilisa-
tion, transformed by thirty centuries of revolutions, nevertheless
manifests in its languages, religions, literatures, philosophies,
the community of blood and of intellect which to this day binds
its offshoots together.[7]

For Taine, as for Arnold, literary history is part of the scientific study of
race. Taine was one of the half dozen most influential European historians and critics of his era. (The ground-shaking nineteenth-century
German philosopher Friedrich Nietzsche called him "the first of living historians.") Matthew Arnold was the most distinguished English
literary critic of the later nineteenth century.[8] By their day, then, race
was a central preoccupation of European history and literary criticism, and not just of the social and biological sciences.

A second idea that took hold in the years after Amo came to Europe
followed from the racial fixation. If your individual character—not
just your body, but your temperament, your habits of life, your artistic
work—was deeply formed by your race, then we could see the shared
nature of a race in each of its members. Each of us not only belonged

to a race, we expressed its nature. The result was that each member of the group was typical: representative, that is, of his or her type.

This form of what we might call "typological" thinking made Amo, in particular, a crucial exemplar in the debates about the capacity of the Negro that took place in the Enlightenment and beyond. For, against this background, Amo's very existence showed something not just about an individual African, but about all Negroes: that the race had the capacity to achieve at the very highest levels in philosophy.

The Abbé Grégoire, the great French revolutionary priest and anti-slavery campaigner, published a survey of the cultural achievements of black people in 1808. He subtitled it "researches on their intellectual faculties, their moral qualities and their literature," and he offered up Amo as evidence for his belief in the unity of the human race and the fundamental equality of black people. Thomas Jefferson had remarked in his *Notes on the State of Virginia* (1785) that he could never "find that a black had uttered a thought above the level of plain narration."[9] Grégoire sent him a copy of his book *On the Literature of Negroes*, including its extended discussion of Amo's life and work, and asked him to think again.

Amo was not the only counterexample to Jefferson's blighted view of the Negro. Grégoire's exemplary Negroes included Angelo Soliman, another West African enslaved as a child, who had been educated by a marchioness in Messina in Sicily, and became the tutor to the heir to the Prince of Liechtenstein in Vienna, joining the same Masonic lodge as Mozart a couple of decades after Amo's rise to eminence. Soliman was famous for taking walks through Vienna arm-in-arm with the emperor.[10] The French revolutionary priest also told the older tale of Juan Latino, the poet and professor of grammar and Latin in sixteenth-century Granada; known as "El negro Juan Latino," he shows up in the first of the burlesque poems that Cervantes wrote at the start of *Don Quixote*. The black professor is mentioned because he has the "gift of tongues" and so could write in Latin, unlike Cervantes, who must write in the Spanish vernacular.

Reading *On the Literature of Negroes,* Jefferson would have been reminded, too, of his countrywoman Phillis Wheatley, who published in 1773 the first book of poetry by an African-American. George Washington had praised Wheatley as "so favoured by the Muses" after receiving a copy of her patriotic poem "His Excellency George Washington."[11] Part of what we should notice is that these wildly diverse lives were brought together only by the question "What are the intellectual capacities of blacks?"

Behind both the racial fixation and the typological thinking was a third habit of mind: we find ourselves face-to-face once more with our natural essentialism, reconstructed now at the heart of scientific theory. Since the late eighteenth century, the conviction has grown and spread that all of us carry within us something derived from the race to which we belong that explains our mental and physical potential. That something, that racial essence, was inherited biologically, transmitted through procreation. If your parents were of the same race, you shared their common essence. If people of different races married, their offspring carried something of the racial essence of each parent.

Of course, even if there had been a racial essence, it wouldn't have meant that Amo's gift for philosophy told you very much about it. No one ever thought that because Plato or Descartes was a European, every European was capable of works of philosophical genius. But Amo's relevance in Grégoire's argument derived largely from the fact that, for black people, the racial essence was thought by many to rule out real intellectual capacity. The philosopher David Hume, one of the beacons of the Scottish Enlightenment, wrote in a footnote in 1753, "There never was a civilized nation of any other complexion than white, nor even any individual eminent either in action or speculation." No empire of Mali, then, no Chinese philosophy, no architectural glories of the Mughal Empire.

Immanuel Kant, the most influential European philosopher of the eighteenth century, famously declared, in 1764—it was not his best moment—that the fact that someone "was completely black from head to foot" was a "distinct proof that what he said was stupid."[12] Amo's existence did refute that view. But it was open to those skeptical of Negro capacity to insist that Amo was a singular anomaly. So Grégoire not only assembled the dozen or more extraordinary counterexamples in his book but reported on a visit to a group of black children brought from Sierra Leone to a school founded in London by William Wilberforce, the great evangelical antislavery campaigner, concluding that, so far as he could tell, "there exists no difference between them and Europeans except that of color."[13]

RACE AS RATIONALE

Part of the background to the debate about the capacity of the Negro was the explosion of African slavery in Europe's New World colonies in the Americas. In Amo's years in Germany, the transatlantic slave trade was rising toward its late-eighteenth-century peak, when some 80,000 people a year were transported in shackles from Africa to the New World. Many historians have concluded that one reason for the increasingly negative view of the Negro through the later eighteenth century was the need to salve the consciences of those who trafficked in and exploited enslaved men and women. As Grégoire put it, bleakly but bluntly, "People have slandered Negroes, first in order to get the right to enslave them, and then to justify themselves for having enslaved them. . . ."[14]

Many in Europe needed, in short, to believe that the subjugation of black people was justified by their natural inferiority. This argument—that some people are natural slaves—has a classical ancestry: it can be found in Aristotle. As in Aristotle's day, this view was supported by pointing to the limited achievements of actual slaves. But, Grégoire and others insisted, you couldn't tell much about what black people were capable of by seeing what most of them achieved in the appalling conditions of New World slavery. Who knew what would happen if all black people were offered the education of Anton Wilhelm Amo? (Or, conversely, if Amo had been sent, like his brother, to work as a slave in the sugarcane fields of Suriname?)

It is, perhaps, worth noting that the discovery that not a single Negro was good at philosophy wouldn't have justified black slavery. As Thomas Jefferson admitted, in responding to the Abbé Grégoire, "Because Sir Isaac Newton was superior to others in understanding, he was not therefore lord of the person or property of others."[15] The slanders against the Negro race may have salved some Christian consciences, but they could never have justified what had been done in enslaving millions of black people.

Still, ideology—enlisted by forms of domination from slavery to colonization—does help explain why, at a time when scientists were discarding notions like phlogiston, supposedly the substance of fire, they made extraordinary efforts to assert the reality of race. There were the physical anthropologists, with their craniometrical devices; there were the ethnologists and physiologists and the evolutionary theorists, who, discounting Darwin, propagated notions of race degeneration and separate, "polygenic" origins for the various races. One illustrious discipline after another was recruited to give content to color. And so, in the course of the nineteenth century, in a hubbub of contentious argument, the modern race concept took hold.

MENDELISM

This theory of the racial essence developed before modern genetics. In 1866, a Czech monk by the name of Gregor Mendel published his proposal that the particulate factors we now call "genes" explained the patterns in the inheritance of the characteristics of organisms.[16]

But the significance of his work would not be appreciated for another thirty years. Modern genetic theory, which treated our biological inheritance as the product of tens of thousands of individual factors, did not really begin until around 1900.

Once you grasped the Mendelian picture, though, you could see an alternative to the idea of a racial essence. There need be no underlying single something that explained why Negroes were Negroes or Caucasians Caucasian. Their shared appearance could be the product of genes for appearance that they had in common. And those genes need play no role in fixing your tastes in poetry or your philosophical ideas. The prejudices that Arnold and Taine represented no longer had a foundation in the sciences. There was no longer a theory to support the racial fixation.

On the older view, if you wanted to say that blacks had rhythm, you would declare that a rhythmic sense was part of the Negro essence. On the new scientific view, if all Negroes liked rhythmic music, it had to be either because they happened to come from places where that taste was taught—a shared environment—or because they shared, alongside the genes for skin color or hair, other genes that made for a taste for rhythm. When chromosomes were discovered, in the early twentieth century, you could understand that genes would mostly be inherited independently of one another; even those on the same chromosome could become separated in the cell divisions that precede the creation of each sperm and each egg.

Another thing became clear through the course of twentieth-century genetics. The vast bulk of our genetic material is shared with all normal human beings, whatever their race. Of course, it turned out that we shared a great deal of our genome with our primate cousins, too, though we alone among the great apes have twenty-three pairs of chromosomes. So what was more important was that the existing variation between populations didn't correspond to the old racial categories. Equally significant was the vast variability *within* the populations of Asia or Europe or Africa. Ninety percent of the world's genetic variation is found in every so-called racial group. Take any two human beings, entirely at random: the continental origin of the majority of their ancestors could play only a relatively small role in accounting for their genetic differences.

All three elements of the older view were put in doubt: the racial fixation and the typological assumption made sense if there was a racial essence. But if there wasn't, then each human being was a bundle of characteristics and you had to have some other reason for supposing that Anton Wilhelm Amo, the African, told you anything more about another black person than he told you about a white person with whom he would also share most of his genes.

It's true that if you look at enough of a person's genes you can usually tell whether they have recent ancestry in Africa or Asia or Europe; and you'll find, naturally, that many have ancestry on two or three continents. (As you've learned, my family is full of such people!) But that's because there are patterns of genes in human populations— which is a fact about groups—not because there are distinctive sets of genes shared by the members of a race, which would be a fact about individuals. Some of the genes that signal my Asante ancestry are different from the ones that identify other people of recent African descent. And many, many people in the world live at the boundaries between the races imagined by nineteenth-century science: between African Negroes and European Caucasians there are Ethiopians and Arabs and Berbers; between the yellow races of East Asia and the white Europeans are the peoples of central and South Asia. Where in India is there a sharp boundary between white and brown and black?

Since the beginning of the twenty-first century, we have made huge strides in understanding the human genome. Statistical techniques allow us to reconstruct the ways in which genes travel (and don't travel) together. So we can find broad patterns of correlation, clusterings of genetic material, that allow us to assign human populations into groups that fade into one another. Because there are no sharp boundaries, some ways of doing this will put together two people who would be separated by another, equally reasonable, way of doing it. Some biologists think that there are reasons to favor some clusterings over others, because they clump more people into a small number of groups, capturing broader features of the statistical landscape of human variability. Those patterns reflect the ways in which human groups have traveled over the last 100,000 years or so, as well as the history of the forces of selection that have shaped local populations. But what, biologically, makes you you, or me me, isn't best explained by tracing our respective ancestries; it's the total genetic package each of us carries *now*: which genes—among the tiny proportion of our genome that varies in ways that have biological significance—we actually have. (It's also increasingly clear that it matters what microorganisms are living in and on us.) There are patterns in populations, but each of us is an individual. To say that these statistical discoveries vindicate the racial theories of the nineteenth century would be like arguing that the statistical correlation between birth month and the length of a career in the National Hockey League confirms the claims of astrology.[17]

It is clear that genes make a difference, alongside environment, in determining your height or the color of your skin. Some people are cleverer or more musical or better poets than others and, no doubt, part of the explanation for that, alongside environment, is in their genes as well. But those genes are not inherited in racial packages. And so, despite the fact that the genetic story is vastly more detailed than it was a century ago, a fundamental fact remains. If you want to think about how the limits of human capability are set by genetic inheritance, it won't help you to think about those nineteenth-century races: Negro, Caucasian, Oriental.

More than this, what actually matters to us about other people depends on connections that pass through language and culture as well as through our physical bodies. After all, whether or not we share a language, as Leibniz knew, makes a profound difference in how we interact with one another. Pick your favorite way of classifying people by their genetic similarities into a small number of groups. In each of those groups, the world's largest languages—English, Chinese, Hindi, for example—will be spoken with equal ease and fluency; in each of them, there will be Christians and Muslims and Buddhists; and, yes, in each of them, there will be both philosophers and psychopaths.

What the new understanding of genetics has made clear is that the old picture of race conflated questions of biology and questions of culture. It wanted to explain every difference between groups in terms of an underlying racial essence, inherited by each generation from the one before. Nowadays, it is clear that one of the most distinctive marks of our species is that our inheritance is both biological *and* cultural. Each generation of human beings in a particular society can build on what was learned by the ones before; by contrast, among our great ape cousins, there is little cultural inheritance, and in most other organisms there is almost none. What makes us the wise species—*sapiens*, remember, is the Latin for "wise"—is that our genes make brains that allow us to pick up things from one another that are *not* in our genes. Amo's ability to wrestle with Descartes required his European teachers, not just his African genes. The extended period of dependency that we call childhood is necessary because to be a fully functioning member of our species you need to have the time to learn the things that make us human.

THE COLOR OF POLITICS

The racial assumptions of the nineteenth century were not just scientific; they were also moral. People didn't only belong to natural racial types; they also had a natural and proper preference for—indeed, they had special obligations to—their own kind. Edward W. Blyden, one of the founders of Pan-Africanism, who was born in the Caribbean but moved to Liberia as a young man, expressed this thought as well as anyone. "Abandoning the sentiment of race," he wrote in a Sierra Leonean newspaper, in 1893, was like trying to "do away with gravitation."[18]

In reality, the history of the world shows that hatred and warfare was as common within the so-called races as it was between them. Over the long haul, indeed, conflict among white Europeans or black Africans or yellow Asians was much more common, since conflict requires contact. There was nothing racial in the fifth-century BCE conflicts between China's warring states, or the sixteenth-century battles that created the Mughal Empire, or between Asante and Denkyira in West Africa at the turn of the eighteenth century, or among the various Amerindian states of Mexico before the arrival of the Spanish.

Still, this dynamic, in which the idea of race becomes the common currency of negation and affirmation, dominance and resistance, would prove dauntingly difficult to withdraw from. That's unfortunate. Because there is little doubt that the race idea was associated with moral disasters from its earliest beginnings. Not only did European racial thinking develop, at least in part, to rationalize the Atlantic slave trade, it played a central role—often a pernicious one—in the development and execution of Europe's nineteenth- and twentieth-century colonial projects; and, with the Nazis, it was central in organizing the systematic genocide of millions and millions of people, Jews and Roma, conceived as inferior races, among them. In the Armenian, Herero, and Rwandan genocides, the language of race played a terrifying role alongside the language of nation. It is hard to think about race without mentioning racism, a word that was coined—somewhat belatedly, you might think, given this history—not to evoke hostile white attitudes to blacks but to describe the anti-Semitism of the German National Socialists.

In 1900, in an address "To the Nations of the World" at the first Pan-African Conference in London, the eminent black intellectual W. E. B. Du Bois proclaimed that the "problem of the twentieth century" was "the problem of the color-line," to wit:

> the question as to how far differences of race—which show themselves chiefly in the color of the skin and the texture of the hair—will hereafter be made the basis of denying to over half the world the right of sharing to their utmost ability the opportunities and privileges of modern civilization. . . .[19]

Du Bois was the beneficiary of the best education that our North Atlantic civilization then had to offer. He qualified for a doctorate in Germany, returning home without it only because he couldn't afford to stay to meet the residence requirements, and receiving (almost as a sort of consolation prize) the first doctorate earned by an African-American at Harvard University, in 1895. A year before the London conference, he had published *The Philadelphia Negro*, the earliest detailed, statistical, sociological study of an American community. Anyone with a respect for scholarship was, and is, bound to take his views seriously.

I'm not sure it would be useful to debate which of the many problems in the disaster-filled hundred years that followed Du Bois's observation should count as *the* problem of the twentieth century. But there's no denying that race, as Du Bois understood it, was central around the world in the moral and political life of that century. Du Bois was not remotely parochial in his interests or his analyses: and when he said that race was to be the problem of the twentieth century, he didn't just mean in his own country, and he didn't just mean his own race. He was talking, as he said, about "over half the world"; elsewhere in the address, he spoke not just of "the millions of black men in Africa, America and the Islands of the Sea," but of "the brown and yellow myriads elsewhere."[20] So Du Bois had very much in mind the ways in which race figured in the European colonial schemes that were reshaping Africa and

Asia as well as its role in the American social injustices he had experienced at first hand.

Indeed, European colonial conquest in Africa was still very much under way when he spoke to the delegates in London. In West Africa, the final British conquest of Kumasi, where I grew up, occurred just a few weeks after Du Bois's London conference; and the Sokoto caliphate, in northern Nigeria, was conquered only in 1903. In the North, Morocco became a French protectorate in 1912, Egypt a British one in 1914. To the east, Ethiopia remained independent until 1936 (and became so again a mere five years later). To the south, the Boer War was still in bloody progress when Du Bois spoke. In all of these African conflicts, notions of race played a crucial role; and after the Berlin Conference of 1884–85, which defined Europe's shared understanding of the terms of its African empires, the status of the subject peoples in the Belgian, British, French, German, Spanish, and Portuguese colonies of Africa—as well as in independent South Africa—was defined in racial terms.[21]

BLOODLINES

Du Bois was not alone in failing to anticipate that race would also play a disastrous role in the history of Europe itself in the mid-twentieth century; but, familiar as he was with German culture at the turn of the century, he was well aware that attitudes to the Jews and the Slavs there had resonances with the antiblack racism he knew from his homeland. Nevertheless, his German training left him touched by the anti-Semitism that was already on the rise during his student years. In 1893, a year after arriving in Berlin, he wrote,

It must be ever remembered that the great capitalists of Germany, the great leaders of industry are Jews; moreover, banded together by oppression in the past, they work for each other, and aided by the vast power of their wealth, and their great natural abilities, they have forced citadel after citadel, until now they practically control the stock-market, own the press, fill the bar and bench, are crowding the professions—indeed there seems to be no limit to the increase of their power. This of course is a menace to the newly nationalized country. . . .[22]

That "of course" would have received more than a murmur of assent in many places in Europe and the Americas. Du Bois was taking for granted here not just the standard grumblings of the enemies of German Jewry but also the idea that the German nation was the home to a German race, a race to which Germany's Jews, however assimilated, could not belong; and in thinking of nations in racial terms, he was following the theories whose rise I have been sketching. These notions persisted well into the twentieth century: during the Second World War, Winston Churchill's doctor wrote in his diaries, apropos of the prime minister's attitude to China: "Winston thinks only of the color of their skin; it is when he talks of India or China that you remember he is a Victorian."[23]

Despite his youthful parroting of anti-Jewish commonplaces, Du Bois was, for most of his adult life, a powerful critic of anti-Semitism along with other forms of racism. He visited Nazi Germany for six months in 1936—taking in a performance of Wagner's *Lohengrin* at Bayreuth—and when he returned he wrote frankly (in one of his country's leading black newspapers, the *Pittsburgh Courier*) that the "campaign of race prejudice . . . surpasses in vindictive cruelty and public insult anything I have ever seen; and I have seen much." And he went on, in distinct contrast to the tone of his 1893 report: "There has been no tragedy in modern times equal in its awful effects to the fight on the Jew in Germany. It is an attack on civilization comparable only to such horrors as the Spanish Inquisition and the African Slave trade."[24] This was more than five years before the creation of the first *Todeslager*, as the Nazis called the camps created specifically for the purposes of mass murder.

The Nazis did not invent modern racially motivated mass murder, though. The first genocide of the twentieth century began in the German colony of South West Africa, which is now Namibia. In 1904, General Lothar von Trotha issued what came to be known as his *Vernichtungsbefehl*—an extermination order—in which he told the Herero that if they did not abandon their lands, he would shoot "every Herero man, with or without weapons" and that he would "accept no more women and children," expelling them or allowing them, too, to be shot.[25] And, as the world now knows, the recurrent mass killings of Armenians in the Ottoman Empire rose to the level of genocide in the period of the First World War, as modern Turkey came into being. The Armenians might not have been one of Du Bois's races, but the Ottomans thought of them as a community of shared ancestry with more than religion and culture in common; one needs little more than this to be thinking in racial terms. As for the Rwandan genocide of 1994, the separation of the country's people into two races, Hutu and Tutsi (with a dash of Twa) was the product of Belgian colonial racial theory. All three were on the same side of the color line: but what Du Bois meant by the problem of the color line didn't have to be literally about color.

Against this somber background, it's worth reminding ourselves, then, that the 6 to 9 million Soviet citizens whose deaths were due to Stalin, or the even greater numbers of Chinese who succumbed in the Great Leap Forward, or the millions of victims of the murderous policies of Pol Pot in Cambodia, or the hundreds of thousands killed in India's partition or the anticommunist campaigns in Indonesia in the 1960s, were mostly the victims of hostilities based on ideology or religion, rather than anything like race.[26]

RACISM'S RANGE

Violence and murder were not the only political problems that Du Bois associated with the color line. Civic and economic inequality between races—whether produced by government policy, by private discrimination, or by the very complex interactions between the two of them—were pervasive features of states at the start of the twentieth century, and they remained so long after that first Pan-African conference was but a distant memory. All around the world, people know of the struggle of African-Americans and of South Africa's nonwhite population for racial equality; but political struggles over racial inequality have been central in the politics of Australia, New Zealand, and most of the other countries of the Americas, as well, whether the racial groups seeking justice were first peoples or the descendants of African slaves or South or East Asian indentured laborers. Over time, as non-Europeans, including many citizens of Europe's former empires in Asia and Africa, have migrated into Europe in increasing numbers, questions of racial inequality in rights, in education, in employment and housing, and in income and wealth have come to the fore there, too. Japanese and Chinese people were, in Du Bois's mind, on the same side of the color line as he was.

But the condescension (and worse) displayed toward China by many Japanese in the decades between the First Sino-Japanese War (1894–95) and World War II is naturally thought of as racial, too. The sheer viciousness of the murder and rape in the massacre in Nanking, capital of the Republic of China, in 1937–38, where tens and perhaps hundreds of thousands of people were killed by Japanese soldiers, is a paradigm of racist violence. The continued denial by many Japanese of the scale, or even the occurrence, of these atrocities mirrors the forms of denial of those who deny the mass murder of Armenians in Turkey or Jews in the Nazi genocide.

Less violent, but as racially grounded, are the anti-African attitudes reported by black visitors to China, who hear themselves described as *hēi guǐ* (black ghosts). Among the hundreds of thousands of Chinese now working in Africa, racial condescension of a sort familiar from the European colonial period is common (and, alas, anti-Chinese attacks have occurred in many African countries in recent years).[27] While these East Asian attitudes must have roots in earlier traditions of the sort of xenophobia that is found historically around the planet, they are no longer independent of racial attitudes that came from the traditions of Europe and North America. Racial discrimination and insult remain global phenomena.

Still, once more, it's worth insisting that ethnoracial inequality is not the only social inequality that matters. In 2013, the nearly 30 million white people below the poverty line in the United States made up slightly more than half the total number of America's poor.[28] Nor is racial discrimination the only significant form of discrimination. Ask the Christians of Somalia or Indonesia, Europe's Muslims, or Uganda's LGBTQ people. Ask women everywhere.

LOCALIZING RACE

Racial concepts work out in particular ways in particular places. In the United States, the social idea that anyone with one black parent was also black meant that a person could be socially black but have skin that was white, hair that was straight, eyes that were blue. As Walter White, the midcentury leader of the National Association for the Advancement of Colored People (a man whose name was one of his many ironical inheritances), wrote in his autobiography: "I am a Negro. My skin is white, my eyes are blue, my hair is blond. The traits of my race are nowhere visible upon me." (In "The Ballad of Walter White," the African-American poet Langston Hughes put it more succinctly: "Now Walter White / Is mighty light.")[29]

In the colonial context, race thinking produced anomalies, too. Treating all Africans in Nigeria, say, as Negroes would combine people with very different biological traits. Rates of multiple births are much higher among Yoruba than among Hausa women, to take a random example, never mind the considerable cultural differences between the two groups.[30] If there were interesting traits of national character, they belonged not to races but to ethnic groups: and people of one ethnic group—Arabs from Morocco to Oman; Jews in the diaspora—could come in a wide range of colors and hair types.

I mentioned that some scholars have sought to reintroduce a biological race concept in recent years, using sophisticated statistical techniques that uncover patterns among individual genotypes that reflect shared ancestry. But none of these arguments would support the claim that the boundaries of the social groups we call races are drawn by biological rather than social means.[31] Discussions of the social significance of race, then, need not be distracted by arguments about whether the groups in question are biological. Members of a socially constructed group can differ statistically in biological characteristics from one another (as rural folk in the United States differ in some health measures from urban people); and whether we should treat someone differently in virtue of the statistical characteristics of a group to which she belongs is always a separate question from whether such group differences exist. As a result, when questions arise about the salience of race in political life, it is seldom a good idea, as Du Bois was one of the first to argue, to turn to questions of biology.

You might think that, because racial difference is not biological, it must be more malleable; but this is a mistake. Whether a biological difference is malleable depends on its nature: skin color, as we all know, can be affected by exposure to the sun; the appearance of hair can be chemically manipulated; differences in susceptibility to disease can be eradicated by vaccination; noses can be altered by surgery. Conversely, as we have learned in the United States, racial disparities in wealth and in many other measures can persist long after the government has given up trying to impose them. In 2009, the median wealth of American white households was twenty times that of black households, almost half a century after the 1965 Voting Rights Act.[32] The recognition that these differences are produced by social processes has not made it any less difficult to alter them.

COLOR INSIDE THE LINES

In the twenty-first century, one might have hoped to see signs that race thinking and the hostilities grounded in race—the problem of the color line—might be vanishing. Yet belief in an essential difference between Us and Them persists widely and continues to be thought by many to be inherited. And, of course, differences among groups defined by common descent can be the basis of social identity whether or not they are believed to be based in biology. As a result, ethnoracial categories continue to be important in politics at the national level, and racial identities shape people's political affiliations.

Once ethnoracial groups are in place, inequalities between them, whatever their causes, provide bases for political mobilization. Many people now know that we are all, in fact, one species, and think that racial differences are, from a biological point of view, illusory; but that seldom undermines the significance for them of racial identities and affiliations. Around the world, people have sought and won affirmative action for their ethnoracial groups. In the United States, in part because of affirmative action, public opinion polls consistently show wide divergences on many questions along racial lines.[33] On American campuses where the claim that "race is a social construct" echoes like a mantra, Asian, black, and white identities continue to shape social experience. Conversely (in part, I suspect, because essentialism is so natural to us), many people around the world simply couldn't be persuaded that race, as we experience it in social life, is a "construct."

When I think about why the racial fixation has proved so durable, I sometimes recall the lost-wax method by which goldweights in Ghana are cast. (You create a wax model, surround it with clay, and melt the wax away by pouring in molten brass.) In this case, the nineteenth-century race concept is the lost wax: the substance may have melted away, but we've intently filled the space it created. In the United States, nativists aim to define the country in terms of color and creed (namely, white and Christian). On the other side of the color line, the persistence of material inequality gives a mission to racial identities, for how can we discuss inequities based on color without reference to groups defined by color?

One reason race continues to play a central role in international politics, as well, is the politics of racial solidarity that Du Bois helped to inaugurate in the black world, in cofounding the tradition of Pan-Africanism. It shows up in diverse ways: African-Americans are more likely than whites to be interested in U.S. foreign policy in Africa; people in Port Harcourt, Nigeria, protested the 2014 killing of Michael Brown by a white police officer in Ferguson, Missouri; black Americans have a special access to Ghanaian passports; Rastafarianism in the Caribbean celebrates Africa as the home of black people; and heritage tourism from North and South America and the Caribbean to West Africa has boomed.[34]

But Pan-Africanism is not the only movement in which groups defined by common ancestry show transnational solidarity: many Jews show an interest in Israeli politics; Chinese follow the fates of Chinese in their diaspora; Japanese follow goings-on in São Paulo, home to more than a million people of Japanese descent—and to perhaps a million people of Arab descent (largely Lebanese), some of whom follow events in the Middle East.[35] Identities rooted in the reality or the fantasy of shared ancestry remain central in our politics, both within and between nations. In this new century, as in the last, the color line and its cousins are still going strong. Race, you might say, has become a palimpsest, a parchment written upon by successive generations where nothing is ever *entirely* erased. Often with the most benevolent of intentions, and sometimes with the least, we keep tracing the same contours with different pens.

GOING HOME

At some point, Amo Afer put aside his own pen. Reaching middle age, he decided that it was time to go home, and, in 1747 he made his way back to the Gold Coast, to the Nzema villages of his birth. It was a bold move. Someone who had been raised in the heartland of the European Enlightenment and had built a scholarly career in some of the most prestigious seats of European learning was now turning his back on the grand experiment he embodied and resolving to make a life in a land he'd last glimpsed as a small child.

We can only guess why. There is some suggestion that increasing color prejudice in this period in Germany—the early stirrings of Europe's racial fixation—may have caused discomfort: a satirical play was performed in Halle in 1747 in which Astrine, a young German woman, refuses the amorous advances of an African philosophy teacher from Jena named Amo. "My soul," Astrine insists, "certainly cannot ever love a Moor."[36] The work demonstrates that Amo was a famous figure in Halle. But the rejection of the Moor is Astrine's, not the author's; and some conjecture that what drove Amo off was not racial prejudice but a broken heart.

We know a little more of what happened to him. A Dutch ship's doctor met him in the mid-1750s at Axim. "His father and a sister were still alive and lived four days' journey inland," the doctor reported.

He also reported that Amo, whom he described as "a great sage," had "acquired the reputation of a soothsayer."[37] Both sage and soothsayer: This is someone who knew that the deliverances of the Enlightenment were no less his own than those of his Nzema ancestors.

Sometime later, Amo moved from Axim and went to live in Fort St. Sebastian, one of a couple of dozen forts and castles on the coast of Ghana that served the slave trade, near the town of Shama, where he is buried. (It's a mere dozen miles from where, a century and a half later, Kwame Nkrumah, the world's best-known Nzema, was born.) Today, we're left with questions: What did the soothsayer tell people he had learned from his long sojourn in the north? And how did he explain his decision to leave behind everything he had built there? It's impossible not to wonder whether his was a flight from color consciousness, a retreat to a place where he would not be defined by his complexion. A place where Amo Afer could be just Amo again; where he didn't need to be *the* African. Indeed, his odyssey asks us to imagine what he seems to have yearned for: a world free of racial fixations. It asks if we could ever create a world where color is merely a fact, not a feature and not a fate. It asks if we might not be better off if we managed to give up our racial typologies, abandoning a mistaken way of thinking that took off at just about the moment when Anton Wilhelm Amo was a well-known German philosopher at the height of his intellectual powers.

FIVE

CLASS

Butlers of my father's generation, I would say, tended to see the world in terms of a ladder—the houses of royalty, dukes and the lords from the oldest families placed at the top, those of "new money" lower down and so on, until one reached a point below which the hierarchy was determined simply by wealth—or the lack of it.

Kazuo Ishiguro, *The Remains of the Day*
(1989)

YOUNGSTER

Michael Dunlop Young was fourteen when he arrived at the institution that set the course of his life. It was called Dartington Hall. Dartington was the brainchild of Leonard and Dorothy Elmhirst, who were among the most influential twentieth-century philanthropists in Britain. Both despised meanness and mercantilism, and sought to change society by changing souls. The experimental boarding school Young attended was embedded in the Utopian community they were building on a large estate in Devon, the picturesque county in England's far South West.

Dartington was no ordinary experiment, in part because the Elmhirsts were no ordinary couple. Leonard, born into a rather straitened branch of the Yorkshire gentry, was educated at Trinity College, Cambridge, and at Cornell, in upstate New York, and became the secretary of Rabindranath Tagore, the Indian Nobel laureate in literature, who had himself grown up in a Utopian community in Bengal. Dorothy was the daughter of William Collins Whitney, an American financier and public servant (he had been secretary of the navy under President Grover Cleveland), and a member of one of the few American families who could confidently claim to belong to an established upper class. One Pilgrim ancestor was the governor of the Plymouth Bay Colony, in the seventeenth century, and the Whitneys had husbanded their position in the social and financial elite for generations. Dorothy's father was, some said, the model for Henry James's Adam Verver in *The Golden Bowl*; like Verver, he was not just astonishingly affluent (he left behind an estate valued, in today's terms, at some $600 million), but attractive, amusing, and astute. Dorothy, for her part, was staunch in her Progressive Era allegiances; she helped create and fund the New School for Social Research in New York and the *New Republic* magazine, which, in the First World War and for generations to come, embodied American liberalism.

Their patronage extended to the architecture at Dartington. Oswald Milne, who had designed the interior at Claridge's Hotel in London, was the architect of the neo-Georgian main school building; William Adams Delano, the architect who supervised the addition of a balcony to the South Portico of the White House, designed a new nursery school; Walter Gropius brought his Bauhaus thinking to the conversion of the theater; and the eminent Swiss modernist William Lescaze designed High Cross Hill, the headmaster's house, which was described unflatteringly, in *Country Life,* as "probably the most extreme instance in England of the functional type of house associated with the name of Corbusier."[1] With their connections and their vision, the Elmhirsts recruited children from a progressive elite: Bertrand Russell sent his daughter Kate there in the early 1930s; his friend the philosopher G. E. Moore and the writers Aldous Huxley and Sean O'Casey followed suit. Freud's grandsons, Lucian and Clement, both spent time there as well.

And who was Michael Young? He was born in England—a year into the First World War, in a village near Manchester—but not to English parents. His father, Gibson, had arrived in England from Australia as a young man to study the violin at the Royal Manchester College of Music. And the reason his family could afford to send him there was that Gibson's grandfather had cashed in a gold nugget he dug up in the midcentury Australian gold rush to found the *Bendigo Advertiser,* in a small town a few hours north of Melbourne. Michael's mother, Edith, was the daughter of an Irishwoman, Louisa Fitzpatrick, and a Scotsman, Daniel Dunlop, a successful businessman and an apostle of the Austrian Theosophist Rudolf Steiner. The time Michael's Celtic grandparents spent in Dublin explains why Daniel Dunlop, like Italo Svevo, left an impression on James Joyce, and receives a mention in *Ulysses*, where he's included in a list with other important figures in Theosophy.[2]

In 1917, two years after he was born, Michael's mother and father moved to Australia, in an attempt to resuscitate their marriage. (She had taken a Russian lover, and the aim was to escape him by leaving England.) Gibson returned to England alone a couple of years later, and his wife and son followed in 1925; by then the marriage was dead. Edith Young became a novelist, living in London's bohemia; Gibson never managed to make much of a living as a violinist, but he went on to have a career as a choral conductor, and then became a music critic for the tabloid newspaper the *Daily Express*, before returning to Australia to be musical director of the Australian Broadcasting Commission.

Young's somewhat nomadic education began in state schools, in Australia and in England, and then (despite the fact that his parents were both socialists) at a couple of private prep schools in Bristol and in Cockfosters, a London suburb, where he felt harried by rules and spankings. The school at Dartington was suggested by his father's sister, Florence, who later married the principal of an illustrious West African school. (It was Prince of Wales College, Achimota, which had to defend its title as the best school in the Gold Coast against Mfantsipim, the school my father went to.) The boy's family connected him, then, to the wide world of the British Empire in the early twentieth century.

Dartington gave Michael both the habitus and the social capital (crudely, the connections) with which to proceed. He flourished at the new school, and the Elmhirsts took him into their family, encouraging and supporting him for the rest of their lives. Since she already had a son called Michael, Dorothy called him Michael Youngster. Through the Elmhirsts, Michael Young was introduced to a transnational elite, staying at the White House with President Franklin D. Roosevelt in

1933, and offering him advice about Cuba; listening in on a conversation between Leonard and Henry Ford, as they crossed the Atlantic together on an ocean liner; meeting, through the network of the rich and powerful who circulated through Dartington, the movers and shakers of a progressive British elite.

Michael Young became one of the central figures in the development of sociology in Britain, and he spent much of his life exploring the role of class in the country in which he was born. He was a prodigious builder of institutions and a promulgator of ideas and arguments, among the architects of the postwar British welfare state. "Remember," Leonard Elmhirst later wrote to him, "that the social sciences is only another term for political dynamite, because psychology and economics must drive right at the heart of human affairs."[3] In his life's pursuits, Young had a wide range of personal experience on which to draw. His parents never had much money (when they first separated, there was talk of giving Michael up for adoption), and, with the exception of the occasional school fees, he couldn't expect much from his more prosperous grandparents. He grew up, then, on the poorer fringes of the solid middle class. But Dartington put him in touch with a world of wealth and power that more than made up for these modest beginnings.[4]

Young, who pioneered the modern scientific exploration of the social lives of the English working class, didn't just aim to study class; he sought to ameliorate the damage he believed it could do. The Dartington ideal was about the cultivation of personality and aptitudes whatever form they took, and if British class structures impeded this ideal, he sought to take measures against them. What would supplant those structures, and the old, caste-like system of social hierarchy? For many today, the answer is "meritocracy"—a term that Young himself coined back in the 1950s. Meritocracy represents a vision where power and privilege would be allocated by individual merit, not by our social origins.

Under the sway of the meritocratic ideal, many people, these days, are committed to a picture of how the hierarchies of money and status in our world should be organized. They are against (of course!) the old ways of allocating status through birth; and think that jobs should go not to people who have connections but to the best qualified, regardless of class . . . or, for that matter, race, ethnicity, gender, sexual orientation, or a whole host of other irrelevant identities. Occasionally, they'll allow for exceptions: for positive discrimination, say, to help undo the effects of previous discrimination. But such exceptions, being motivated by the desire to undo earlier breaches of the rule, are provisional: when the bigotries of sex, race, class, and caste are gone, the exceptions will cease to be warranted. They reject the old class society. Their thoughts about class define what they think is right against a picture of the bad old days.

In my chapters on creed and country, I've pointed out that we have a tendency to exaggerate the continuities of such entities over time. When it comes to class, I'm going to argue the opposite—that the continuities here are far greater than we often think. In moving toward the meritocratic ideal, we imagined that we'd moved beyond the old encrustations of inherited hierarchies. As Michael Young knew, that's not the real story.

CLASS DISMISSED?

At the start of this book, I set out three conceptual features that identities share. The first was a set of labels and the rules for ascribing them to people. The second: the label had meaning for those who bear it, so that it sometimes shaped their behavior and their feelings, in ways they might or might not be aware of. And the third: the label had significance for the way its bearers were treated by others. (That's why identity has both a subjective and an objective dimension.) In all three domains—labeling, norms, treatment—there can be contest and contention, and this fact will be obvious in the case of class. I'm going to explore difficulties in each of these domains: difficulties about labeling, about what class means to its bearers, and about how we treat the various classes we label and so recognize. Along the way, I'm going to take part in some of the contest and contention about class.

First, then: what do we write on those labels and how do we ascribe them? What are we talking about when we're talking about class? There's no widely accepted answer. The very idea of class can seem recent, historically speaking. In England, the term gained wide currency only in the nineteenth century, as conservatives reacted to the upheavals of the French Revolution. But tracking a concept by tracking a term can invite confusion. And something like this concept is age-old. The ancient Greeks and Romans were certainly aware of social hierarchies. Feudal Europe saw itself as divided into the "estates of the realm"—although there were different ideas of how many estates there were and where to draw the lines. The clergy and the nobility usually counted for two; the peasants, merchants, and shopkeepers could be lumped together or split up in various ways.

Modern theories of class start with Karl Marx's mid-nineteenth-century writings, and in his highly stylized picture of the British economy in the early days of industrial capitalism, he described two main classes, defined by their "relations to the means of production." There were the capitalists, who owned the factories; and the workers, who earned wages for making things. Marx called the capitalist class the bourgeoisie, taking up a word that had once referred to the shopkeepers and artisans who lived in towns (*les bourgs*, in French). The workers he called the proletariat. And part of his point, which showed up in the nineteenth-century rise of the working men's associations and then of labor unions, was that these classes were identities: they had normative significance for the people who were in them. People *thought* of themselves as and *acted* as members of the working class; they displayed class solidarity, they took pride in the achievements of their kind. Class as identity is implicit in Marx's notion that the proletariat could be both the "object" and the "subject" of history, both the acted-upon and the self-aware actor. E. P. Thompson, a historian in this Marxian tradition, pressed this idea further in his classic *The Making of the English Working Class*, when he wrote, "The working class made itself as much as it was made." Less epigrammatically: "Class happens" when shared experience leads some men "to feel and articulate the identity of their interests . . . as against other men." In this case, those others were "their rulers and employers."[5]

Needless to say, the basic two-way division of Marxian thought left out large numbers of people. There was still the old aristocracy, the nobility. There were small farmers, landowners, and peasants, in the countryside. There were landlords earning rent, and professionals, like barbers, lawyers, doctors, and nurses. Then there was what Marx called the petty bourgeoisie, the shopkeepers and others who ran small businesses, providing goods and services. There were also civil servants of all levels, academics, soldiers, police officers, domestic servants, and the managers, who supervised the proletariat at work. Marx was born to a middle-class German Jewish family in Prussia. Both his grandfathers were rabbis; his father was a successful lawyer, who owned a vineyard, a member of the prosperous middle classes. Where did Marx himself fit in?

Writing a couple of generations later, the German sociologist Max Weber (himself the child of a rather prominent Berlin-based politician) pointed toward a richer conception. Not in his specific treatment of "class," which he defined narrowly, as a purely objective, economic fact about people, but in his larger account of social stratification. That account encompassed, as well, the idea of a status group (a *Stand*) that involved "positive or negative estimations of honor"; and a third concept, which he called party, that reflected your relation to power, and so your ability to achieve your goals. Critically, he saw these three categories as entwined. Wealth had a complex relation to status distinctions; and power, too, could confer status, and be secured by wealth. He saw that "status honor is normally expressed by the fact that above all else a specific style of life can be expected from all those who wish to belong to the circle." (Weber had a strong sense of honor himself; he once challenged an academic antagonist of his wife's—she was also a social theorist—to a duel.)[6]

What evolved from this account was a concept of class that draws from each of Weber's three buckets. We don't think you can specify someone's class from his or her tax return. A Jesuit cardinal's vow of poverty doesn't mean he must live like the poor, nor does it consign him to a lower class. A penniless graduate student is differently situated from the janitor of his dormitory. And, of course, the literature of the nineteenth century is full of poor relations, like Charlotte Brontë's Jane Eyre or Jane Austen's Dashwood girls, who need a job or a husband or a patron to support them, but have a claim to "gentle birth." Conversely, being in possession of a fortune doesn't make you upper class. In *Doctor Thorne*, one of his Barsetshire novels, Anthony Trollope wrote about a character, Sir Roger Scatcherd, who is rich, titled, and the owner of a grand estate. Upper class? Not by his accounting or anybody else's: he's an ex-convict and stonemason who made his fortune, and procured his title, by his feats as a railway contractor. So why not say that class is simply a matter of status? That would be tempting, but the economic dimension here is anything but incidental or contingent, and not every form of status relates to class status. (The elite members of a football team have an advantage in honor, as well as in earnings, over its benchwarmers, but class isn't the right way to describe the arrangement.) Heritability is part of the picture; so is the prospect of upward or downward mobility. The connection between class and wealth, though complex, is indissoluble.

You can start to see why class became the four-color-map problem of the social sciences. The more variables we try to account for, the harder it is to solve. Indeed, given the uncertainties about precisely how class identities might be defined or demarcated, a number of sociologists have, over the decades, sought to banish the term—to abolish "class," if not class. But, like Svevo's character Zeno, who is constantly trying, and failing, to give up smoking, we haven't quite bridged the vow to the deed. In the postwar era, social scientists have widely adopted the term "socioeconomic status" to designate what's ordinarily meant by class, but they have merely tucked away the perplexities into the "socio" part, like a child hiding her spinach in a napkin.

The mortifying truth is that, by whatever designation, social hierarchy is so baked into our culture and history that even our everyday terms of praise and censure are rooted in it, as the eminent literary critic (and Svevo biographer) P. N. Furbank has observed.[7] The term "honest" is linked to the term "honor," and *honestus* once designated a social cohort, Romans of "high birth." When Horace wrote, in the first poem of Book Three of his *Odes*, that a candidate for office was *generosior*, he meant that the man was of a better family; our word "generous" derives from the Latin. *Gentil* meant "highborn" in medieval French, from whence it came into English. (Recall Chaucer's Prologue to the *Canterbury Tales*, and the "verray, parfit, gentil knight.") "Courteous" meant having the manners of the court. "Boor" comes from the Old French *bovier*, which means a cowherd, from the genitive, *bovis*, of *bos* in Latin, which means an ox or a cow. In the Middle Ages, a churl, from which "churlish" descends, was a person of "low birth," as was a *vilain*, in Norman French, which came from the Latin *villa*, a country house, and hence referred to someone who worked there, a farmhand. By the early fourteenth century, "mean," which came from a German root meaning "common, shared by all," had come to refer to people who were, as Dr. Johnson's dictionary put it, "of low rank." We see this connection in the lines of Marvell's 1650 "Horatian Ode upon Cromwell's Return from Ireland," where he says about Charles I at his execution: "He nothing common did or mean / Upon that memorable scene. . . ." Class is at once elusive and inescapable.

SHOULDERS BARED

Nor, of course, are class systems peculiar to Europe. In Kumasi, in Ghana, we lived just down the hill from the palace of the King of Asante, or, in Twi, the Asantehene. When I was a child, Otumfuo Sir Osei Agyeman Prempeh II lived up at Manhyia, as his residence is known. One of Prempeh's wives was my grandfather's sister: and so my grandfather was brother-in-law to the king, and some of my father's cousins were *ahenemma*, princes and princesses.

On many a Sunday in my childhood, after church, my mother, my sister, and I would be driven up to the palace, where we sat on a veranda in the leafy shade of the hanging plants that kept it cool, waiting quietly for an audience with my great-uncle. He would appear from the interior of the house, impeccably swathed in his kente—the silken toga worn on special occasions by the Asante elite—and we would rise to greet him and wait until he was seated to sit down ourselves again. He and my mother would chat for a few minutes, while we children drank sodas served by his steward, displaying, as we had promised, our very best manners. Prempeh II had the charisma of years of rule about him; he seemed to me at once both genial and awe-inspiring, connecting our modern world to a storied past. It did not occur to me until much later how rare a privilege these regular private audiences might have been.

When I was about sixteen, Prempeh II went, as we say obliquely, "to his village," the fourteenth Asantehene to go to sleep with his ancestors. He was succeeded by a man I had known all my life as Uncle Matthew, the husband of my aunt Victoria, my father's favorite "sister," and someone whose children were the closest of my Asante kin.[8] When I was a child, I could take his hand as we walked around the house; now he was invested with majesty, and I was bound to uncover my shoulder in his presence, and remove my shoes, as signs of respect. Otumfuo Opoku Ware II, as he became known, lived in the much larger palace he built next door to the building where we had sat with his predecessor, returning Manhyia to a grandeur that had not been on display since the British destroyed the old palace at the end of the Anglo-Asante Wars.

Because my father was the head of their family—remember, we are matrilineal and their mother was his sister—my father oversaw the educations of these royal children, discussed their school reports with them, and played a large role in their lives. And we grew up together. Belonging to the royal family was about blood, ancestry, and honor, not so much about wealth—at least not obviously.[9] There were cousins aplenty who were not especially rich, living in modest homes, sleeping two or three or four to a room; but who (like the scrimping, landless relations of English aristocrats) knew how to comport themselves in grand circles. In the later nineteenth century, in Asante as in Britain, a military aristocracy and a court aristocracy were joined by men and women whose wealth came from trade rather than land and the command of people; they were called *asikafoo*, gold people, money men. But the true aristocracy consisted of the royal family and the paramount chiefs, who had long-remembered lineages, titles, *and* the land that came with them.

Where there is nobility, alas, there is always its opposite—those stigmatized, rather than exalted, by their origins. Once, when I was a child, I asked my father in a room full of people how we were related to a woman whom I knew and liked, and who lived in one of the family houses. I thought of her, in fact, as one of my multitudinous "aunts." My father brushed the question aside crossly. Only later, when we were alone, did he explain that you should never inquire after people's ancestry in public. She was, as every adult in the family knew, the descendant of a family slave, and this meant that she was of lower status than the rest of us. As children, we were required to be courteous to all adults, even those of lower status. But that didn't mean they weren't inferior. I am not here reporting my father's thoughts or mine about this woman's status. My father was trying to avoid embarrassing her; he almost certainly did not think her ancestry an embarrassment himself. But she was often treated by people I knew in ways that reflected a conception of her as having an inferior status. And I suspect that the most important truth here is that this is how she thought of herself. She believed that she was somewhere below a world of superior others. Accepting the class system has meant seeing such forms of self-deprecation as natural.

Privilege could bring the power to injure subordinates in more active ways than mere contempt. In nineteenth-century Kumasi, social rank was visible in the differing penalties exacted for adultery. If you got involved with one of the wives of the Asantehene, the king, you could expect an agonizing, drawn-out death. If a high-status man interfered with a commoner's wife, by contrast, a less-than-burdensome fine would suffice.[10] Gender and class come together in familiar ways here, even though this was a society where royal women had enormous power and authority, and women who were not royal could amass great fortunes through trade. But the basic point holds: the upper classes had enormous social privilege that gave them power over the lives of others.

A similar dynamic involving upper-class privilege in England in the same period is illustrated in a story I once found in the diary of Frances, Lady Shelley. She recounted a day in 1819 that her husband spent hunting birds with the Duke of Wellington, who, as it happens, was not much of a shot. After "wounding a retriever" and "peppering" a gamekeeper's shoes, Wellington ended a catalogue of mishaps by shooting an old woman, who had been unwise enough to do her washing by the open window of her cottage on the estate. "I'm wounded, Milady," the woman screamed. "My good woman," Lady Shelley replied, "this ought to be the proudest moment of your life. You have had the distinction of being shot by the great Duke of Wellington!"[11]

THE AMERICAN WAY

Many Americans, like most English people, have a hobbyist's knowledge of the old British class order from watching shows like *Downton Abbey* on television. But in America, it is regarded as quaint and even alien, like a *National Geographic* documentary about an unfamiliar tribe; as strange, in some respects, as the world of the Asante court. From the very beginning, the United States repudiated the very idea of a titled aristocracy. The first article of the American Constitution declares forthrightly: "No title of nobility shall be granted by the United States." Here in America our only titles are the democratic Mr., Mrs., and Ms., the academic Professor, the professional Doctor, and the official Your Honor, Senator, and Congressman and Congresswoman. (When John Adams proposed in the Senate that the president of the United States should be called "Highness," Thomas Jefferson wrote to James Madison that this was "the most superlatively ridiculous thing I ever heard of." Presidents have been plain Mr. President ever since.) A courteous stranger is likely to address you as "Sir" or "Ma'am," in the spirit of recognizing the equal standing of all people. Thomas Paine, one of the American Revolution's great theorists, had written that what he called "pompous titles conferred on unworthy men . . . over-awe the superstitious vulgar, and forbid them to inquire into the character of the possessor."[12]

But his reference to "the superstitious vulgar" underlines the fact that the American Founders' hostility to the moral corruption associated with hereditary titles did not reflect a rejection of class distinctions. In the early republic, the new political elite was actually full of men concerned to preserve their status as gentlemen, for example, by giving and accepting challenges to duels. Alexander Hamilton, the country's first secretary of the treasury and creator of its national

banking system, died, famously, in a duel with Vice President Aaron
Burr; he had dueled nearly a dozen times before. Dueling, an affair
of honor, was a practice limited, by definition, to gentlemen. Indeed,
part of Hamilton's reason for accepting the challenge may have been
his insecurity, as the illegitimate son of a Scottish immigrant to the
Caribbean, about his own status. Rejecting titles certainly did not
mean abandoning the idea of honor, or the notion that some people
were born into it. One of the best books on the political culture of the
early American republic is entitled *Affairs of Honor*.[13]

In America, as in England, at the start of the nineteenth century
there were gentlemen and ladies, on the one hand, and the lower
orders, on the other. In fact, many people in the early republic were
assigned to lower places in various hierarchies by their birth. As
Thomas Jefferson wrote in an 1816 letter to his fellow Virginian
Samuel Kercheval, in a pure democracy some people would "yet be
excluded from their deliberations, 1, infants, until arrived at years
of discretion. 2. Women, who, to prevent depravation of morals and
ambiguity of issue, could not mix promiscuously in the public meetings of men. 3. Slaves, from whom the unfortunate state of things
with us takes away the right of will and of property."[14] As a matter of
law, then, slaves and women were denied the franchise; but the supposedly democratic U.S. Constitution did not guarantee the vote to
all white men, either. Many were denied the vote because they could
not meet property requirements (which were also in place for voters
in England until 1918) or because they could not afford to pay the poll
tax. The effect of these rules was to enhance the political power of the
well-off. The franchise in national elections was extended to blacks
after the Civil War and to women in 1920; using the poll tax to deny
the vote was barred only in 1964.[15]

Still, wealth was more evenly distributed in America in the nineteenth century than it was in Europe, as Alexis de Tocqueville noted,
and much of the wealth was held by people who had acquired it themselves. "Wealth," he wrote, "circulates there with incredible rapidity,

and experience teaches that it is rare to see two generations reap the rewards of wealth." The result, among what he called the Anglo-Americans (i.e., the white population), was that social relations were more equal than in the societies of the Old World. Democracy, for Tocqueville, was, as much as anything else, a condition of society in which men addressed each other as equals. It was only indirectly a matter of the franchise. As he observed in *Democracy in America*, "What is most important for democracy, is not that there are no great fortunes; it is that great fortunes do not rest in the same hands. In this way, there are the rich, but they do not form a class."[16]

That wasn't necessarily the experience from inside. The instability of the class structure, not its nonexistence, may have been a lever of the country's political history. When America started to become a manufacturing center, a few decades into the nineteenth century, the scions of well-established Northern families began to feel socially and politically displaced. They had been raised to be a ruling elite, the American historian David Herbert Donald has argued, but found no followers; power was shifting from the agricultural world to an emerging business world, where "too gentle an education, too nice a morality were handicaps." And so this cohort, who came of age in the 1830s, became reformers—something Donald sees as an effort to reclaim their lost social dominance. "Some fought for prison reform; some for women's rights; some for world peace; but ultimately most came to make that natural identification between moneyed aristocracy, textile manufacturing, and Southern slave-grown cotton," he argues. "An attack on slavery was their best, if quite unconscious, attack upon the new industrial system. . . . Reform gave meaning to the lives of this displaced social elite."[17] A class-based analysis of motives is seldom flattering; but these moral ideals gained genuine traction. They kept alive the picture of a politics of equals that some took to be implicit in the American republic.

Which isn't to say such a politics was actually achieved. And if a politics of equals was elusive, so was the ideal of a society of equals.

Race complicates and divides everything in America, but among whites, as among blacks, there were hierarchies of status associated with distinctions of habitus between those who came from uneducated families in which men and women worked with their hands and those who came from educated families and did not earn a living from manual labor. An American sociologist, writing in the early 1970s, discusses a Boston pipefitter who makes twice as much as the schoolteacher next door: "when they meet, the pipe fitter calls the schoolteacher 'Mister' and is called in turn by his first name."[18] (I fear this reverence for teachers may have since diminished.)

With the massive increase in college education after the Second World War, which came earlier for whites than for blacks, and the growth of occupations for which a college education was—or, at any rate, was regarded as—necessary, a substantial divide grew up between those whose formal education ended with high school and those who went on. For a period, that divide was increasingly a matter of individual income and style of life, and less likely to be decided by the family from which you came. You can think of this, with some justice, as the democratization of opportunity. But don't for a moment imagine that it meant the erasure of hierarchy.

RECIPROCATIONS

To speak of the upper classes or of the lower classes is to invoke a system in which the latter are supposed to owe a kind of social deference to the former; and to speak of the middle classes is to imagine them as placed between these two, looking down, like the upper classes, toward the lower; looking up, like the lower classes, toward the upper. A class system inevitably involves elements of hierarchy, in which relations among classes are asymmetrical. This does not mean that people higher up the hierarchy are free to treat those below in any way they like: there are forms of respect that, so to speak, look downward as well as upward. But in general, there will be a pattern in which those in the higher ranks of a system of status—those with higher standing—receive deference from those of lower status, and can expect their needs and interests to receive more weight as well.

Speaking of a *system* here is going to be a bit misleading, though. Not everyone will accept the hierarchy that is presupposed by others. As I said at the start of this book, labels are contested and so is the normative significance of having them. People at one place in the hierarchy will often have a very different view of what matters from those supposedly much higher up or lower down.

In a 1957 study, *Family and Kinship in East London,* which Michael Young published with Peter Willmott (cofounder with him of the Institute for Community Studies), working-class families in Bethnal Green, in London's East End, expressed complicated attitudes toward white-collar workers. On the one hand, when discussing their children, they would say things like, "I don't want him to be in manual work. I'd sooner he worked with his brains than his hands." But their comments could have a sting in their tail: "I'd like him to take up chemistry. It's completely unproductive and therefore well paid." And many of them had a view of the relative prestige of various occupations that would have astonished (and appalled) most people in the classes officially above them. Young and Willmott write:

> A sizeable minority of men in Bethnal Green take a very different view from white-collar people about the status of manual work, placing jobs such as company director and chartered accountant towards the bottom of the scale and manual jobs, like agricultural labourer, coal miner and bricklayer towards the top. These men regard business managers with disfavour because "They're not doing anything. They get their money for walking around," and, as for civil servants—"I could find other

ways of using my money." Agricultural labourers, on the other hand, they value highly because "you can't do without grub"; coal-miners because "without coal, industry stops"; and brick-layers because "you've got to have food and after that you've got to have houses."

Still, a majority of them accepted the truth that the economic pros-pects of their children would be better if they escaped the standard state schools and got themselves into "a grammar or technical school, anything other than what one woman called the 'ordinary.' "[19] They could mock the hierarchy, espousing values that were at odds with those of the classes "above" them, but they couldn't pretend the peck-ing order didn't exist.

That's because one of the central human goods is respect: both self-respect and the respect of others. Respect, at its most general, involves a positive attitude to a person, which is elicited by something about them—that's why we speak of "due respect." Understanding a society's codes entails grasping what kinds of facts about people are seen to entitle them to this positive attitude and to the correspond-ing forms of "respectful" treatment. In social life, one central form of respect is the deference that we grant people whose identities give them a higher social standing than ours: and this deference is at the heart of systems of social class like those I've known in Asante, in England, and in the United States. Class involves a system of status and rights to respect associated with the family you were born into. Because honor is fundamentally a matter of socially ascribed rights to respect, class, in its earliest forms, was critically about the distribu-tion of honor as a birthright.[20] As the distribution of honor becomes less associated with birth, as opposed to personal achievement, we may imagine that we have left class behind, or else transformed it beyond recognition. Have we?

Consider what, in the eighteenth century, was called "condescen-sion." It occurred when a person of higher status generously treated a person of lower status in a way that presupposed that they were equals. ("Voluntary submission to equality with inferiors," was Samuel Johnson's definition.) It was a kindness and, when it worked, it pleased the beneficiary as much is it gratified the self-regard of the benefactor. The phenomenon reminds us that ladies and gentlemen were enmeshed in networks of reciprocal attitudes not just to each other but also to those they regarded as their inferiors.

In Fanny Burney's 1778 epistolary novel *Evelina*, we're told that a well-born character

> thinks it incumbent upon her to support the dignity of her ancestry. Fortunately for the world in general, she has taken it into her head, that condescension is the most distinguishing virtue of high life; so that the same pride of family which renders others imperious, is with her the motive of affability.

You might suppose that nothing so clearly marks a rupture between that age and our own than this discarded notion that condescension is virtuous.

By the time Jane Austen was writing, the term could already prompt discomfort or derision. When Mr. Collins, in *Pride and Prejudice*, published in 1813, extolls the "affability and condescension" of Lady Catherine, readers were thereby reminded that this clergyman was at once snobbish and obsequious. The intellectual historian Don Herzog tells of an encounter between the Duke of Devonshire and John Payne Collier, his librarian, in the early 1830s. The duke brought the librarian lunch in the library at Chatsworth, his home, which remains one of the most magnificent country houses in England. In his diary, Mr. Collier wrote:

> He always does his utmost to lessen the distance between us, and to put me at my ease, on a level with himself . . . I do not call it condescension (he will not permit the word), but kindness,

and I should be most ungrateful not to make all the return in my power.[21]

In denying that he was condescending to Collier, the duke was treating him in a way that presupposed they were equals. Since neither Collier nor the duke really believed that, the denial was itself a form of higher-level condescension. You could condescend by pretending not to.

In our more democratic age, we cannot admit to condescending; nor can we confess the pleasure we feel in the condescension of our betters. We cannot own up to these sentiments because we dare not admit that we think we *are* better than others, let alone that anyone is better than us. Give up the assumption that the Duke of Devonshire is his librarian's superior—an assumption that entailed condescension whenever His Grace treated Collier as an equal—and you can no longer conceive of such condescension as a gift. Nowadays we notice people treating others as inferiors only when we think they shouldn't. When people treat others as inferiors appropriately—as when I say to a five-year-old, "You clever thing, you"—no one would see condescension.

Yet the background assumption of hierarchy is still available, however loath we are to admit it.[22] It shows up in the fact that people will admit to resenting insolence, which is a sort of mirror image of condescension: treating a superior as an equal, or even as an inferior. And, in fact, something like eighteenth-century condescension is a common enough practice still; we have simply lost the name for it. When the president of a university stops to talk courteously to a student after a lecture, he or she is talking down a hierarchy of academic status and the student is likely to be charmed by that. Lay Catholics and nuns gain the same sort of gratification from the considerate attentions of a cardinal; the security guard from the museum trustee who remembers her name; the traffic-court judge from the politesse of a Supreme Court justice. In reporting events like these, it is natural for the beneficiary to describe the behavior of the superior as thoughtful or kind or humble or down-to-earth, and to suggest that it was not to be assumed.

When inferiors approach superiors, then, condescension, in this eighteenth-century sense, is precisely what they hope for: they want the superior to pretend to be their equal, and the gratification they take when he or she does is proof of that tacitly ascribed superiority. What would upset them most is the opposite response: that is, contempt. Contempt can be hate-filled or dismissive, intense or mild, amused or angry; but, like condescension, it requires the background system of status. Its natural expression—it is important that it has a natural expression—tends toward the sneer.

The eponymous heroine of Fanny Burney's 1782 novel *Cecilia* reminds us of a crucial point about this family of practices and feelings associated with hierarchy, through a remark about contempt. Delvile, her lover, has told her that they must elope if they are to marry, because "my family . . . will never consent to our union!"

> "Neither, then, Sir," cried Cecilia, with great spirit, "will I! . . . I will enter into no family in opposition to its wishes, I will consent to no alliance that may expose me to indignity. Nothing is so contagious as contempt!—The example of your friends might work powerfully upon yourself, and who shall dare assure me you would not catch the infection?"[23]

The possibility that one person's contempt will spread to his neighbors reflects the social nature of these emotions and attitudes. That is how they work. We care about our standing among our fellows, which is reflected in the patterns of their respect and their contempt. And these contagious evaluations remain central forces in the social shaping of human behavior. Again, what's critical is that these are the evaluations of our betters. A scientist, with a large laboratory to run, learns that some of the junior staff think he's an arrogant jerk, and he rolls his eyes, wondering why they don't grasp that he simply has high standards; he learns that a Nobel laureate in his field considers him a lightweight, and he doesn't sleep for a week. Within networks of hierarchy, people distinguish sharply between bearing the resentment of someone of lower status and bearing the contempt of someone of higher status. One annoys; the other wounds.

What's familiar about class is that the forms of respect that are offered to those higher up reflect not just their own, individual properties, but those of the identity group—the social class—to which they belong. Here, as with every identity, we see that people's responses to us are shaped not just by our own acts, attitudes, achievements, and offenses, but also by complex facts about the groups to which we belong.

THE IDENTITY OF LABOR

Systems of honor involve socially ascribed rights to respect; but we shouldn't imagine that they repose only among the relatively advantaged; peasants as well as aristocrats have their honor codes. And the enlistment of honor is one way in which groups have contested patterns of contempt from others.

"Poverty looks grim to grown people; still more so to children: they have not much idea of industrious, working, respectable poverty," Jane Eyre reflects at one point. Brontë's novel was published in 1847, two years after Friedrich Engels's *Conditions of the Working Class in England,* a devastating indictment of the damage wrought by factory labor. Changes were afoot. In England, during the later years of the eighteenth century and the first half of the nineteenth century, people in what had once been called the "lower orders" developed a growing sense of self-respect, something that manifested itself in the development of a self-conscious working class. No longer defined negatively by their lower place in a system of status—by what they were not—the members of the working men's associations of Britain came to view manual labor as a source not just of income but of pride. This way of thinking, as is evident from the fact that these groups were called *Men's* Associations, saw men and women of the working classes as having different roles. But working-class women didn't just look after and raise workingmen; they also worked themselves. (This is one of the many places where intersectionality matters.) And even if their work was not pleasant or interesting, working people of both sexes could be proud both of what they produced and of what they earned through their labor. Through such refashioned social identities, they could then mobilize to resist exploitation and challenge derogation.

By the middle of the twentieth century, when I was growing up, dividing all the personnel of a modern economy into a working class, a lower, middle, and upper middle class, and an upper class—to use a taxonomy that emerged in the second half of the nineteenth century—seemed to involve a complex mixture of income and of status, which itself derived from a complex mixture of considerations.[24] My maternal grandmother might have had the money, the accent and idiom, the manners, and even the title of an aristocrat, but, as the granddaughter of a pharmacist who had made a fortune from patent medicine, she was firmly upper-middle-class. As in America, there were economic distinctions that were about more than how much you earned. Workers tended to get hourly wages and overtime if they worked more than a certain number of hours per week; the middle classes received salaries, not hourly wages (though the fees of some professionals—lawyers, for example—could be hourly as well). But, once you moved away from the tiny aristocracy, the key elements of status had, above all else, to do with a style of speech and behavior—the habitus—that came from education.

Just as happened in the United States, college attendance leapt in Britain after the Second World War, and one of the key indicators of class was increasingly a matter of whether you had been to university. The middle-class status of meagerly compensated librarians reflected a vocational requirement for an education beyond secondary school; that the better-paid assembly-line workers were working-class reflected the absence of such a requirement. And, again, jobs that required little muscle and kept your hands clean were associated with middle-class status, pretty much regardless of income. Working-class consciousness—legible in the very name of the British Labour Party, founded in 1900—spoke of class mobilization, workers securing their interests; the emerging era of education spoke of class mobility, blue collars giving way to white. Would mobility undermine class consciousness?

Such issues were on Michael Young's mind when the Dartington Hall alumnus was in a position to do something about it. That didn't happen overnight. He had studied law and sat in on the occasional course at the London School of Economics. (There he first crossed paths with my maternal grandfather, Stafford Cripps, who was, Young wrote, "dressed in barrister-black with a smart, spotted tie, the last person you would imagine to be a socialist.")[25] Eventually, he decided to take a degree in economics at the LSE. He was well supplied, then, with credentials and connections.

He was also, as they say, a man of the left. When he finished his economics degree, he went to work for a nonpartisan research and policy think tank called PEP, for "Political and Economic Planning," that had been conceived at a meeting at Dartington while Young was a student there. (The Elmhirsts helped fund PEP.) Unable to serve in the armed forces because of his asthma, he spent the Second World War writing and thinking about policy—but also learned something about industry, by working for a year as a manager in a munitions factory—before returning to run PEP. In 1942, at a meeting at Dartington, Young once again saw my grandfather, who was by then serving in Churchill's war cabinet and pondering his postwar future. My forebear was an independent Member of Parliament at the time, having parted ways with the Labour Party. (He had defied its leadership by helping to form an alliance across the political spectrum to oppose fascism in the face of the government's appeasement.) Young was among those who persuaded him to reapply to join his old party. That was why, when the Labour Party won the first election after the war, Grandfather was able to serve as Chancellor of the Exchequer.

Michael Young had drafted large parts of the manifesto on which the Labour Party won that election, after leaving PEP for the party's research department in 1945. The manifesto, *Let Us Face the Future*, announced that "its ultimate purpose at home" was "the establishment of the Socialist Commonwealth of Great Britain—free, democratic, efficient, progressive, public-spirited, its material resources organised in the service of the British people."[26] The party sought to raise the school-leaving age to sixteen, increase adult education, improve public housing, make public secondary school education free, create a national health service, provide social security for all, guarantee full employment, and take fuel and power, public transportation, and iron and steel into public ownership. The manifesto did not lack ambition, as you can see, and the party achieved more of its aims than many believed possible.

As a result, the lives of the English working class were beginning to change radically for the better. Unions and labor laws reduced the hours worked by manual laborers, increasing their possibilities of leisure. Rising incomes made it possible for them to buy televisions and refrigerators. (Men spent more evenings at home in front of the telly, drinking beer kept cool at home, rather than with their mates at the pub.) These sorts of changes—described in *Family and Kinship in East London,* based on the work for which Young received a Ph.D. in sociology from London University in 1954—were going on toward the bottom of the income hierarchy. Changes, partly driven by new estate taxes, were going on at the top, as well. In 1949, my grandfather, as Labour Chancellor of the Exchequer, introduced a tax that rose to 80 percent on estates of a million pounds and above.[27] (If you're wincing for the unfortunate rich, that's 34 million pounds in 2017 inflation-adjusted sterling.) For a couple of generations after this, these efforts at social reform both protected members of the working classes and allowed more of their children to make the move up the hierarchy of occupations and of income, and so, to some degree, of status. Young was acutely conscious of these accomplishments; he was acutely conscious, too, of their limitations.

CAPITAL: CULTURAL, SOCIAL, AND HUMAN

To understand what such reforms meant, and didn't mean, we'll want to have another go at sorting through some of the elements that go into fixing the social meaning of class. Earlier, I asked why, given that class wasn't reducible to money, we couldn't just leave economics out of the analysis. One reason is that everyone has a use for money, and, usually, the desire for more than they currently have, in ways that echo status competition. (In the early years of the past century, the social theorist L. T. Hobhouse, when asked in a seminar at the London School of Economics what was the ideal standard of living, answered, "Ten per cent more than you have."[28]) At the same time, the stereotype of the nouveau riche is ancient and global, running, as it does, from Roman skepticism about the *novus homo*, the new man, first in his family to be elected consul, to the not-so-gentle satire of Kevin Kwan's *Crazy Rich Asians* in Singapore, despised (as usual) by the old money . . . in this case the long-established Chinese families with their priceless antiques discreetly hidden away on invisible estates.

But if wealth—financial capital—is one thing and class another, there have always been ways of using one to get the other. In both Asante and England, if you did get rich, you could take measures to see that the next generation of your family had the manners, the hexis and habitus, of an aristocrat—in England, by sending your sons to the right school and getting your daughters a governess or, in Asante, by finding your children positions, or spouses, at court. There's also an intrinsic association between class and money: the behavioral indicators of status are those most associated with a lineage of long-possessed wealth. And though upper-class status doesn't always entail having money, it does entail some social proximity to money. Real poverty, it has been observed, is about social isolation as much as it is about material deprivation; the poor don't have the sort of friendship networks that the advantaged draw upon.[29] That's why we may balk at calling a penniless graduate student "poor." Class is one way that you benefit from the money in the pockets of friends and acquaintances.

Indeed, you miss something important about our class system if you think that it is just about inequality. That's because class creates equals as well as unequals. A class identity, like any identity, creates an in-group, and it comes with mechanisms by which fellow members recognize one another. Nancy Mitford, daughter of an English peer and sister of the Duchess of Devonshire, scandalized members of her class by revealing, in an essay on "The English Aristocracy," some of the vocabulary by which they recognized one another. Since what she had to say was bound, as she acknowledged, to seem snobbish, she chose to distance her analysis by putting it in the mouth of Alan Ross, a professor of linguistics: "The Professor, pointing out that it is solely by their language that the upper classes nowadays are distinguished (since they are neither cleaner, richer, nor better-educated than anybody else) has invented a useful formula: U (for upper class) -speaker versus non-U speaker."

Mitford borrowed some of Ross's examples:

Toilet paper: non-U for U lavatory paper.
Wealthy: non-U for U rich.

And she added a couple of her own:

> Sweet: non-U for U pudding.
> Dentures: non-U for U false teeth.[30]

The non-U choices here naturally read as euphemism: the idea was that the non-U—the striving, insecure middle classes—sought strenuously to signal their refinement; the upper classes did not need to. Such patterns of behavior are part of a dimension of class that goes beyond hierarchy: for class membership, like ethnicity, comes with social enmeshments. The poor relations of the English upper classes, like Jane Eyre, had something that poor people from other classes did not: connections. They had not financial but social capital. Jane, as an orphan badly treated in a great house, is once asked whether she would join poor relations if she knew they would be kind to her, and demurs. "I was not heroic enough to purchase liberty at the price of caste," she reports. Jane's adjacency to privilege (conferred, albeit insecurely, by her mother's "gentle" birth) is what connects her to the education that allows her to become a governess, which is the job that brings her to Thornfield Hall, the home of Mr. Rochester. It's made possible by the links that her class makes possible, by the bonds that tie her to her own class and connect her with others in it.[31]

To speak somewhat abstractly, Jane Eyre takes her social capital and turns it, through education and upbringing, into cultural capital: the habitus and the bodily hexis of an educated woman of her class and time. There were jobs that Jane Eyre wouldn't have considered doing—factory labor as a seamstress, for example—because they were inconsistent with her class. (She was perfectly happy to sew at home.) This habitus makes her not just a suitable teacher but also a suitable companion of her young pupil. Her posture and the way she speaks, her ability to talk about history, or play the piano and paint watercolors, all identify her class and distinguish her from the maids and valets who surround her and the farmhands who work on the estate.

And her education provides her with something else. Not just status and connections but skills: the knowledge that makes her a suitable teacher for her pupil. That knowledge is valuable, then, beyond the status and respect it can bring. She can also put it into use to make a living. It is part of what an economist would call her human capital, her knowledge, her abilities, and the physical attributes that affect the value of her labor.[32]

The fact that financial, social, and cultural capital are distinct is one reason why efforts to reduce class to any single hierarchy don't work. I said that Weber's account of social stratification left us with a quandary: it wouldn't put hatch marks on a ruler and provide a system by which everyone could be assigned a class rank. The account that I favor isn't meant to solve that problem. On the contrary, it's meant to show why it can't be solved. The Oxford philosopher Isaiah Berlin often talked about values as being "incommensurable": you couldn't measure the value of freedom and the value of equality on the same scale. Something like this is true of these different vectors of capital.

Still, some forms of clustering, or segmentation, can be more illuminating than others, so long as we're clear that we aren't (in a phrase we owe to Plato) "carving nature at the joints." In the largest study of class in Britain ever undertaken, the Great British Class Survey of 2011, which used measures of all three forms of capital, the English sociologist Mike Savage and his colleagues concluded that there were now not three but seven classes in their society today. There was still an elite at the top, equipped with money, connections, and education, able to transmit financial, social, and cultural capital to their children. This top 6 percent of the population has an average income of more than £89,000 ($115,000), education at elite universities like Oxford and Cambridge, and a network of social connections to one another and into the old aristocracy. And there's still a well-defined place at the bottom: 15 percent of the British population is now what Savage and his colleagues called the "precariat," with low incomes (typically around £8,000, or a little over $10,000, after taxes), irregular, unstable employment, few savings, and few social connections to the classes above them. Only about 3 percent of the children of the precariat get a college education.[33]

But between these two classes, Savage identified five distinct groups, clusters of financial, social, and cultural capital, which are not easily ranked against each other: emergent service workers, like chefs and production assistants, who go to gigs, play sports, and use gyms and social media; a traditional working class, like truck drivers and office cleaners, who mostly don't do these things; a class of newly affluent workers; a technical middle class; and an established middle class, who work in the professions and in upper management. These groups don't have a shared sense of what activities confer standing—reading versus computer games, classical versus contemporary popular music, cricket versus soccer, and so on—and the relative prestige of their occupations is also far from agreed upon. Class in Britain isn't a ladder. It's a mountain, with multiple paths for ascent and descent. It rises, though, from a single valley to a single peak.

THIS SIDE UP

People sometimes say that in America, by contrast, everyone is middle class. But this, it turns out, is not currently what Americans themselves think. In 2014, Americans were offered these four options in one of the regular National Opinion Research Center surveys: lower class, working class, middle class, and upper class. Almost 8 percent said they were lower-class, 47 percent that they were working-class, and 2.7 percent declared themselves upper-class; less than half, only 42.4 percent, to be precise, claimed middle-class status. Even among those with graduate degrees, three-quarters of whom did say they were middle-class, 1.7 percent said they were lower-class, 16.4 percent that they were working-class, and about 8 percent that they were upper-class.[34]

A different set of choices, to be sure, might have elicited a different array of responses. And social scientists don't own the nomenclature for class identity. Many Americans would still proudly invoke the working-class identity that is marked by the expression "blue-collar." "Redneck," an old and disparaging term for those whites whose necks were burned by the sun as they worked outside in agriculture, can now be claimed, at least jocularly, as a class identity, too, though, like so much else in American society, it is an identity inflected with a racial meaning. (That's intersectionality again.) Many people of wealth and education and professional standing would admit to being upper-middle-class, though only a few would claim, as we saw, to belong to an upper class. Still, as these results remind us, the fact that Americans don't talk very much about class doesn't mean there isn't a good deal of class consciousness. Twenty-first-century systems of social standing, in the country where I now live, look very similar to the patterns that shaped the worlds I grew up in. One (but, yes, only one) strand of the populist explosion that tipped Donald Trump into power was an expression of resentment against a class defined by its education and its values: the cosmopolitan, degree-laden people who dominate the media, the public culture, and the professions in our country. Populists think that liberal elites look down on ordinary Americans, ignore their concerns, and use their power to advantage themselves. They may not call them an upper class, but the indices populists use to define them—money, education, connections, power—would have picked out the old upper and upper middle classes of the last century.[35]

Resentment of this sort, as Nietzsche taught us, can be a reaction against a sense of inferiority. There are, naturally, Americans who reject the system of values that looks down on those with less education, and some who regard the "liberal elites" with contempt rather than resentment, too. Yet many white working-class voters feel a sense of subordination, derived from a lack of formal education, and that can play a role in their politics. You could hear this in some of the conversations with working-class men in Boston recorded in the early 1970s by Richard Sennett and Jonathan Cobb. Here is a young man talking to his college-educated interviewer:

> "Um, let me try to explain to you why I was so nervous at the beginning of the interview," said a house painter. "It's not you, you're all right—but you see . . . um . . . whenever I'm with educated people, you now, or people who aren't my own kind . . . um . . . I feel like I'm making a fool of myself if I just act natural, you know?"[36]

Sennett and Cobb's classic study was memorably titled *The Hidden Injuries of Class*. Such injuries have persisted. In a best-selling 2016 account of growing up as what he himself calls a "hillbilly," J. D. Vance reports many moments of just such anxiety as a rare white working-class student at Yale Law School.[37]

We've repeatedly seen that the significance of identities is always being contested. So this sense of inferiority is perfectly consistent with feeling superior in other ways. J. D. Vance is entitled to feel prouder of his achievements than those who had them served up to them on an upper-middle-class platter. It is no accomplishment to have been born on the finish line. Attitudes and values are part of what distinguish classes. Working-class men often think that middle-class and upper-class men are unmanly or undeserving. Remember the working man in Bethnal Green who wanted his son to take up chemistry because "it's completely unproductive and therefore well paid."

Still, a significant portion of what we call the American white working class has been persuaded that, in some sense, they do not deserve the opportunities that have been denied to them. They may complain that blacks and other racial minorities are unfairly advantaged in the competition for work and the distribution of government benefits. (And some men may believe that the women are being unfairly advantaged, too.) Nevertheless, they do not think that it is wrong either that they do not get jobs for which they believe they are not qualified or that the jobs for which they are qualified are typically less well paid. They think that blacks and other minorities are getting handouts, but they don't think the solution is to demand handouts for themselves. They are likely to regard the treatment of racial minorities as an exception to the right general rule: they think that America mostly is and certainly should be a society in which opportunities belong to those who have earned them.

People continue to rank the occupations that come with a large measure of cultural capital higher than those that are typical of the working and lower-middle classes. In a 2012 survey of occupational prestige, Americans ranked professors close to big-city mayors, a little below physicians and above lawyers.[38] We academics occupy a strange place in the contemporary class system. Our extended educations give us a great deal of cultural capital, and this can sometimes translate into connections and money—social and financial capital—as well. But many Americans with doctoral degrees have little money, and work long hours in jobs with few perks. These men and women may seek to join labor unions. Nevertheless, their cultural capital means that they are very unlikely to be identified as straightforwardly working-class. Education can, in fact, lead to jobs that are only moderately remunerative but that carry a great deal of cachet—as journalists and editors at major media outlets or in publishing. And so some Americans find themselves regularly at social events with the much richer people who have parlayed their educations (or their connections) into the higher reaches of business and finance.

If there is something wrong in this whole picture, many Americans think, it isn't that there's status for the educated and high incomes for some occupations; it's that the distribution of the education and the money is not arrived at fairly. If class means respecting those who have worked hard to get educations or to get rich, what would be wrong with that? What matters is not equality but that the unequal shares are deserved.

If it's a contemporary sentiment, it's also an ancient one. Socrates, in the fifth century BCE, chastised those who claimed a superior birth, charging that those who take pride in ancestry are too ill educated "to consider that every man has had thousands and ten thousands of progenitors, and among them have been rich and poor, kings and slaves, Hellenes and barbarians, innumerable." His point was not that almost everyone has both kings and slaves among their ancestors—which may well be true—but that the natural object of honor is not ancestry but personal merit. Horace, the son of a freed slave, made a similar point four centuries later when he praised Maecenas, the richest of the Roman patrons of the Augustan age, for thinking "it's no matter who your parents are, so long as you're worthy."[39] A century or so after Horace's birth, Seneca wrote in his letters that "if there is anything good in philosophy, it's this: it doesn't inspect your pedigree."[40] True, class can get you respect, but if it comes merely from ancestry, it's hard to see why anyone, including you, should think of it as something you are really entitled to. Shouldn't we care most about the forms of esteem that reflect things we ourselves have achieved? This ideal may not be new, but it has achieved its greatest influence under a modern term: meritocracy.

THE NEW RULING CLASS

It's worth recalling, though, that the word "meritocracy" was invented in a work of satire, Michael Young's *The Rise of the Meritocracy*. Published in 1958, the book was not a sociological tract but a work of fiction, purporting to be a sociological analysis written in 2033, looking back at the development of a new British society. In that distant future, unlike the class society of the 1950s, riches and rule were earned, not inherited. The new ruling class was determined by the formula "I.Q. + effort = merit."[41] Narrating from the perspective of that future, Michael Young's fictional alter ego draws conclusions from over half a century of fictional social experience:

> Today we frankly recognize that democracy can be no more than an aspiration, and have rule not so much by the people as by the cleverest people; not an aristocracy of birth, not a plutocracy of wealth, but a true meritocracy of talent.[42]

This is the first appearance of the word "meritocracy," and the book aimed to show what a society governed on this principle would look like. Young's dystopian vision is of a world in which, as wealth increasingly reflects the innate distribution of natural talent, and the wealthy increasingly marry one another, society sorts into two main classes, in which everyone accepts that they have more or less what they deserve. This was an England in which

> the eminent know that success is a just reward for their own capacity, their own efforts. . . . As for the lower classes, their situation is different. Today all persons, however humble, know they have had every chance. They are tested, again and again. . . . If they have been labeled "dunce" repeatedly, they cannot any longer pretend; their image of themselves is more nearly a true, unflattering reflection.[43]

The older class systems I've described were sometimes called systems of caste. My ancestors in Asante and in England had a status they did not ask for and could not easily escape. In this one respect, the old classes *were* like the castes of India. You were born into a structure (in India, an exceedingly complex structure) of status hierarchies.

Occasionally, by some mixture of talent and effort and good fortune, you might rise through the ranks; occasionally, through ineptitude or laziness or bad luck, you could fall. The social revolutions of the late eighteenth century in France and in North America began a long process of gradually displacing an existing hereditary ruling class. The equality of the French Revolution was, as much as anything else, about removing the obstacles in the way of those who did not belong to the aristocracy of the *ancien régime*. Napoleon may have reintroduced a monarchy, but, as his Irish surgeon on St. Helena recounted, he saw it as governed by the ideal of the *"carrière ouverte au talents* (the career open to talents), without distinction of birth or fortune, and this system of equality is the reason that your oligarchy hate me so much."[44]

We've seen that in the early American republic, too, the old hereditary distinction remained between gentlemen and ladies, on the one hand, and a class below them. But in all these places, this caste-like element of status declined in the two centuries that followed. Progressive politics was guided over the late twentieth century by the desire not just to reduce the hereditary hierarchies of status but to make available to all, whatever their "birth or fortune," an education that would allow them to develop their talents.

As Michael Young recognized, however, this ideal was bound to conflict with a force in human life as inevitable and as compelling as the idea that some individuals are more deserving than others, namely, the desire of families to pass on advantages to their children. As he said in *The Rise of the Meritocracy,* "Nearly all parents are going to try to gain unfair advantages for their offspring."[45] And when you have inequalities of income, one thing people can do with extra money is to pursue that goal.

There is nothing wrong with cherishing your children. But a decent society governed by the ideal of merit would have to limit the extent to which this natural impulse permitted people to undermine that ideal. If the economic rewards of social life depended not just on your individual talent and effort but also on the financial and social inputs of your parents, you would no longer be living by the formula that "I.Q. + effort = merit."

Young's apprehensions have proved well founded. Consider the fact that, between 1979 and 2013, the top fifth of American households enjoyed a $4 trillion increase in pretax income—a trillion dollars more than came to all the rest. No amount of money or status can guarantee that your children will all end up where you are, to be sure: only 37 percent of the childen born into that top fifth will stay there, according to the most comprehensive study now available. Still, in a book provocatively titled *Dream Hoarders*, Richard V. Reeves, of the Brookings Institution, observes, "There has been no increase in inequality below the eightieth percentile. All the inequality action is above that line."

Among the "hoarding mechanisms" by which the top fifth of the population is claiming most of the growth in the social product for themselves, he points to "exclusionary zoning in residential areas" and "unfair mechanisms influencing college admissions."[46] As one legal scholar has explained, exclusionary zoning bundles an expensive house together with the chance to live in a "good neighborhood" and send your kids to a good public school. Poor children who attend elite schools will enjoy incomes close to those of their rich classmates. Yet, researchers have found, many elite schools—including Brown, Dartmouth, Penn, Princeton, and Yale—take more students from the top 1 percent of the income distribution than from the bottom 60 percent.[47]

"American meritocracy," the Yale law professor Daniel Markovits, drawing on similar research, argues, "has thus become precisely what it was invented to combat: a mechanism for the dynastic transmission of wealth and privilege across generations." To the extent that you can predict that disproportionately many of the children of the elite will—and disproportionately many of the children of the precariat will not—achieve a position in the top tier of wealth, power, and privilege, you have something too much like the intergenerational transmission of status that marks systems of caste. In Markovits's view, "Meritocracy now constitutes a *modern-day aristocracy*, one might even say, purpose-built for a world in which the greatest source of wealth is not land or factories but human capital, the free labor of skilled workers."[48]

These problems received some attention in the United States after the election in 2016 of Donald Trump; some people think the alienation of poorer whites from the "coastal elites" is in part a result of the former's recognition that the latter have fixed the game to the advantage of their families. But the problem is not particularly American. In China, too, wealth and status is 80 percent determined, using one measure, by the wealth and status of your parents. (For women, it's even more.)[49] And that is a society whose ruling party officially set out nearly a century ago to abolish class. In Britain, the alienation of the precariat from the cosmopolitan elites who mostly live in London—an alienation that manifested itself in the pattern of voting on Brexit—reflects a similar concentration of our three kinds of capital in a self-perpetuating upper class.

Michael Young, who lived to be eighty-six, saw what was happening. Writing at the start of the new century, a year before his death in 2002, he lamented that educational institutions had been enlisted into a newly calcifying form of social stratification. "With an amazing battery of certificates and degrees at its disposal," he observed, "education has put its seal of approval on a minority, and its seal of disapproval on the many who fail to shine from the time they are relegated to the bottom streams at the age of seven or before." What should have been mechanisms of mobility had become fortresses of privilege. He looked at the educated elites who had come to dominate the British government, and compared it with the 1945 Labour cabinet of Clement Attlee: Ernest Bevin, the foreign secretary, had left school at the age of eleven, and worked as an errand boy and a drayman before he became active in the Bristol dockworkers union;

Herbert Morrison, deputy prime minister, left school at fourteen and worked as a shop assistant and switchboard operator before getting involved in local council politics. These were the members of the "Big Five" (a group that also included my grandfather, Hugh Dalton, and Attlee himself) who sought to alleviate social inequalities whose burdens they knew from direct experience.

In other realms, too, Young saw an emerging cohort of mercantile meritocrats who "can be insufferably smug, much more so than the people who knew they had achieved advancement not on their own merit but because they were, as somebody's son or daughter, the beneficiaries of nepotism. The newcomers can actually believe they have morality on their side. So assured have the elite become that there is almost no block on the rewards they arrogate to themselves."[50] Inequality rose as salaries and fees soared and stock-option schemes proliferated; and the carapace of "merit," Young argued, had only inoculated the winners from shame and reproach.

Class had co-opted meritocracy, it seemed, and Young grieved. It was personal, to him. For no social scientist did more than he to try to expose and heal the injuries of class. "Michael Young resembled Cadmus," Noel Annan, the historian of the British intelligentsia, memorably wrote of him. "Whatever field he tilled, he sowed dragon's teeth and armed men seemed to spring from the soil to form an organization and correct the abuses or stimulate the virtues he had discovered."[51] After leading PEP, he founded a hugely effective consumer advocacy organization. His ideas guided the creation in 1965 of the Open University, with lectures broadcast on radio and television by the BBC, providing distance learning over the next half century to more than one and a half million students.[52] And at the age of eighty he founded the School for Social Entrepreneurs in Bethnal Green, the London borough where, decades earlier, he had carried out the research for his doctoral dissertation. Now he looked around and saw the rollback of his life's work: and it was happening as he had predicted.

Yet if a new dynastic system was taking shape, you might conclude that meritocracy has faltered because it isn't meritocratic enough. If talent is capitalized efficiently only in high tax brackets, you could conclude that we've simply failed to achieve the meritocratic ideal. You will seek to push more rigorously for merit, making sure that every child has the educational advantages and is taught the social tricks that successful families now hoard for their children. So isn't that the right response?

CLASS ACTION

Not according to Michael Young. He saw that there would be a problem even if the top class didn't exploit its advantages to give their children chances that were denied to others'. The problem wasn't just with how the prizes of social life were distributed; it was with the prizes themselves. A system of class filtered by meritocracy would, in his view, still be a system of *class*: it would involve a hierarchy of social respect, granting dignity to those at the top, but denying respect and self-respect to those who did not inherit the talents and the capacity for effort that, combined with proper education, would give them access to the most highly remunerated occupations. That is why the authors of his fictional "Chelsea Manifesto"—which, in *The Rise of the Meritocracy,* is supposed to serve as the last sign of resistance to the new order—ask for a classless society:

> The classless society would be one which both possessed and acted upon plural values. Were we to evaluate people, not only according to their intelligence and their education, their occupation and their power, but according to their kindliness and their courage, their imagination and sensitivity, their sympathy and generosity, there could be no classes. . . . Every human being

would then have equal opportunity, not to rise up in the world in the light of any mathematical measure, but to develop his own special capacities for leading a rich life.[53]

Class identities in a meritocracy reduce people to a single measure of worth, the argument runs: and only someone with a very limited vision could suppose that human worth reduces to a single measure. And so the manifesto proposes an alternative vision in which we recognize many forms of excellence.

This vision, in which each of us takes our allotment of talents and pursues a distinctive set of achievements and the self-respect that they bring, was one that Michael Young had learned from his schooling at Dartington Hall. Each of the students there was encouraged to seek his or her own path. Young tells the story, perhaps, he admits, apocryphal, of the "small Dartington girl who said, 'Oh dear, do I have to do what I want to do all over again today?' "[54] Above all, the students at Dartington were taught to think of each other as equals. Some people were better at pottery or poetry or carpentry or chemistry or geography or gardening. None of these achievements made you more important.

This profound commitment to the social equality of people with a variety of talents can sound quixotic, but it draws on a deeper philosophical picture. The central task of ethics is to ask: what is it for a human life to go well? The answer, I believe, is that living well means meeting the challenge set by three things: your capacities, the circumstances into which you were born, and the projects you yourself decide are important. Making a life, my friend the philosopher and legal scholar Ronald Dworkin once wrote, is "a performance that demands skill," and "is the most comprehensive and important challenge we face."[55] But because each of us comes equipped with different talents and is born into different circumstances, and because people choose their own projects, each of us faces his or her own challenge, one that is, in the end, unique. So there is no sensible answer to the question of whether one person meets her challenge better than another. Did Bertrand Russell have a better life than Mozart? The only sane answer is that Russell was a better philosopher and Mozart a better musician. I know what it is for my life to go better or worse, but it doesn't make sense to ask whether my life is better than yours. And that means there is no comparative measure, no single scale of human worth. As a result, a system of selection for jobs and educational opportunities cannot be designed by considering who is most worthy of those opportunities, because, as Michael Young argued through his Chelsea Manifesto, there isn't a single scale of merit on which to rank them. Indeed, because each of us faces a distinct challenge, what matters in the end is not how we rank against others at all. We do not need to find something we are best at; what is important is simply that we do *our* best. Each of us, as Herder once wrote, expressing one of the great leitmotifs of Romanticism, has his own measure.[56] John Stuart Mill expressed something like the same thought when he wrote, in the marvelous third chapter of *On Liberty*, that to have a character is to be a "person whose desires and impulses are his own—are the expression of his own nature, as it has been developed and modified by his own culture. . . ."[57] And if you have a character, if you have your own measure, the most important standards you have to meet are distinctively yours.

The ideal of meritocracy, then, confuses two different concerns. One is a matter of efficiency; the other is a question of human worth. If we want people to do difficult jobs that require talent, education, effort, training, and practice, we are going to need to be able to identify candidates with the right combination of talent and willingness to exert themselves, and provide them incentives to train and practice. So we design schools and universities, and select people to fill the places in them. If the institutions are working properly, they aren't merely handing out credentials (which is always a danger); they are building human capital. We then allow for entrepreneurship, social and commercial; and we offer jobs with salaries and other advantages—

interesting work, respect and autonomy in your job, vacations, pensions, health care—and select people to fill them as well. We open careers, in Napoleon's formulation, to developed talent.

But in the end, there will be a limited supply of educational and occupational opportunities, and we will have to have ways of allocating them. As intelligent machines dominate more and more activities, the supply may grow scarcer. At school and work, we will have to use some principles of selection to match people to positions. Those principles should be designed so that the educational system produces a supply of people who have the right trainings, and the jobs end up being done by people who are prepared to do them.

Of course, both the jobs and the schools must do more than make people useful to others. Work needs to have meaning; education needs to prepare you for life as a citizen and a private person—as someone living a valuable human life—and not just as someone earning a living. Such considerations, too, must be taken into account in selecting people for schools and colleges and the world of work. If these principles of selection have been reasonably designed, we can say, if we like, that the people who meet the criteria for entering the schools or getting the jobs "merit" those positions. This is, to enlist some useful philosophers' jargon, a matter of "institutional desert." People deserve these positions in the sense in which people who buy winning lottery tickets deserve their winnings: they got them by a proper application of the rules.

WORTH AND REWARDS

Institutional desert, however, has nothing to do with the intrinsic worthiness of the people who get into college or who get the jobs, any more than lottery winners are people of special merit and losers are somehow less worthy. Even if we are going to reward hard work, the capacity for hard work is itself the result of natural endowments and upbringing. So neither talent nor effort, the two things that would determine rewards in the world of the meritocracy, is itself something earned. Someone who, as *The Rise of the Meritocracy* bluntly put it, has been repeatedly "labeled 'dunce,'" still has capacities and aptitudes, and the challenge of making a meaningful life.

The only decent way to select people for educational and occupational opportunities is to ask what schools and jobs are properly aiming to do and then decide whose admission will best advance those aims. The aims of a school or a college are complex; and most jobs have a variety of dimensions that make it hard to identify one person as uniquely best suited to do them. It would be a bad idea to admit to your college only students who will flourish in literature or only those who will triumph in mathematics. And if you're training doctors it's worth looking for people who will happily end up in different places, since doctors are needed everywhere. If you're looking for litigators to join your law firm, their temperament as well as their record at trial will matter, because their behavior will affect the contributions of others. Given a bunch of candidates with different track records and different temperaments, there's rarely going to be one way to balance these concerns; usually there are going to be many reasonable principles of selection. But there are constraints on what sorts of principles of selection are morally permissible. Social origin is not, in itself, a permissible basis for excluding people from places in colleges. Nor is race, gender, or religion. In a world poisoned by prejudices directed at certain identities, it may nevertheless be a good idea to take these identities into account in designing the selection process, if it contributes to ending those forms of prejudice. And, as long as we do so in a rational, morally permissible way, it may turn out that some working-class and black people, some women, some Muslims, will deserve, institutionally speaking, places that some otherwise equally qualified upper-class or white or Christian or male people will not.

It will be unhelpful at that point to insist that these others are equally deserving. It's true that the lives of those who get the opportunities aren't worth more than the lives of those who don't. But this is not, to repeat the point, because we have some scale of human worth on which we have weighed them and judged them equivalent. It is because there is no such scale. True, then, that the lives of the less successful are not less worthy. But not because they are *as* worthy or *more* worthy. There is simply no sensible way of comparing the worth of human lives.

Here, I think, is a better picture. Money and status are social rewards that can encourage people to do the things that need doing. It will be a matter of luck whether you inherit the capacities whose development will be rewarded in the society into which you are born; and of more luck whether the capacities you actually develop turn out to be highly rewarded. You can respond to messages from the market and seek training, of course. And a well-designed society will elicit and deploy developed talent efficiently.

But I know that my relatively high place in the current system of class in Ghana would have been insecure in nineteenth-century Asante, since I am confident I didn't inherit the temperament of a successful general. Einstein's mathematical and physical intuitions wouldn't have been much use among the Amazonian Nukak. And Mozart's success would have been unlikely in a society where the only musical instrument was the drum.

The English poet Thomas Gray, in his well-loved 1751 "Elegy Written in a Country Churchyard," wrote about the talent wasted in a society that fails to train all its young:

Full many a gem of purest ray serene,
The dark unfathom'd caves of ocean bear:
Full many a flow'r is born to blush unseen,
And waste its sweetness on the desert air.

Gray's society had not, of course, achieved universal education, let alone imagined the removal of barriers to success based purely on accidents of birth. So perhaps below the gravestones, he imagined, there rested, as a result, some "mute inglorious Milton," or "some Cromwell guiltless of his country's blood." One thinks, too, of Virginia Woolf's powerful imagining (in *A Room of One's Own*) of a Judith Shakespeare, the Bard's "extraordinarily gifted" twin sister.

> She was as adventurous, as imaginative, as agog to see the world as he was. But she was not sent to school. She had no chance of learning grammar and logic, let alone of reading Horace and Virgil. She picked up a book now and then, one of her brother's perhaps, and read a few pages. But then her parents came in and told her to mend the stockings or mind the stew and not moon about with books and papers.

Gray, Woolf, and not a few others have—with power and justice—conjured a sense of natural talent stifled and stilled.

The vista of the country churchyard may tempt us, further, to suppose that, in the absence of penury and restraint, people offered adequate educations will find a level set by their natural talents: each natural poet will find her inner Milton, each tyrant his waiting inner Cromwell. What's missing here, though, is the massive contingency of human life. Not knowing who could be a Milton, we do not know which parents should immerse their children in the world's great ocean of poesy; to prepare the next Einstein, you'd need to know what talents it will take to make the next great breakthroughs in physics. If we knew *that*, we wouldn't need the next Einstein.

I have relished my life in philosophy, which began, I think, by the pure chance of having a few friends and a couple of teachers whom I met at a moment in my life when I was thinking about my religious faith and my place in the world. One reason I could read and appreciate Kant, Camus, Sartre, and Ayer at that moment is that I had spent a great deal of my childhood reading books, some of them quite challenging, from my parents' library, at my mother's urging. But a different school, different friends, different parents, a different library (or none at all) and I would have had a different life.

I love the life I have happened upon; but there are surely many other lives I could have had and loved. (No doubt the same was true of Milton and Cromwell, too.) And most people would have multifarious possible rewarding lives, if we made a world that respected a life well lived: a life in which a person gave others their due, had rewarding relationships with family, friends, and fellow citizens, and pursued projects they had elected with passion and purpose. The social rewards of wealth and honor are inevitably going to be unequally shared, because that is the only way they can serve their role as incentives for human behavior. But we do not need to deny the dignity of those whose luck in the genetic lottery and in the historical contingencies of their situation has left them less rewarded.

However the dice fall, people will inevitably want to share both money and status with those they love, seeking to get their children financial and social rewards. Inheritance laws permit us to transfer money to our children; class lets us transfer status through the educational system, enlarging their cultural capital, and permits us, by sharing connections, to enhance their social capital. But we shouldn't secure our children's advantages in a way that denies a decent life to the children of others. Each child should have access to a decent education; each should be able to regard him or herself with self-respect. Historically, we have used inheritance taxes to help even out the opportunities, because, while being able to give money to your children incentivizes a parent, it doesn't incentivize the child. Further democratizing the opportunities for advancement is something we know how to do, even if the state of current politics in Britain and the United States has made it increasingly unlikely that it will be done. But we also need to work to do something that we do not yet quite know how to do: to eradicate contempt for those who are disfavored by the ethic of effortful competition. Those who seek to cultivate class consciousness typically think about workers engaged in collective actions on their own behalf; those who seek to dampen class consciousness think about the social prerogatives of the privileged, the injuries extracted from the less privileged. Young rightly sought to enlist both vectors. So should we.

LORD DARTINGTON

"It is good sense to appoint individual people to jobs on their merit," Young wrote. "It is the opposite when those who are judged to have merit of a particular kind harden into a new social class without room in it for others."[58] The goal isn't to eradicate hierarchy and to turn every mountain into a salt flat; we live in a plenitude of incommensurable hierarchies, and the circulation of social esteem will always advantage the better novelist, the more important mathematician, the savvier businessman, the faster runner, the more effective social entrepreneur. We can't fully control the distribution of economic, social, and human capital, or eradicate the intricate moiré patterns that emerge from these overlaid grids. But class identities don't have to internalize those injuries of class; it remains an urgent collective endeavor to revise the associated labels, norms, and treatments in the service of what we can call moral equality.

If that sounds utopian, bear in mind that nobody was more practical-minded than Michael Young, institution-builder par excellence. It's true that the stirrings of Young's conscience responded to the personal as well as the systemic; he would routinely hand over the contents of his wallet to a homeless person he encountered on the street. Dying of cancer in a hospital ward, he worried whether the contractor-supplied African immigrants who wheeled around the food trolleys were getting minimum wage. But his compassion was welded to a sturdy sense of the possible. He didn't merely dream of reducing inherited privilege; he devised concrete measures to see that it happened, in the hope that all citizens could have the chance to develop their "own special capacities for leading a rich life." He had certainly done exactly that himself. In the imaginary future of *The Rise of the Meritocracy*, there was still a House of Lords, but it was occupied solely by people who had earned their places there through distinguished public service. If anyone had merited a place in that imaginary legislature, it would have been Michael Young.

That was decisively not true of the House of Lords Michael Young grew up with, which was probably one reason why his patron Leonard Elmhirst declined a peerage when offered one in the 1940s; in the circles he moved in, he made clear, "acceptance would neither be easy for me to explain nor easy for my friends to comprehend."[59] It is more than a little ironic, then, that when Michael Young, the great egalitarian, was offered a peerage, in 1978, he took it. Naturally, he chose for himself the title Baron Young of Dartington, honoring the institution he had served as a trustee since the age of thirty. As you would expect, he used the opportunity to speak about the issues that moved him in the upper house of the British Parliament. But there is a further, final irony. A significant reason he had accepted the title ("guardedly," as he told his friends) was that he was having difficulties meeting the expense of traveling up to London from his home in the country. Members of the Lords not only got a daily allowance if they attended the House; they got a pass to travel free on the railways. Michael Young entered the aristocracy because he needed the money.[60]

SIX

CULTURE

Here's what our books have taught us:
That Greece once had the greatest reputation
For chivalry and learning.
Then chivalry went to Rome,
And so did all of learning,
Which now has come to France.

Chrétien de Troyes, *Cligès*
(1176?)

A "CULTURE" WAR

Like many Englishmen who suffered from tuberculosis in the nineteenth century, Sir Edward Burnett Tylor went abroad on medical
advice, seeking the drier air of warmer regions. Tylor came from a
prosperous Quaker business family, so he had the resources for a
long trip. In 1855, in his early twenties, he left for the United States,
traveling on in the early part of the next year to Cuba, where he met
another rich English Quaker, Henry Christy; and they ended up rid-
ing together through Mexican towns and countryside, visiting Aztec
ruins and dusty pueblos.

Christy was already an experienced archeologist. Under his tute-
lage, Tylor learned how to work in the field. He grew impressed by
what he called "the evidence of an immense ancient population,
shown by the abundance of remains of works of art."[1] Tylor published
an extensive account of his Mexican journey when he returned to
England, but that sojourn fired in him an enthusiasm for the study
of faraway societies, ancient and modern, that lasted the rest of his
life. In 1871, he produced his masterwork, *Primitive Culture,* which
can lay claim to being the first work of modern anthropology. Over
the decades, as his beard morphed from a lustrous Garibaldi to a vast,
silvery cumulonimbus that would have made Gandalf jealous, Tylor
added to his knowledge of the world's peoples through study in the
museum and the library.

Primitive Culture was, in some respects, a quarrel with another
book that had "culture" in the title: Matthew Arnold's *Culture and*

Anarchy, a collection that had appeared just two years earlier. (Yes, this is the same Matthew Arnold we met a couple of chapters back as an exemplar of the racial fixation.) For Arnold, the poet and literary critic, culture was the "pursuit of our total perfection by means of getting to know, on all the matters which most concern us, the best which has been thought and said in the world." Arnold wasn't interested in anything as narrow as class-bound connoisseurship—the postprandial flute duet, the recited Keats sonnet. He had in mind a moral and aesthetic ideal, which found expression in art and literature and music and philosophy.[2]

But Tylor thought that the word could mean something quite different, and in part for institutional reasons, he was able to make sure that it did. For Tylor was eventually appointed to direct the University Museum at Oxford, and then, in 1896, he became Oxford's first professor of anthropology. It is to Tylor more than anyone else that we owe the idea that anthropology is the study of something called "culture," which he defined as "that complex whole which includes knowledge, belief, arts, morals, law, customs, and any other capabilities and habits acquired by man as a member of society."[3] Civilization was merely one of culture's many modes.

Nowadays, when people speak about culture, it's usually either Tylor's or Arnold's notion that they have in mind. The two concepts of culture are, in some respects, antagonistic: Arnold's ideal was "the man of culture" and he would have considered "primitive culture" an oxymoron; Tylor's model denies that a person could be devoid of culture. Yet, in ways we'll explore, these contrasting notions of culture are locked together in our concept of Western culture, which many people think defines the identity of modern Western people. In this final chapter, I'm going to talk about culture as a source of identity, and to try to untangle some of our confusions about the culture, both Tylorian and Arnoldian, of what we've come to call the West.

You may have heard this story: someone asked Mahatma Gandhi what he thought of Western civilization, and he replied: "I think it would be a very good idea." Like many of the best stories, alas, this one is probably apocryphal; but also like many of the best stories, it has survived because it has the flavor of truth. I have been arguing that many of our thoughts about the identities that define us are misleading, and that we would have a better grasp on the real challenges that face us if we thought about them in new ways. In this last chapter I want to make an even more stringent case about a "Western" identity: whether you claim it, as many in Europe and the Americas might, or rebuff it, as many elsewhere around the world do, I think you should give up the very idea of Western civilization. It's at best the source of a great deal of confusion, at worst an obstacle to facing some of the great political challenges of our time. I hesitate to disagree with even the Gandhi of legend, but I believe Western civilization is not at all a good idea, and Western culture is no improvement.

One reason for the confusions that "Western culture" spawns comes from confusions about the West. We have used the expression "the West" to do a variety of very different jobs. Rudyard Kipling, England's poet of empire, wrote, "Oh, East is East and West is West, and never the twain shall meet," contrasting Europe and Asia, but ignoring everywhere else.[4] During the Cold War, "the West" was one side of the Iron Curtain; "the East" its opposite and enemy. This usage, too, effectively disregarded most of the world. Often, in recent years, "the West" means the North Atlantic: Europe and her former colonies in North America. The opposite here is a non-Western world in Africa, Asia, and Latin America—now dubbed "the Global South"—though many people in Latin America will claim a Western inheritance, too. This way of speaking takes notice of the whole world, but lumps a whole lot of extremely different societies together; at the same time, it delicately carves around nonindigenous Australians and New Zealanders and South Africans, so that "Western" here can look simply like a euphemism for white.

And, as everyone knows, we also talk today of the Western world to contrast it not with the South but with the Muslim world. Muslim thinkers themselves sometimes speak in a parallel way, distinguishing between Dar al-Islam, the home of Islam, and Dar al-Kufr, the home of unbelief.[5] This contrast is the one I want to explore in this final chapter. European and American debates today about whether Western culture is fundamentally Christian inherit, as we'll see, a genealogy in which "Christendom" was replaced by "Europe" and then by the idea of "the West."

CREATING THE EUROPEAN

For the Greek historian Herodotus, writing in the fifth century BCE, the inhabited earth was divided into three parts. To the east was Asia, to the south was a continent he called Libya, and the rest was Europe. He knew that people and goods and ideas could travel between the continents with little hindrance: he himself traveled up the Nile as far as Aswan, and on both sides of the Hellespont, the traditional boundary between Europe and Asia. Herodotus, the "father of history," admitted to being puzzled, in fact, as to "why the earth, which is one, has three names, all women's."[6] Still, for the Greeks and their Roman heirs, these continents were the largest significant geographical divisions of the world. It is a division we have inherited.

Now, here's the important point: it wouldn't have occurred to Herodotus to think that these three names corresponded to three kinds of people, Europeans, Asians, and Africans. He was born at Halicarnassus, Bodrum in modern Turkey. But being born in Asia Minor didn't make him an Asian; it left him a Greek. And the Celts—about whom he says only that they live "beyond the pillars of Hercules" in the far west of Europe—were much stranger to him than the Persians or the Egyptians, about whom he knew rather a lot. Herodotus uses the word "European" only as an adjective, never as a noun. It was a place, not an identity. For more than a millennium after his day, no one else spoke of Europeans as a people either.

Then the geography Herodotus knew was radically reshaped by the rise of Islam, which burst out of Arabia in the seventh century, spreading with astonishing rapidity north and east and west. After the Prophet's death in 632 CE, the Arabs managed in a mere thirty years to defeat the two great empires to their north, Rome's residue in Byzantium and the Persian empire that reached through central Asia as far as India.

The Umayyad dynasty, which began in 661, pushed on west into North Africa and east into Central Asia. In early 711, its army crossed the Strait of Gibraltar into Spain, which the Arabs called al-Andalus, and attacked the Visigoths who had ruled much of the Roman province of Hispania for two centuries. Within seven years, most of the Iberian Peninsula was under Muslim rule; not until 1492, nearly eight hundred years later, was the whole peninsula under Christian sovereignty again.[7]

The Muslim conquerors of Spain had not planned to stop at the Pyrenees, and they made regular attempts in the early years to continue moving north. But at Tours, in 732, Charles Martel, Charlemagne's grandfather, defeated the forces of Abd al-Rahman al-Ghafiqi, the governor of al-Andalus, and that turned out to be the decisive battle in ending the Arab attempts at the conquest of Frankish Europe. Edward Gibbon, surely overstating somewhat, observed that if the Arabs had won at Tours, they could have sailed on up the Thames. "Perhaps," he added, "the interpretation of the Koran would now be taught in the schools of Oxford, and her pulpits might demonstrate to a circumcised people the sanctity and truth of the revelation of Mahomet."[8]

What matters for our purposes is that the first recorded use of a word for Europeans as a kind of person seems to have come out of this history of conflict. A Latin chronicle, written in 754 in Spain, refers to the victors of the Battle of Tours as *"Europenses,"* Europeans.

Simply put, the very idea of a "European" was first used to contrast Christians and Muslims.[9]

Nobody in medieval Europe would have used the word "Western" to contrast Europeans with Muslims. For one thing, the western-most point of Morocco, home of the Moors, lies west of all of Ireland. The Muslim world stretched from west of Western Europe into Central and South Asia; much of it, if the points of the compass matter, was south of Europe. And, as we've just seen, parts of the Iberian Peninsula—which was uncontroversially part of the continent that Herodotus called Europe—were under Arab or Berber Muslim rule from 711 to 1492. The natural contrast was not between Islam and the West, but between Christendom and Dar al-Islam, each of which regarded the other as infidels, defined by their unbelief.

Neither of these was the name of a single state: the Muslim world divided politically into two major states—Umayyad and Abbasid—in 750, and gradually split further over the centuries as it spread farther east. Christendom was divided among even more rulers, although in Europe the great majority of them respected to some degree the authority of the popes in Rome. Each of the two religions covered vast areas—the Umayyad empire at its height extended for over 4.3 million square miles and comprised nearly 30 percent of the world's population; Charlemagne's Holy Roman Empire covered some 460,000 square miles in Western Europe, and the Byzantine Empire (the eastern heir to the Roman Empire) was only a little smaller at the time of Charlemagne's death, in 814.

At the end of the eleventh century, the First Crusade opened up another military front between European Christians and the Muslim world. In 1095, at Clermont in France, Pope Urban II, at the urging of Alexios I Komnenos, emperor of Byzantium, declared that anyone who, "for the sake of devotion, but not for money or honor," set out to liberate Jerusalem from Muslim control would no longer need to do any other penance for their sins. What followed was a series of invasions of the Holy Land by Christian armies, from all over Europe, which recaptured Jerusalem in 1099 and set up a number of crusader states there and in other parts of Palestine and Syria. Meanwhile, over the next three hundred years, the Turks who created the Ottoman Empire gradually extended their rule into parts of Europe: Bulgaria, Greece, the Balkans, and Hungary. Eastern Europe and Asia Minor were now a patchwork quilt of Muslim and Christian states, created and maintained by ferocious warfare and mired in intolerance. Only in 1529, with the defeat of Suleiman the Magnificent's army by the Holy Roman emperor's forces at Vienna, did the reconquest of Eastern Europe begin. It was a slow process. It wasn't until 1699 that the Ottomans finally lost their Hungarian possessions; Greece became independent only in 1830, Bulgaria even later.

We have, then, a clear sense of Christian Europe (Christendom) defining itself through opposition. And one approach to understanding talk of Western culture is to think of it as a way of talking about the culture in Tylor's sense—the socially transmitted "knowledge, belief, arts, morals, law, customs," and other capabilities—derived from Christian Europe.

THE GOLDEN NUGGET

The educated people of Christian Europe, however, inevitably inherited many of their ideas from the pagan societies that preceded them. Thus, even though the divide between the West and Islam began with a religious conflict, not everything in Western civilization is supposed to be Christian. This itself is a very old idea. At the end of the twelfth century, Chrétien de Troyes, born a hundred or so miles southwest of Paris, celebrated these earlier roots: "Greece once had the greatest reputation for chivalry and learning," he wrote. "Then chivalry went to Rome, and so did all of learning, which now has come to France." The idea that the best of the culture of Greece was

passed by way of Rome into Western Europe in the Middle Ages gradually became a commonplace. In fact, this process had a name. It was
called the *translatio studii,* the transfer of learning. And this, too, was
an astonishingly persistent idea. More than six centuries later, Hegel,
the great German philosopher, told the students of the high school
he ran in Nuremberg, "The foundation of higher study must be and
remain Greek literature in the first place, Roman in the second."[10]

So from the late Middle Ages through Hegel until now, people have
thought of the best in the culture of Greece and Rome as a European
inheritance, passed on like a precious golden nugget, dug out of
the earth by the Greeks, and transferred, when the Roman Empire
conquered them, to Rome, where it got a good polish. Eventually, it
was partitioned among the Flemish and Florentine courts and the
Venetian Republic in the Renaissance, its fragments passing through
cities such as Avignon, Paris, Amsterdam, Weimar, Edinburgh, and
London, and finally reunited in the academies of Europe and the
United States. This priceless treasure is no doubt nestled now somewhere here in the American academy, where I work . . . perhaps in
the university library right around the corner. And its content is the
West's Arnoldian culture, not the everyday habits of life that make up
much of what Tylor had in mind.

There are many ways of embellishing the story of the golden nugget. But they all face a historical challenge—at least if you want to
make the golden nugget the core of a Western civilization opposed
to Islam. For the classical inheritance it identifies was shared with
Muslim learning. In ninth-century Baghdad, in the Bayt al-Hikmah,
the palace library set up under the Abbasid caliphs, the works of Plato,
Aristotle, Pythagoras, and Euclid were translated into Arabic. They
became the basis of a tradition of scholarship that the Arabs called
falsafa, adapting the Greek word for philosophy. In the centuries that
Petrarch called the Dark Ages, when Christian Europe made little
contribution to the study of Greek classical philosophy, and many of
the texts were lost to view, these works, and the capacity to interpret

them, were preserved by Muslim scholars. And a good deal of what we now know of the texts of classical philosophy and how to read them we know only because that knowledge was recovered by European scholars in the Renaissance from the Arabs.

In the mind of its Christian chronicler, as we saw, the Battle of Tours pitted Europeans against Islam; but the Muslims of al-Andalus, bellicose as they were, did not think that fighting for territory meant that you could not share ideas. Even in its prosperous heyday, under Abd al-Rahman III, who ruled from 912 to 966 and proclaimed himself Caliph of Córdoba, al-Andalus was hardly a paradise of pluralism, to be sure; the character of the autocratic state was not to be challenged. Still, by the end of the first millennium, in Córdoba (then the largest city of Europe) and other cities of the Caliphate, Jews, Christians, and Muslims, Arabs, Berbers, Visigoths, Slavs, and countless others created the kind of cultural goulash—a spicy mixture of various distinct components—that generates a genuine cosmopolitanism.[11] The caliph himself, who, like his father, had a mother from the Christian north, was blue-eyed and fair-haired; mixing in al-Andalus was not merely cultural.

There were no recognized rabbis or Muslim scholars at the court of Charlemagne; in the cities of al-Andalus, by contrast, there were bishops and synagogues. Racemundo, Catholic Bishop of Elvira, was Córdoba's ambassador to Constantine VII, the Byzantine ruler, in Constantinople, and to Otto I, the Holy Roman emperor, in Aachen. Hasdai ibn Shaprut, leader of Córdoba's Jewish community in the middle of the tenth century, was not only a great medical scholar, he was the chairman of the caliph's medical council; and when the Emperor Constantine in Byzantium sent the caliph a copy of Dioscorides' *De materia medica,* the caliph took up ibn Shaprut's suggestion to send for a Greek monk to help translate it into Arabic. The knowledge they acquired made Córdoba one of the great centers of medical knowledge of Europe as well as of the Muslim world.[12]

The translation into Latin of the works of ibn Rushd, born in

Córdoba in the twelfth century, was crucial for the European redis-
covery of Aristotle. Ibn Rushd came from a distinguished family—his
father and grandfather held the office of chief judge in Córdoba—but
though trained, like them, as a Muslim legal scholar, he devoted most
of his intellectual energy to recovering Aristotle's original ideas from
the encrustations of ideas associated with Platonism. He was known
in Latin as Averroes, or more commonly just as "The Commentator,"
because of his extensive commentaries on Aristotle. Around 1230,
for example, Aristotle's *De anima* (On the Soul), which had been
unknown in Latin, the language of scholarship throughout the Middle Ages and after, was translated into Latin from the Arabic, along
with Averroes's commentary, probably by the court astrologer of the
Holy Roman emperor, Frederick II, one of whose titles was King of
Jerusalem. (The translation was finished while Frederick was recovering from the disastrous failure of the Fifth Crusade and preparing
for the Sixth.) The *De anima* became an important part of the philosophy curriculum in medieval European universities. So the classical traditions that are meant to distinguish Western Civ. from the
inheritors of the caliphates are actually a point of kinship with them.

Even the later boundaries of Christendom turn out to be more
complicated than we usually recall. In the heyday of the Ottoman
Empire, our battle lines were, we imagine, to the East. But in the late
sixteenth century, Queen Elizabeth I of England allied with the Ottoman Sultan Murad III, in part because of her Protestant isolation from
the great powers of continental Europe. (Some in her court shared
Murad's skepticism about whether Roman Catholicism succeeded in
avoiding idolatry. The Bishop of Winchester declared that the pope
was "a more perilous enemy unto Christ, than the Turk; and Popery
more idolatrous, than Turkery.")[13] And the Franco-Ottoman alliance,
which persisted sporadically through three centuries—from the time
of Suleiman the Magnificent through the time of Napoleon—saw
Christian and Muslim soldiers fighting alongside each other, largely
united by their Hapsburg enemies.[14]

The golden-nugget story imagines Western culture as the expression of an essence that has been passed from hand to hand on its historic journey. And we've seen the pitfalls of this sort of essentialism in these pages again and again. In the second chapter, we saw how the scriptures of a religion were supposed to determine its unchanging nature. In the third, it was the nation, bound together through time by language and custom. In the fourth, it was a racial quiddity shared by all blacks or all whites. In the last chapter, we saw how unhelpful it is to look for the essence of a class.

In each case, people have supposed that an identity that survives through time and across space must be underwritten by some larger, shared commonality; an essence that all the instances share. But that is simply a mistake. What was England like in the days of Chaucer, "father of English literature," who died more than six hundred years ago? Take whatever you think was distinctive of it, whatever combination of customs, ideas, and material things that made England characteristically English then. Whatever you choose to distinguish Englishness now, it isn't going to be *that*. Rather, as time rolls on, each generation inherits the label from an earlier one; and, in each generation, the label comes with a legacy. But as the legacies are lost or exchanged for other treasures, the label keeps moving on. And so, when some of those in one generation move elsewhere from the territory to which English identity was once tied—move, for example, to a *New* England—the label can even travel beyond the territory. Identities can be held together by narratives, in short, without essences: you don't get to be called "English" because there's an essence this label follows; you're English because our rules determine that you are entitled to the label—that you are connected in the right way with a place called England.

So how did people in New York and old York; in London, Ontario, and London, England; in Paris, Texas, and Paris, France, get connected into a realm we call the West and gain an identity as participants in something called Western culture?

HOW THE WEST WAS SPUN

In English, the very idea of the "West," to name a heritage and object of study, doesn't really emerge until the 1880s and 1890s, during a heated era of imperialism, and gains broader currency only in the twentieth century. So you can wonder about an age-old concept with such a recent name. For that matter, talk of "civilizations," in the plural, is pretty much a nineteenth-century development, too. When scholars in the late nineteenth century offered a view of Western civilization, it was somewhat at odds with our own: they would say Western civilization was rooted in Egypt and Phoenicia; or that Greek seaport towns were the cradle because they brought together elements from Egyptian, Syrian, Persian, and Indian civilizations; or that civilization traveled from East to West.[15]

The kindred term "Western culture," too, is surprisingly modern—certainly more recent than, say, Edison's phonograph. We've seen precursor ideas in the concepts of "Christendom" and "Europe," of course. In the previous chapter, I pointed out, apropos of "class," that the history of a term isn't always a guide to the history of its referent, but in this instance there is a true intimacy between the label and what it labels. It's significant that Tylor, say, never spoke of Western culture. And, indeed, he had no reason to, since he was profoundly aware of the internal cultural diversity even of his own country. In 1871 he reported evidence of witchcraft in rural Somerset. A blast of wind in a pub had blown some roasted onions stabbed with pins out of the chimney. "One had on it the name of a brother magistrate of mine, whom the wizard, who was the alehouse-keeper, held in particular hatred," Tylor wrote, "and whom apparently he designed to get rid of by stabbing and roasting an onion representing him."[16] Primitive culture, indeed.

The Decline of the West, written by Oswald Spengler around the time of the First World War, was the work that introduced many readers around the world to the concept. (He actually titled it *Der Untergang des Abendlandes,* literally, the decline of the evening lands—those lands nearest the setting sun. The term had once referred to the western provinces of the Roman Empire.) Yet his conception of the West was startlingly different from the one that's now commonplace. Spengler scoffed at the notion that there were continuities between Occidental culture and the classical world. "The word 'Europe' ought to be struck out of history," he further avowed. "There is historically no 'European type.'"[17] For him, critically, the West was defined by contrast to the culture of the classical world, to the culture of the ancient Christians (and Jews and Muslims), and to the "semi-developed" culture of the Slavs. For others, though, the Ottoman incursions remained imaginatively key. During a visit to the Balkans in the late 1930s, Rebecca West recounted her husband's sense that "it's uncomfortably recent, the blow that would have smashed the whole of our Western culture." The "recent blow" in question was the Turkish siege of Vienna in 1683.

If the notion of Christendom was an artifact of a prolonged series of military struggles against Muslim forces, our modern concept of Western culture largely took its present shape in the late 1940s and the 1950s, during the Cold War. In the chill of battle, we forged a grand Plato-to-NATO narrative about Athenian democracy, the Magna Carta, the Copernican Revolution, and so on.[18] Western culture was, at its core, individualistic and democratic and liberty-minded and tolerant and progressive and rational and scientific. Never mind that premodern Europe was none of these things, and that until the past century democracy was the exception in Europe, something that few stalwarts of Western thought had anything good to say about. The idea that tolerance was constitutive of something called Western culture would certainly have surprised Edward Burnett Tylor, who, as a Quaker, had been barred from attending England's great universities.

(Tylor's university appointments at Oxford occurred after the passage of the Universities Tests Act in 1871, which allowed people who were not Anglican to enter Oxford and Cambridge.) Indeed, it's possible to feel that if Western culture were real, we wouldn't spend so much time talking it up. Settling over us like a low-hanging fog, "culture," however qualified, has been required to do a great deal of work. I admit I have sometimes wondered whether the concept of culture, like the luminiferous ether that nineteenth-century physicists posited as the medium through which light waves traveled, explains rather less than we might hope.

Still, such historical and intellectual vagaries did not discourage genuinely distinguished scholars from accepting something like that Plato-to-NATO narrative. "The essence of Western culture, the basis of its success, the secret of its wide influence, is liberty," the French political theorist Raymond Aron declared in the 1950s. More recently, the intellectual historian Gertrude Himmelfarb has maintained that justice, reason, and the love of humanity "are, in fact, predominantly, perhaps even uniquely, Western values."[19]

Once Western culture could be a term of praise, it was bound to become a term of dispraise, too. Critics of Western culture, producing a photographic negative—light areas exchanged for dark—emphasizing slavery, subjugation, racism, militarism, and genocide, were committed to the very same essentialism, even if they saw a nugget not of gold but of arsenic.

MIRROR, MIRROR

In ways we've seen, the assertion of an identity always proceeds through contrast or opposition; and such critics are sometimes preoccupied with another supposed cultural clime, that of Africa. In a battle against the Victorian ideologies of "Eurocentrism," some critics have therefore rallied behind "Afrocentrism." Yet Afrocentrists have not always been certain whether Western culture is a burden to be jettisoned or a prize to be claimed. Starting in the 1950s, Cheikh Anta Diop, the Senegalese man of letters, argued strenuously that Greek civilization had African origins. (He maintained that its achievements derived from a more advanced Egyptian civilization, and that the ancient Egyptians were black.) His followers were left with certain awkward implications. If the West was spawned by Greece, which was spawned by Egypt, then wouldn't black people inherit the moral liability of its legacy of ethnocentrism? Other Afrocentrists, favoring a separate development, were happy to disclaim Greece, while elevating the civilizational achievements that were peculiarly African. Either way, this lineage-based model of culture confronts a challenge. If the ideology of "Western culture" posits an implausible unity, equally enrobing Alexander and Alfred and Frederick the Greats, the ideology of Afrocentrism had to make similar claims for the cultural unity of Africa.

Where might such a unifying essence repose? Many took inspiration from Janheinz Jahn's *Muntu: African Cultures and the Western World*, a work that appeared in the United States to great acclaim in the early 1960s. Its author was a German literary scholar who, in part owing to his friendship with the Senegalese poet and statesman Léopold Sédar Senghor, became an enthusiast for Négritude, a movement that stressed the cultural and racial kinship putatively shared by people of African descent. Curiously, though, he discovered the power core of African culture on the other side of the continent, in the concept of "NTU." It's the last syllable of the Kinyaruanda-Bantu words "Muntu" (person), "Kintu" (thing), "Hantu" (place and time), and "Kuntu" (modality). "NTU," Jahn concluded, "is the universal force as such." For the African, force and matter are integrally bound up, and it is in the "cosmic universal force" of NTU that "Being and beings coalesce." At the heart of the African conceptual world, then, was a truth that

Western rationalists had grown estranged from: a profound recognition of the harmony and coherence of all things.[20]

I recall, when I first encountered these arguments, being drawn into a fantasy in which an African scholar returns from London to Lagos with the important news that she has uncovered the key to Western culture. Soon to be published, *THING: Western Culture and the African World*, a work that exposes the philosophy of ING, written so clearly on the face of the English language. For ING, in the Euro-American view, is the inner dynamic essence of the world. In the very structure of the terms do*ing* and mak*ing* and mean*ing*, the English (and thus, by extension, all Westerners) express their deep commitment to this conception: but the secret heart of the matter is captured in their primary ontological category of th-*ing*; every th-*ing*—or be-*ing*, as their sages express the matter in the more specialized vocabulary of one of their secret societies—is not stable but ceaselessly changing. Here we see the fundamental explanation for the extraordinary neophilia of Western culture, its sense that reality is change.

I am caricaturing a caricature, of course. At such levels of abstraction, almost everything and its opposite can be claimed of almost anything we might call a culture. When non-Western cultures are extolled for their collectivism, cooperation, and spiritual enlightenment, it is typically in order to criticize the West for complementary vices such as rampant materialism, selfish individualism, and rapacious exploitation. This move is itself a familiar part of Western Europe's cultural repertory. Ventriloquizing the perspective of non-Western interlopers has often served the purposes of social commentary, notably in fictional epistolary works like Montesquieu's 1721 *Persian Letters* (in which one of his Persian travelers tartly reports that "there's never been a kingdom where there were as many civil wars as in that of Christ") or Oliver Goldsmith's 1761 *Citizen of the World* (in which a Chinese philosopher visiting London marvels that, while "their compacts for peace are drawn up with the utmost precision and ratified with the greatest solemnity . . . the people of Europe are almost continually at war").[21] The aim is, in Burns's phrase, to "see ourselves as others see us," or as we imagine they might.

ORGANIC TEMPTATIONS

Simply as a matter of scale, talk of "Western culture" has an immediate implausibility to overcome. It places at the heart of identity all manner of exalted intellectual and artistic achievements—philosophy, literature, art, and music, the things Arnold prized and humanists study. But if Western culture was there in Troyes in the late twelfth century when Chrétien was alive, it had little to do with the lives of most of his fellow citizens, who didn't know Latin or Greek and had never heard of Plato. Today in the United States the classical heritage plays no greater role in the everyday lives of most Americans. Look around at our modern metropolises, which must count as centers of Western civilization if anything does, and you will see great museums, great libraries, great theater, great music in every genre. Are these Arnoldian achievements what hold us city-dwellers together? Of course not. What holds us together, surely, is Tylor's broad sense of culture: our customs of dress and greeting, the habits of behavior that shape relations between men and women, parents and children, cops and civilians, shop assistants and consumers. Intellectuals like me have a tendency to suppose that the things *we* care about are the most important things. I don't say they don't matter. But they matter less than the story of the golden nugget suggests.

So how have we bridged the chasm here? How have we managed to persuade ourselves that we're rightful inheritors of Plato, Aquinas, and Kant, when the stuff of our existence is more Justin Bieber and Kim Kardashian? Well, by fusing the Tylorian picture and the Arnoldian one, the realm of the everyday and the realm of the ideal. And the key to this was something that was already present in Tylor's work.

Remember his famous definition: it began with culture as a "complex whole."[22] What you're hearing there is something we can call *organicism.* A vision of culture not as a loose assemblage of disparate fragments but as an organic unity, each component, like the organs in a body, carefully adapted to occupy a particular place, each part essential to the functioning of the whole. The Eurovision Song Contest, the cutouts of Matisse, the dialogues of Plato are all parts of a larger whole. As such, each is a holding in your cultural library, so to speak, even if you've never personally checked it out. It's your heritage and possession. Organicism explained how our everyday selves could be dusted with gold.

The trouble is that there just isn't one great big whole called culture that organically unites all these parts. There *are* organic wholes in our cultural life: the music, the words, the set design, and the choreography of an opera are meant to fit together. It is, to use Richard Wagner's term, a *Gesamtkunstwerk,* a total work of art. But the Tylorian cultures of the North Atlantic were not made together. They are not an organic whole. Spain, in the heart of the West, resisted liberal democracy for two generations after it took off in India and Japan in the East, the home of Oriental despotism. Jefferson's cultural inheritance—Athenian liberty, Anglo-Saxon freedom—did not prevent the United States from creating a slave republic. Nor, for that matter, did the Christian heritage of hostility to adultery keep him from having children with Sally Hemings, his slave. At the same time, Franz Kafka and Miles Davis can live together as easily, perhaps even more easily, than Kafka and the waltz king Johann Strauss, his fellow Austro-Hungarian. (Those bleakly comic parables don't keep 3/4 time.) You will find hip-hop in the streets of Tokyo and Takoradi and Tallinn. The same is true in cuisine. In my youth, Britons swapped their fish and chips for chicken tikka masala.[23] (This was a very wise exchange.)

Once we abandon organicism, we can take up the more cosmopolitan picture in which every element of culture—from philosophy or cuisine to the style of bodily movement—is separable in principle from all the others; you really can walk and talk in a way that's recognizably African-American *and* commune with Immanuel Kant and George Eliot, as well as with Bessie Smith and Martin Luther King Jr. No Muslim essence stops individual inhabitants of Dar al-Islam from taking up anything from the Western Civ. syllabus, including democracy. No Western essence is there to stop a New Yorker of any ancestry taking up Islam. Wherever you live in the world, Li Po can be one of your favorite poets, even if you've never been anywhere near China.

PROPERTY CRIMES

In some of the darker recesses of the Internet, enthusiasts for the idea of North America or Europe as the home of the White Race celebrate the achievements they claim for the West as somehow theirs. They claim National Socialism and Shakespeare, eugenics and Euclid, democracy and Dante. The far-right German movement Pegida (Patriotic Europeans Against the Islamization of the West) has called for the "preservation and protection of our Christian-Jewish Western culture," offering a pleasant compound in which a hyphen masks a history of massacres, expulsions, and mass murder.[24] I will let white nationalists have Nazism and eugenics for themselves; but I begrudge nobody the things I also love, because, like Arnold, I can love what is best in anyone's traditions while sharing it gladly with others. Yet if they believe that something in them, some racial essence, somehow connects them with an organic kernel, a *Geist*, that pervades Western culture, they understand neither race nor civilization. For what is best in Arnoldian culture cuts across color, place, and time. One of

Goethe's great poetic cycles is the *West-östlicher Divan*: it is inspired by the poetry of the fourteenth-century Persian poet Hafez, whose tomb in Shiraz is still a place of pilgrimage. (*Diwan* is the Persian word for a collection of poetry, so Goethe's title, "West-eastern Collection," is explicitly meant to bridge the gap.) Matsuo Basho, the magnificent haiku master of the seventeenth century, was shaped to a large degree by Zen Buddhism, and so an Indian—Siddhartha Gautama, the Buddha—is part of Basho's heritage. Kurosawa's *Throne of Blood*—its dark castle walls on Mount Fuji swathed in mist—is a powerful cinematic rendering of *Macbeth*.

That's why we should resist using the term "cultural appropriation" as an indictment. All cultural practices and objects are mobile; they like to spread, and almost all are themselves creations of intermixture. Kente in Asante was first made with dyed silk thread, imported from the East. We took something made by others and made it ours. Or rather, they did that in the village of Bonwire. So did the Asante of Kumasi appropriate the cultural property of Bonwire, where it was first made? Putative owners may be previous appropriators.

The real problem isn't that it's difficult to decide who owns culture; it's that the very idea of ownership is the wrong model. The Copyright Clause of the United States Constitution supplies a plausible reason for creating ownership of words and ideas: "To promote the progress of science and useful arts, by securing for limited times to authors and inventors the exclusive right to their respective writings and discoveries." But the arts progressed perfectly well in the world's traditional cultures without these protections; and the traditional products and practices of a group—its songs and stories, even its secrets—are not best understood as its property, or made more useful by being tethered to their putative origins.

For centuries, the people on the Venetian island of Murano made a living because glassmakers there perfected their useful art. Their beads, with multicolored filaments, some made of gold, were among the artistic wonders of the world. To keep their commercial advantage, the Venetian state forbade glassmakers from leaving with their secrets; the penalty for revealing them to outsiders was death. Good for Murano and its profits: bad for everyone else. (As it happens, lots of the skilled artisans escaped anyway and brought their knowledge to a wider European world.) Venetian beads were already being imported into the Gold Coast by the turn of the seventeenth century, arriving across the Sahara, where they had been an important part of the trade on which the empire of Mali had risen to commercial success centuries earlier. Crushed and sintered to make new beads, they developed into the distinctive *bodom* you still see today in Ghana, beads my mother and my stepgrandmother collected and made into bracelets and necklaces.[25] What sorts of progress would have been advanced by insisting that the Venetians owned the idea of glass beads, and policing their claim? Unfortunately, the vigorous lobbying of huge corporations has made the idea of intellectual property go imperial; it seems to have conquered the world. To accept the notion of cultural appropriation is to buy into the regime they favor, where corporate entities acting as cultural guardians "own" a treasury of IP, extracting a toll when they allow others to make use of it.

This isn't to say that accusations of cultural appropriation never arise from a real offense. Usually, where there's a problem worth noticing, it involves forms of disrespect compounded by power inequities; cultural appropriation is simply the wrong diagnosis. When Paul Simon makes a mint from riffing on mbaqanga music from South Africa, you can wonder if the rich American gave the much poorer Africans who taught it to him their fair share of the proceeds. If he didn't, the problem isn't cultural theft but exploitation. If you're a Sioux, you recognize your people are being ridiculed when some fraternity boys don a parody of the headdress of your ancestors and make whooping noises. But, again, the problem isn't theft, it's disrespect. Imagine how an Orthodox Jewish rabbi would feel if a gentile pop-music multimillionaire made a music video in which he used the Kaddish to mourn a Maserati he'd totaled. The offense isn't appropriation; it's the insult entailed by trivializing something another group holds sacred. Those who parse these transgressions in terms of ownership have accepted a commercial system that's alien to the traditions they aim to protect. They have allowed one modern regime of property to appropriate *them*.

CULTURE AS PROJECT

Although Tylor's notion of culture helped create our own, it wasn't exactly ours. Unlike so many of his colleagues, he saw culture as something you acquired and transmitted, and not as a feature of your racial inheritance. He did not use "culture" in the plural, however; he was a progressivist (like Arnold, in this respect) who thought in terms of stages, advancing from savagery to the happier state of civilization. Still, his fascination with the cultural range of humanity acknowledged, precisely, the humanity of those he studied, in a way that refashioned a discipline. Culture wasn't vaporous to him. He loved the material artifacts that he collected, although his vast beard once got entangled with a bow he was demonstrating to his students, and his attempts to start fires with flints did not always end well. When he retired from Oxford, he gave the university's committee for anthropology his enormous library on the topic: whatever your origins, he was convinced, you could enter deeply into other forms of life, but you had to put in the work.

We must, as well. This project can start with the recognition that culture is messy and muddled, not pristine and pure. That it has no essence is what makes us free. To be sure, the stories we tell that connect Plato or Aristotle or Cicero or St. Augustine to the contemporary American or European world have some truth in them. These grand arcs are sustained by self-conscious traditions of scholarship and argumentation. Remember those medieval Christians digging back through Averroes looking for Aristotle; or Chrétien claiming chivalry from Rome. The delusion is to think it suffices that we have *access* to these values, as if they're songs in a Spotify playlist we've never quite listened to. These thinkers may be part of our Arnoldian culture, but there's no guarantee that what is best in them will continue to mean something to the children of those who now look back to them, any more than the centrality of Aristotle to Muslim thought for hundreds of years guarantees him an important place in Muslim communities today.

Values aren't a birthright: you need to keep caring about them. Living in the West, however you define it—being Western, however you define *that*—provides no guarantee that you will care about Western Civ. The values that European humanists like to espouse belong as much to an African or an Asian who takes them up with enthusiasm as to a European. By that very logic, they *don't* belong to a European who hasn't taken the trouble to understand and absorb them. The same is true, naturally, of what we term non-Western cultures. The story of the golden nugget suggests that we can't help caring about the traditions of "the West" because they are ours: in fact, the opposite is true. They are ours only if we care about them. A culture of liberty, tolerance, and rational inquiry: that *would* be a good idea. But these values represent choices to make, not tracks laid down by a Western destiny.

In 1917, the year of Edward Burnett Tylor's death, what we've been taught to call Western civilization had stumbled into a death match with itself: the Allies and the Central Powers hurled bodies at each other, marching young men to their deaths in order to "defend civilization." The blood-soaked fields and gas-poisoned trenches must have shocked Tylor's evolutionist, progressivist hopes, and confirmed Arnold's worst fears about what civilization really meant. Arnold and Tylor would have agreed, at least, on this: culture isn't a box to be checked on the questionnaire of humanity; it's a process you join, in living a life with others.

CODA

And now what will become of us without
   barbarians?
Those men were some kind of solution.

C. P. Cavafy,
"Waiting for the Barbarians" (1898)

Perhaps you know this poem? Constantine Cavafy—if you'll permit me to introduce just one more character in closing—was a writer whose every identity came with an asterisk, a quality he shared with Svevo. Born two years after Svevo, he died only a few years after him. Cavafy was a Greek who never lived in Greece. A government clerk of Eastern Orthodox Christian upbringing in a tributary state of a Muslim empire that was under British occupation for most of his life, he spent his evenings on foot, looking for pagan gods in their incarnate, carnal versions. He was a poet who resisted publication, save for broadsheets he circulated among close friends; a man whose homeland was a neighborhood, and a dream. Much of his poetry is a map of Alexandria overlaid with a map of the classical world—modern Alexandria and ancient Athens—in the way that Leopold Bloom's Dublin neighborhood underlies Odysseus's Ithaca. No single sentence captures this Alexandrian genius better than E. M. Forster's evocation of him as "a Greek gentleman in a straw hat, standing absolutely motionless at a slight angle to the universe."[1] And I conjure Cavafy, here, at journey's end, because I want to persuade you that he is representative precisely in all his seeming anomalousness.

Poems, like identities, never have just one interpretation. But in Cavafy's "Waiting for the Barbarians" I see a reflection on the promise and the peril of identity. All day the anticipation and the anxiety build as the locals wait for the barbarians, who are coming to take over the city. The emperor in his crown, the consuls in their scarlet togas, the silent senate and the voiceless orators wait with the assembled masses to accept their arrival. And then, as evening falls, and they do not appear, what is left is only disappointment. We never see the barbarians. We never learn what they are actually like. But we do see the power of our imagination of the stranger. And, Cavafy hints, it's possible that the mere prospect of their arrival could have saved us from ourselves.

As we have seen throughout these pages, the labels we adhere to, the labels that adhere, willy-nilly, to us, work through and in spite of the mistakes we make about them. Cavafy was not exactly gay, not exactly Greek or Egyptian, not exactly Orthodox or pagan. But each of these labels tells you something about him, if you listen carefully to his own inflection of these modes of being. And Cavafy's Alexandria, like Svevo's Trieste, like the marvelous city I live in, was exactly the sort of cultural hodgepodge that could provide the space for him to be each of these things in his own way, negotiating with his friends and acquaintances, struggling with his city; it allowed him to shape a self that was not merely captured but also liberated by the identities that enmeshed him. In my final chapter, I argued that our largest cultural identities can free us only if we recognize that we have to make their meanings together and for ourselves. You do not get to be Western without choosing your way among myriad options, just as you do not get to be Christian or Buddhist, American or Ghanaian, gay or straight, even a man or a woman, without recognizing that each of these identities can be lived in more than one way.

Cavafy's own community—cosmopolitan Alexandria—has long since vanished; the end of the British protectorate and the rise of Arab nationalism made the city less hospitable to its motley crew of strangers. In Naguib Mahfouz's 1967 novel *Miramar*, an Alexandrian Greek, mistress of the eponymous *pensione*, reflects of her people, "They're gone, every one of them." Mr. Amer, an aging Egyptian friend and tenant, tries to console her. "*We* are your people now," he says. "That sort of thing is happening everywhere."[2] It is, indeed. But so, alas, is a move in the other direction: a choice for an imaginary purity, a clinging to an unreal essence, an insistence on a single significance for labels whose meanings need to be kept open and contestable. If essentialism is a misstep in the realms of creed, color, country, class, and culture, as it is in the domain of gender and sexuality, then it is never true that identity leaves us no choices. The existentialists were right: existence precedes essence; we are before we are anything in particular. But the fact that identities come without essences does not mean they come without entanglements. And the fact that they need interpreting and negotiating does not mean that each of us can do with them whatever we will.

For these labels belong to communities; they are a social possession. And morality and political prudence require us to try to make them work for us all. Over the course of my lifetime, I have watched, learned from, and participated in the reshaping of what it means to be women and men (and yes, sometimes neither) in the various interconnected places I have lived my life. Without the reshaping of gender that has increasingly liberated us all from old patriarchal assumptions, I could not have lived my life as a gay man, married to another man, making a life, in public and in private ways, together. This life has been made possible through other people's struggle, in ways both large and small, and by my taking small risks with friends, employers, and family. If I had stayed in Ghana, where I grew up, I would, like other lesbian and gay Ghanaians, have a long road still to travel. But in the meanwhile, women in Asante, who were always more autonomous than in many other parts of the world, have seen their options grow and prosper, in part by recognizing that much that was once assumed impossible for women, because they were women—because of what a woman essentially was—could be *made* possible; and that a world of empowered women is enriching for men as well.

There is a liberal fantasy in which identities are merely chosen, so we are all free to be what we choose to be. But identities without demands would be useless to us. Identities work only because, once they get their grip on us, they command us, speaking to us as an inner voice; and because others, seeing who they think we are, call on us, too. If you do not care for the shapes your identities have taken, you cannot simply refuse them; they are not yours alone. You have to work with others inside and outside the labeled group in order to reframe them so they fit you better; and you can do that collective work only if you recognize that the results must serve others as well.

In the poem "Walls," Cavafy writes:

Without reflection, without sorrow, without shame,
they've built around me great, high walls.
And I sit here now and despair.
I think of nothing else: this fate consumes my mind:
because I had so many things to do out there.[3]

We all have many things to "do out there" in the world. And the problem is not walls as such but walls that hedge us in; walls we played no part in designing, walls without doors and windows, walls that block our vision and obstruct our way, walls that will not let in fresh and enlivening air.

The modes of identity we've considered can all become forms of confinement, conceptual mistakes underwriting moral ones. But they can also give contours to our freedom, as working-class and LGBTQ and national and religious identities have done in struggles all around the world. Women, negotiating intersectionality, have worked together across class and language and religion and nation in the global struggle against oppression and inequality. Social identities connect the small scale where we live our lives alongside our kith and kin with larger movements, causes, and concerns. They can make a wider world intelligible, alive, and urgent. They can expand our horizons to communities larger than the ones we personally inhabit. And our lives *must* make sense at the largest of all scales as well. We are denizens of an age in which our actions, in the realm of ideology as in the realm of technology, increasingly have global effects. When it comes to the compass of our concern and compassion, humanity as a whole is not too broad a horizon.

We live with 7 billion fellow humans on a small, warming planet. The cosmopolitan impulse that draws on our common humanity is no longer a luxury; it has become a necessity. And, in encapsulating that ancient ideal, I can draw on someone who's a frequent presence in courses in Western Civ., the dramatist Terence: a slave from Roman Africa, a Latin interpreter of Greek comedies, a writer from classical Europe who called himself, like Anton Wilhelm Amo, "the African." Here's how Publius Terentius Afer, writing more than two millennia ago, put it:

Homo sum, humani nihil a me alienum puto.
I am human, I think nothing human alien to me.

Now there's an identity that should bind us all.

Acknowledgments

This book began with the 2016 Reith Lectures for the BBC, under the title "Mistaken Identities," and I am extremely grateful to Gwyneth Williams, controller of BBC Radio 4, who first discussed with me the prospect of my giving them and then helped me to shape my ideas for them. I owe a profound debt, as well, to Hugh Levinson and Jim Frank, who edited and produced the series. All of these radio professionals know how much they improved the first drafts I sent them; as does Bob Weil, my editor, whose copious and enthusiastic notes guided my final revisions. Henry Finder, my spouse, is always my first and best reader, and though I once promised we would share all our worldly goods, I'm afraid that I must claim all the faults that remain in this book for myself.

The actual writing began in the summer of 2016 at the Rockefeller Foundation's Bellagio Center, where a few mostly uninterrupted weeks of work allowed me to draft three of the four lectures and begin the fourth. I am very grateful to the staff of the center, who make sure that visitors are fed three delicious meals a day and left otherwise to their own devices. Over the weeks I was there, a variety of other guests, from all over the world, provided stimulus in conversations over meals and in seminars. I am especially grateful to the dozen or so people who responded to my first run-through of the lecture on religion.

The lectures were delivered in London, Glasgow, Accra, and New York, on a cosmopolitan circuit suggested by the BBC. So I heard responses from a range of audiences with different preoccupations, and was helped to see new angles that I have tried to capture in rewriting and extending the initial arguments. Sue Lawley, the program's host, did her usual, highly professional job of guiding the discussions that followed each of the lectures. It was a pleasure spending time with her and with each of the audiences.

Henry Louis Gates Jr. introduced me to the issues discussed in the chapter on color many years ago, since he had explored them in his 1978 Cambridge doctoral thesis *The History and Theory of Afro-American Literary Criticism, 1773–1831: The Arts, Aesthetic Theory, and the Nature of the African*. I am grateful for his friendship over the last forty years, but, for the purposes of this book, I am especially grateful for our many conversations about the race concept.

In developing the arguments of the talks into a book, I have added a chapter on class, which seemed to me an obvious absence in the lectures, and expanded my discussion of gender. I learned a great deal about Singapore while visiting there as a participant in the Foresight Conference of the Centre for Strategic Futures, in the Office of the Prime Minister, in July 2017. I'm particularly grateful to Han Fook Kwang for his summary at that meeting of the early history of identity policy in Singapore. I was also enlightened through conversations with a number of people I met outside the group, including some vigorously, if discreetly, dissenting voices.

I was blessed, as I hope this book makes clear, in the families that I was born into. My English grandmother and Ghanaian stepgrandmother gave me much love but also taught me so much more than I think they realized. My parents are presences throughout this book, and I have thanked them often before. But without my sisters, my life would have been so much less rewarding, because they are smart and interesting and loyal, and, of course, because without them I would not have the wonderful nephews and nieces whose fates I follow as they take on the world. So Isobel, Adwoa, and Abena, thank you.

The book is dedicated to your grandchildren; they are, as the dedication says, my hope for the future, not having children or (therefore) grandchildren of my own. I hope the world they are growing into will be one of constantly evolving identities that give them and their generation the combination of freedom and constraint that make the best in human life possible. Olanitan, the first of them, carries a Yoruba name, which means "one with a rich history." Born, like me, in London—as the son of a Nigerian mother and a father whose grandparents were English, Ghanaian, and Nigerian—and growing up, at least for now, in Nigeria, he has inherited connections to even more places than my sisters and I were endowed with. His cousins will swap out Nigeria for Norway, but add in Namibia and Russia. There are those who think that this must leave them rootless: I count them, rather, lucky to have roots in so many places, and urge them all to do their part in shaping to good purpose the identities they inherit. They will have my assistance, if they need it, and, in any case, my blessing.

There is, as always, a great deal more to be said on each of the topics I have taken up. Each has complexities I haven't been able to probe. T. S. Eliot once wrote that "the larger part of the labour of an author" was "the labour of sifting, combining, constructing, expunging, correcting, testing . . ."[4] You could always do more, as this suggests, but at some point you have to stop. I take comfort in the fact that—as I argued in my last book, *As If: Idealization and Ideals*—imperfect pictures are the only serviceable tools we have for making sense of the world. But part of the point of a book like this is to allow its readers to build their own pictures. As I said at the outset, my aim is to start conversations, not to end them.

Adinkra

Adinkra symbols (seen throughout this book) are used by the Akan people of Ghana to express complex beliefs, concepts, or aphorisms. In use for hundreds of years, these images are typically found on printed textiles, carved wooden objects, architectural features, and jewelry.

SANKOFA
"go back and get it"
learning from the past

ANANSE NTONTAN
"spider web"
wisdom and creativity

NYAME NTI
"by God's grace"
faith

NKYINKYIM
"twisting"
initiative, dynamism, versatility

SUNSUM
"the soul"
spirituality and purity

OHENE ADWA
"the king's stool"
state, chieftaincy

NSEREWA
wealth and abundance

Notes

ONE Classification

1. When I quote literary classics in the text, as in the epigraphs, I won't put a reference in a note: in the age of the Internet, you'll be able to find these passages and their contexts without publishing details. When I refer to the Christian Bible, I'll use the King James translation and usually give the book. For the Quran, I'll use *The Holy Qur'an* (Classics of World Literature), trans. Abdullah Yusuf Ali (London: Wadsworth Editions, 2001). Where I have used translations, I have acknowledged the translator in the notes; where there is no translator mentioned, the translation is mine.
2. Erik H. Erikson, "Autobiographic Notes on the Identity Crisis," *Daedalus* 99 no. 4 (Fall 1970): 743, 747; Sue Erikson Bloland, *In the Shadow of Fame* (New York: Viking, 2005), 65.
3. Erik H. Erikson, *Childhood and Society*, 2nd ed. (New York: W. W. Norton, 1985; originally published 1950), 282.
4. Alvin W. Gouldner, "Cosmopolitans and Locals: Toward an Analysis of Latent Social Roles—I," *Administrative Science Quarterly* 2 no. 3 (December 1957): 282–283.
5. Paul Dundas, *The Jains*, 2nd ed. (New York: Routledge & Kegan Paul, 2002), 158–159.
6. Kwame Anthony Appiah, *In My Father's House: Africa in the Philosophy of Culture* (New York: Oxford University Press, 1992).
7. In North India, the term *kinnar* does much the same work; in Tamil-Nadu, in the south, they'll often use *aravani*. *Report of the Expert Committee on the Issues Relating to Transgender Persons* (Ministry of Social Justice and Empowerment, Government of India), Appendix 2, http://socialjustice.nic.in/writereaddata/UploadFile/Binder2.pdf.
8. *Ibid.*, 102.

9. *Hijras* are not typically intersexes, it should be pointed out, although some intersexes were likely to identify as *hijras*, at least in the past.

10. Arundhati Roy, *The Ministry of Utmost Happiness* (New York: Knopf, 2017), 23.

11. Carolyn Apple, "A Navajo Worldview and Nádleehí: Implications for Western Categories," in *Two-Spirit People: Native American Gender Identity, Sexuality, and Spirituality*, ed. Sue-Ellen Jacobs, Wesley Thomas, and Sabine Lang (Champaign: University of Illinois Press, 1997), 174–191.

12. M. Blackless *et al.*, "How Sexually Dimorphic Are We? Review and Synthesis," *American Journal of Human Biology* 12 no. 2 (March 2000): 151–166. And cf. "How Common Is Intersex," Intersex Society of North America, http://www.isna.org/faq/frequency. Scientific estimates depend on which conditions count as intersexual, and range widely, from .05 to 1.7 percent.

13. Kimberlé W. Crenshaw, "Mapping the Margins: Intersectionality, Identity Politics, and Violence Against Women of Color," *Stanford Law Review* 43 no. 6 (July 1991): 1241–1299.

14. See, e.g., "The Habitus and the Space of Life-Styles," in Pierre Bourdieu, *Distinctions* (Cambridge: Harvard University Press, 1987), 169 *et seq.*; and John B. Thompson, "Editor's Introduction," in Pierre Bourdieu, *Language and Symbolic Power* (Cambridge: Polity Press, 1991), 12.

15. Pierre Bourdieu, *The Logic of Practice* (Stanford: Stanford University Press, 1980), 69–70; Thompson, in Bourdieu, *Language and Symbolic Power*, 13.

16. "... *un nouveau parler des intellectuels, un peu hésitant, voire bredouillant, interrogatif ('non?') et entrecoupé*"; "... *l'ancien usage professoral (avec ses périodes, ses imparfaits du subjonctif, etc.)*," Pierre Bourdieu, *Ce que parler veut dire: L'économie des échanges linguistiques* (Paris: Fayard, 1982), 56.

17. *The Encyclopedia of African-American Popular Culture*, ed. Jesse Carney Smith (Santa Barbara, CA: Greenwood, 2011), 3:1089.

18. Bourdieu, *Language and Symbolic Power*, 86–89.

19. Thompson, in Bourdieu, *Language and Symbolic Power*, 17–18.

20. Claude Steele, *Whistling Vivaldi: And Other Clues to How Stereotypes Affect Us* (New York: W. W. Norton, 2010), 7. The graduate student in question, Brent Staples, went on to be a well-known *New York Times* columnist.

21. Susan Gelman, "Psychological Essentialism in Children," *Trends in Cognitive Sciences* 8 no. 9 (September 2004): 404–409.

22. Sarah-Jane Leslie, "The Original Sin of Cognition: Fear, Prejudice, and Generalization," *Journal of Philosophy* 114 no. 8 (August 2017): 393–421.

23. Marjorie Rhodes, Sarah-Jane Leslie, and Christina M. Tworek, "Cultural Transmission of Social Essentialism," *Proceedings of the National Academy of Sciences* 109 no. 34 (August 21, 2012): 13526–13531. The idea that some racial prejudice arises from the normal operation of basic cognitive

mechanisms is the thrust of Sarah-Jane Leslie's argument in "The Original Sin."

24. Graham Robb, *The Discovery of France: A Historical Geography* (New York: W. W. Norton, 2007), 43–47. Robb sorts through various old conjectures—were the Cagots descendants of Visigoths, or Saracen invaders, or Cathar heretics, or lepers?—and theorizes that they may have originated simply as a medieval carpenter's guild, stigmatized by rival guilds. In the nineteenth century, the widely traveled Irish writer Thomas Colley Grattan described them as "a rejected caste, enveloped in a mystery which no research can penetrate," and proposed, "We might, by imagining the possibility of their amelioration, lead to plans for their relief; and instead of useless efforts to account for their miseries, make practical attempts to remove them. . . . While contemplating with shame, the narrow circle into which man may imprison his fellow man, we have at least the consolation of knowing that he possesses in himself the power of dissolving the shackles he has forged; and of buying the memory of his own injustice, in an oblivious flood of charity and atonement." Thomas Colley Grattan, *High-ways and By-ways: The Cagot's Hut* (London: Henry Colburn & Richard Bentley, 1831), 46, 48–49. See also Sean Thomas, "The Last Untouchable in Europe," *The Independent on Sunday*, July 27, 2008, http://www.independent.co.uk/news/world/europe/the -last-untouchable-in-europe-878705.html.

25. Muzafer Sherif *et al.*, *The Robbers Cave Experiment: Intergroup Conflict and Cooperation* (Middletown, CT: Wesleyan University Press, 1988; originally published by the Institute of Group Relations, University of Oklahoma, 1961), 95–116. I discussed this experiment in my book *The Ethics of Identity* (Princeton: Princeton University Press, 2005), 84–85.

26. Sherif *et al.*, *op. cit.*, 116.

TWO Creed

1. Robert Emory, *History of the Discipline of the Methodist Episcopal Church*, revised by W. P. Strickland (New York: Carlton & Porter, 1857), 55.

2. Philo of Alexandria, "On Monarchy. Book 1," in *The Works of Philo Judaeus*, vol. 3, trans. C. D. Yonge (London: Henry G. Bohn, 1855), 182; and *On the Creation: Allegorical Interpretation of Genesis 2 and 3*, trans. F. H. Colson and G. H. Whitaker (Cambridge: Harvard University Press, 1929), 135.

3. Gore Vidal, *Julian* (New York: Vintage International, 2003; originally published 1964), 331.

4. http://www.alifta.net/fatawa/fatawaDetails.aspx?languagename=en&View=Page&PageID=12069&PageNo=1&BookID=7.

5. See, for example, Robert Frykenberg, "The Emergence of Modern 'Hinduism' as a Concept and as an Institution: A Reappraisal with Special

Reference to South India," in *Hinduism Reconsidered*, ed. G. D. Sont-
heimer and H. Kulke (Delhi: Manoh, 1989), 29–49; Richard King, "Ori-
entalism and the Modern Myth of 'Hinduism,'" *Numen* 46 no. 2 (1999):
146–185; Harjot Oberoi, *The Construction of Religious Boundaries: Culture,
Identity, and Diversity in the Sikh Tradition* (Chicago: University of Chicago Press, 1994), 16–18; Pankaj Mishra, "The Invention of the Hindu,"
Axess Magazine, June 2004; and Wendy Doniger, *The Hindus: An Alternative History* (New York: Penguin Press, 2009). Firmly on the other side
is David N. Lorenzen, "Who Invented Hinduism?" *Comparative Studies in
Society and History* 41 no. 4 (October 1999): 630–659.

6. *"Tantum religio potuit suadere malorum"* (So potent was Religion in per-
suading to do wrong). Lucretius, *On the Nature of Things*, trans. A. E. Stall-
ings (New York: Penguin, 2007), Book 1, line 101. Valuable discussions
about the formation of the religion concept can be found in Wilfred
Cantwell Smith, *The Meaning and End of Religion* (New York: Macmillan,
1963); Talal Asad, *Genealogies of Religion: Discipline and Reasons of Power
in Christianity and Islam* (Baltimore: Johns Hopkins University Press,
1993); Brian C. Wilson, "From the Lexical to the Polythetic: A Brief History of the Definition of Religion," in *What Is Religion? Origins, Defini-
tions, and Explanations*, ed. Thomas A. Idinopulos and Brian C. Wilson
(Leiden: Brill, 1998), 142–162; Daniel Dubuisson, *The Western Construction of Religion: Myths, Knowledge, and Ideology*, trans. William Sayers
(Baltimore: Johns Hopkins University Press, 2003); and Brent Nongbri,
Before Religion: A History of a Modern Concept (New Haven: Yale University Press, 2013).

7. Robert Wright's illuminating *The Evolution of God* (New York: Little,
Brown, 2009) describes "scriptural determinists" as "people who think
that scripture exerts overwhelming influence on the religious thought of
believers, and that their social and political circumstances matter little
if at all." At the beginning of chap. 8, he notes one deployment of this:
"'Scriptural determinism' sounds like an arcane academic paradigm, but
it is deployed by nonacademics in a consequential way. After the terror-
ist attacks of September 11, 2001, as Americans tried to fathom the forces
at work, sales of several kinds of books rose. Some people bought books
about Islam, some bought books about the recent history of the Middle
East, and some bought translations of the Koran. And, of course, some
bought more than one kind of book. But people who bought *only* translations of the Koran were showing signs of scriptural determinism. They
seemed to think that you could understand the terrorists' motivation simply by reading their ancient scriptures—just search the Koran for passages advocating violence against infidels and, having succeeded, end the
analysis, content that you'd found the essential cause of 9/11."

8. I once tested Google Translate with a line of Mallarmé's *"L'après-midi*

d'une faune": *"Assoupi de sommeils touffus"* came back as "Sleepy with bushy sleep." (It actually means something like "made drowsy with thick slumbers.")

9. I discuss these scholarly issues in more detail in "Respecting Gay People: Justice and the Interpretation of Scriptural Traditions," in *Justice Through Diversity? A Philosophical and Theological Debate,* ed. Michael Sweeny (Lanham, MD: Rowman & Littlefield, 2016), 551–572.

10. "καὶ ὃς ἂν κοιμηθῇ μετὰ ἄρσενος κοίτην γυναικός ... ," Leviticus 20:13. For Classical Greece: K. J. Dover, *Greek Homosexuality* (Cambridge: Harvard University Press, 1989; originally published 1978); for Rome: Craig Williams, *Roman Homosexuality: Ideologies of Masculinity in Classical Antiquity* (New York: Oxford University Press, 1999).

11. My understanding of the issues of the history of the biblical texts that I address by way of example here derives largely from Lee Martin McDonald, *The Biblical Canon: Its Origin, Transmission, and Authority* (Grand Rapids, MI: Baker Academic, 2007). I rely on him for most historical claims about texts, though I have examined some of those to which he refers. What matters for my purposes is only that these are views that a reasonable Christian might hold, not that they are uncontroversially true. But this reading is very much a Protestant reading, and I am not going to discuss the (somewhat different) current Roman Catholic views about the formation of the biblical canon.

12. Lee Martin McDonald says that part of what Paul writes here could come from the so-called *Ascension of Isaiah*: "This angel said to me, 'Isaiah, son of Amoz, [it is enough for you], for these (are) great things, for you have observed what no one born of flesh has observed.'" Although the *Ascension* itself was composed after the time of Paul, it may have incorporated earlier texts. See *Ascension of Isaiah* 11:34, from *The Old Testament Pseudepigrapha,* trans. M. A. Knibb, in *Apocalyptic Literature: A Reader,* ed. Mitchell G. Reddish (Nashville: Abingdon Press, 1990), 280–290.

13. Jerome Murphy-O'Connor, "The Non-Pauline Character of 1 Corinthians 11:2–16?" *Journal of Biblical Literature* 95 no. 4 (December 1976): 615.

14. See Jeffrey S. Siker, ed., *Homosexuality in the Church: Both Sides of the Debate* (Louisville, KY: Westminster John Knox Press, 1994).

15. Islamic jurisprudence can get caricatured in the way many Westerners think about sharia. Sharia is divine guidance for leading a devout life; fiqh, its human implementation, is devised by scholars who, drawing from the Koran and the hadith, regularly debate and disagree about issues like abortion and matrimonial laws. (Fiqh scholars generally say that Muslims must uphold the law of non-Muslim countries where they live.) Fiqh-devised statutes can be retrograde or progressive. The approach is not so different from the Natural Law theory that derives from Aquinas and is held by at least one (and perhaps two) of the United

States Supreme Court Justices who are sitting as I write. In this Aquin-ian tradition, natural law ultimately comes from He who created human nature, and is how humans, through reason, participate in Eternal Law. (In Aquinas's formulation: "the natural law is nothing else than the rational creature's participation in the eternal law." *Summa I–II, Q. 91, Art. 2*.) But because natural law is known by human reason, prop-erly used, it is accessible to anyone, whatever their religious views. One might bear in mind, too, that the late Justice Antonin Scalia avowed that the Ten Commandments were a "symbol of the fact that government derives its authority from God." Margaret Talbot, "Supreme Confidence," *New Yorker*, March 28, 2005, 53.

16. Rabba Hurwitz's position is, to be sure, not accepted by the Rabbini-cal Council of America, the main Modern Orthodox organization. The number of female Anglican clerics is discussed in George Arnett, "How Much of the Church of England Clergy Is Female?" *The Guardian*, Febru-ary 11, 2014, https://www.theguardian.com/news/datablog/2014/feb/11/how-much-church-of-england-clergy-female.

17. *The Vimalakirti Sutra*, trans. Burton Watson (New York: Columbia Uni-versity Press, 1997), 91.

18. Philo, *Supplement II; Questions and Answers on Exodus*, trans. Ralph Mar-cus (Cambridge: Harvard University Press, 1953), 40–41.

THREE Country

1. Jan Morris, *Trieste and the Meaning of Nowhere* (New York: Simon & Schuster, 2001), 3.

2. Just as his father's being German didn't have much to do with Germany, Schmitz's being Jewish didn't have much to do with Judaism; see Neil Davidson, *James Joyce, Ulysses, and the Construction of Jewish Identity* (Cambridge: Cambridge University Press, 1996), chap. 7.

3. Georg Wilhelm Friedrich Hegel, "*In dem Dasein eines Volkes ist der substantielle Zweck, ein Staat zu sein und als solcher sich zu erhalten; ein Volk ohne Staatsbildung (ein* Nation *als solche) hat eigentlich keine Geschichte . . . ,*" in Hegel, *Enzyklopädie der philosophischen Wissenschaften im Grundrisse* (1830), sec. 549.

4. Millard adds: "Documenting one's own descent from Edward III is, however, another matter!" https://community.dur.ac.uk/a.r.millard/genealogy/EdwardIIIDescent.php.

5. Saadat Hasan Manto, "Toba Tek Singh," http://www.wordswithoutborders.org/article/toba-tek-singh.

6. Canada, Australia, and South Africa received independence under the British Crown in 1867, 1901, and 1910, respectively. New Zealand had been effectively self-governing since 1853. (Newfoundland joined Canada

in 1949.) Ireland was an independent dominion from 1922 until 1939, and then separated entirely from the British Crown.

7. Sudan became independent earlier, in 1956, but it was, strictly speaking, not a British colony but an Anglo-Egyptian condominium.

8. *"inferretque deos Latio, genus unde Latinum, / Albanique patres, atque altae moenia Romae."* *Aeneid*, Book I, ll.6–7. " 'ξυνελών τε λέγω τήν τε πᾶσαν πόλιν τῆς Ἑλλάδος παίδευσιν εἶναι . . ." (In sum, I say that as a city we are the school of Hellas . . .), Thucydides *History of the Peloponnesian War* 2.41.

9. *"Graecia capta ferum victorem cepit et artes intulit agresti Latio . . ."* (Greece, made captive, took her savage victor captive and brought the arts to rustic Rome . . .), Horace *Epistles* 2.1.

10. Robert Burns, "Scots' Prologue for Mr. Sutherland," http://www .robertburns.org/works/298.shtml.

11. Stanley Price, "Schmitz to Svevo to Bloom," *Jewish Quarterly* 63 no. 1 (January 2016): 32–35.

12. As cited in P. N. Furbank, *Italo Svevo: The Man and the Writer* (Berkeley: University of California Press, 1966), 19. And see Victor Brombert, "Svevo's Witness," *American Scholar* 6 no. 3 (Summer 1991): 425–432.

13. Lady Isabel Burton, *The Life of Captain Sir Richard F. Burton*, vol. 2 (London: Chapman & Hall, 1893), 499.

14. Davidson, *op. cit.*, 161–162.

15. *"Svevo poteva scrivere bene in tedesco; preferì scrivere male in italiano."* Umberto Saba, *Scorciatoie e raccontini* (Torino: Giulio Einaudi: 2011; originally published 1946), 100.

16. Sherry Simon, *Cities in Translation: Intersections of Language and Memory* (Abingdon, UK: Routledge, 2011), 71; and Brombert, *op cit.* Brombert notes that Svevo's elementary school was directed by Trieste's chief rabbi, and that his Bavarian boarding school, though secular, had a Jewish headmaster and a significant clientele among the children of German-Jewish businessmen.

17. Italo Svevo, *Zeno's Conscience*, trans. William Weaver (New York: Vintage International, 2003), 109. There is no very good English rendering of *coscienza*, which can mean both "consciousness" and "conscience."

18. See Eugen Weber, "Who Sang the Marseillaise?" in *My France: Politics, Culture, Myth* (Cambridge, MA: Belknap Press, 1991), 92–102.

19. The more than 1 million people of Japanese descent in the Brazilian city of São Paulo almost outnumber the non-Japanese legal residents who live among the 125 million Japanese. There are about a quarter of a million illegal immigrants in Japan as well. See "Japan Web Site Irks Illegal Aliens," *Taipei Times*, May 7, 2004, 5, http://www.taipeitimes.com/ News/world/archives/2004/05/07/2003154450. I discuss these matters in "Misunderstood Cultures: Islam and the West," in *Toward New*

Democratic Imaginaries: Istanbul Seminars on Islam, Culture, and Politics, ed. Seyla Benhabib and Volker Kaul (Basel, Switzerland: Springer International Publishing, 2016), 201–210.

20. http://www.triest-ngo.org/the-free-territory-of-trieste/. And cf. Tara Isabella Burton, "Trieste: The Italian City That Wants a Divorce," BBC News, October 31, 2014, http://www.bbc.com/news/magazine-29822594.

21. Sometimes these families are referred to as Peranakan Chinese, using a Malay word that means "descendant," which connotes remote ancestry from China. After spending a few hours in the Peranakan Museum in Singapore, the one thing I came away with was a firm conviction that what exactly makes you Peranakan—their ancestors include at least Malays, Indians, and Chinese—is contested and hard to explain. The most identifiable Peranakan product is probably its excellent cuisine.

22. Article 153. (1) "It shall be the responsibility of the Yang di-Pertuan Agong [the Malaysian Head of State] to safeguard the special position of the Malays and natives of any of the States of Sabah and Sarawak and the legitimate interests of other communities in accordance with the provisions of this Article."

23. The Statutes of the Republic of Singapore, chap. 290, "Sedition Act," sec. 3 (1) (e).

24. Lai Ah Eng and Mathew Mathews, "Navigating Disconnects and Divides in Singapore's Cultural Diversity," in *Managing Diversity in Singapore: Policies and Prospects,* ed. Mathew Mathews and Chiang Wai Fong (London: Imperial College Press, 2016), 3–41; and "Recent Muslim Marriages Buck Divorce Trend," *Straits Times,* April 7, 2015, http://www.straitstimes.com/singapore/recent-muslim-marriages-buck-divorce-trend.

25. Kwame Anthony Appiah, *The Ethics of Identity* (Princeton: Princeton University Press, 2005), 105.

26. "Mixed and Match: Interracial Couples Say Love Is Truly More Than Skin Deep," *Straits Times,* May 3, 2015, http://www.straitstimes.com/lifestyle/mixed-and-match-interracial-couples-say-love-is-truly-more-than-skin-deep.

27. Jan-Werner Mueller, *What Is Populism?* (Philadelphia: University of Pennsylvania Press, 2016), 3–4.

28. Svevo, *op. cit.,* 404.

29. *"L'oubli, et je dirai même l'erreur historique, sont un facteur essentiel de la création d'une nation."* Renan also wrote: *"Une nation est une âme, un principe spirituel."* (A nation is a soul, a spiritual principle.) Ernest Renan, *Qu'est-ce qu'une nation?* 2nd ed. (Paris: Calmann-Lévy, 1882), 8. For an illustrated account of some of the conflictual truths papered over in Singapore's public history, see Sonny Liew, *The Art of Charlie Chan Hock Chye* (New York: Pantheon Graphic Novels, 2016).

30. *"L'existence d'une nation est (pardonnez-moi cette métaphore) un plébiscite de tous les jours . . . ,"* Renan, *op. cit.*, 27.

31. Robert Burns, "Robert Bruce's March to Bannockburn," http://www .robertburns.org/works/428.shtml.

32. Furbank, *op. cit.*, 104–105.

FOUR Color

1. William E. Abraham, "Anton Wilhelm Amo," in *A Companion to African Philosophy*, ed. Kwasi Wiredu (Oxford: Basil Blackwell, 2004), 194. Pioneering research into Amo's life was done by Norbert Lochner—see Norbert Lochner, "Anton Wilhelm Amo: A Ghana Scholar in Eighteenth-Century Germany," *Transactions of the Historical Society of Ghana* 3 no. 3 (1958): 169–179—and by Abraham, who first published on the subject in the early 1960s. See also Marilyn Sephocle, "Anton Wilhelm Amo," *Journal of Black Studies* 23 no. 2 (December 1992), 182–187; and Paulin Hountondji, "Un philosophe Africain dans l'Allemagne du XVIIIe siècle: Antoine-Guillaume Amo," *Les Études philosophiques* 1 (January–March 1970), 25–46; as well as briefer discussions in Benjamin Simon, *From Migrants to Missions: Christians of African Origin in Germany* (Frankfurt am Main: Peter Lang, 2010), 8–10; and Albert S. Gerard, "Modern African Writing in Latin," in *European-Language Writing in Sub-Saharan Africa*, ed. Albert S. Gérard (Budapest: Coordinating Committee of a Comparative History of Literatures in European Languages, 1986), 54–56.

2. *"Es wird aber auch dieser Name allen Schwarzen, als den Negers, und andern Afrikanische Völkern von dieser Farbe gegeben." Großes vollständiges Universal-Lexikon aller Wissenschaften und Künste, welche bisher durch menschlichen Verstand und Witz erfunden und verbessert worden* (Leipzig und Halle: Verlegte Johan Heinrich Zedler, 1739), vol. 21, Mi–Mt, http:// www.zedler-lexikon.de/. This encyclopedia began publication in Halle in 1731, under the aegis of Johann Peter von Ludewig, chancellor of the university, who authorized Amo's dissertation defense of his book on the rights of Moors. The definition that follows is odd because "Moor" could still refer in Amo's day to the North African Arabs and Berbers who conquered Spain in the eighth century. Johann Gottfried Kraus, rector of the University of Wittenberg, uses the word in this sense in his congratulations to Amo on receiving his doctoral degree. "When the Moors crossed into Spain, . . ." Abraham, *op. cit.*, 193.

3. *"Sed quaero a Te et Toto orbe differentiam genericam inter hominem et Simiam, quae ex principiis Historiae naturalis. Ego certissime nullam novi."* Letter to Johann Georg Gmelin, Uppsala, Sweden, February 25, 1747, http:// linnaeus.c18.net/Letters/display_txt.php?id_letter=L0783.

4. It's perhaps worth saying that this probably isn't how the three sons of

Noah were interpreted in earlier Jewish traditions. My point is that this is how they would have been read by Christians in the eighteenth and nineteenth centuries. See David M. Goldenberg, "The Curse of Ham: A Case of Rabbinic Racism?" in *Struggles in the Promised Land*, ed. Jack Salzman and Cornel West (New York: Oxford University Press, 1997), 21–51.

5.   Matthew Arnold, *On the Study of Celtic Literature and on Translating Homer* (New York: Macmillan, 1883), 67.

6.   *Ibid.*, 87.

7.   Hippolyte Taine, *History of English Literature*, trans. H. Van Laun (London: Chatto & Windus, 1897), 17.

8.   *"des ersten lebenden Historikers,"* Friedrich Nietzsche, *Werke*, vol. 7 (Leipzig: Naumann, 1905), 225.

9.   Query 14 of Thomas Jefferson, *Notes on the State of Virginia* (1785).

10. See Kwame Anthony Appiah, *"Den Toten die Ehre erwiesen,"* in the catalog for the exhibition *"Angelo Soliman: Ein Afrikaner in Wien,"* ed. Phillip Blom (September 29, 2011– January 29, 2012), Wien Museum.

11. "From George Washington to Phillis Wheatley, 28 February 1776," https://founders.archives.gov/documents/Washington/03-03-02-0281.

12. Immanuel Kant, *Observations on the Beautiful and Sublime and Other Writings*, ed. Patrick Frierson and Paul Guyer (Cambridge: Cambridge University Press, 2011), 61. Kant's views on racial hierarchy seem to have shifted over time, however; see Pauline Kleingeld, "Kant's Second Thoughts on Race," *Philosophical Quarterly* 57 no. 229 (October 2007): 573–592.

13. "... il n'existoit de différence que celle de la couleur," Henri Grégoire, *De la littérature des nègres* (Paris: Chez Maradan, 1808), 176, http://gallica.bnf .fr/ark:/12148/bpt6k844925/f189.

14. *"On a calomnié les nègres, d'abord pour avoir le droit de les asservir, ensuite pour se justifier de les avoir asservis . . .,"* Grégoire, op. cit., 74.

15. Thomas Jefferson, letter to Henri Grégoire, February 25, 1809, http:// teachingamericanhistory.org/library/document/letter-to-henri-gregoire/.

16. J. G. Mendel (1866), "Versuche über Pflanzenhybriden," *Verhandlungen des naturforschenden Vereines in Brünn*, Bd. IV für das Jahr 1865, *Abhandlungen*: 3–47. http://www.biodiversitylibrary.org/item/124139#page/133.

17. Beth Carter, "Want to Play in the NHL? Better Hope You Were Born in the Right Month," *Wired*, March 4, 2013, https://www.wired.com/2013/03/ nhl-selection-bias/.

18. E. W. Blyden, *Sierra Leone Weekly News*, May 27, 1893, as cited in Eliezer Ben-Rafael and Yitzhak Sternberg with Judit Bokser Liwerant and Yosef Gorny, *Transnationalism: Diasporas and the Advent of a New Disorder* (Leiden: Brill, 2000), 598.

19. W. E. B. Du Bois, "To the Nations of the World," in *Lift Every Voice: African American Oratory, 1787–1900*, ed. Philip Sheldon Foner and Robert

James Branham (Tuscaloosa: University of Alabama Press, 1998), 906–907. I'm following here my own earlier discussion in Kwame Anthony Appiah, "The Problem of the Color Line: Race in the Modern World," *Foreign Affairs* 94 no. 2 (March–April 2015): 1–8. Henry Louis Gates Jr. has pointed out to me that Frederick Douglass used the phrase before Du Bois in "The Color Line," *North American Review* 132 (June 1, 1881): 567–577.

20. Du Bois, *op. cit.*

21. Mahmood Mamdani, *Citizen and Subject: Contemporary Africa and the Legacy of Late Colonialism* (Princeton: Princeton University Press, 1996).

22. W. E. B. Du Bois, "The Present Condition of German Politics," *Central European History* 31 no. 3 (1998): 170–187.

23. Lord Moran cited in Richard Toye, *Churchill's Empire: The World That Made Him and the World He Made* (New York: Henry Holt, 2010), 33.

24. Cited in David Levering Lewis, *W. E. B. Du Bois, 1919–1963: The Fight for Equality and the American Century* (New York: Henry Holt, 2000), 400.

25. "*Innerhalb der Deutschen Grenze wird jeder Herero mit und ohne Gewehr, mit oder ohne Vieh erschossen, ich nehme keine Weiber und Kinder mehr auf, treibe sie zu ihrem Volke zurück oder lasse auf sie schießen.*" As cited in *Der Spiegel*, December 1, 2004, http://www.spiegel.de/spiegel/print/d-29665604.html.

26. Timothy Snyder, "Hitler versus Stalin: Who Killed More?" *New York Review of Books* (March 10, 2011), http://www.nybooks.com/articles/2011/03/10/hitler-vs-stalin-who-killed-more/.

27. Howard W. French, *China's Second Continent: How a Million Migrants Are Building a New Empire in Africa* (New York: Knopf, 2014), 15.

28. https://www.census.gov/hhes/www/poverty/data/incpovhlth/2013/table3.pdf.

29. Walter F. White, *A Man Called White* (Athens: University of Georgia Press, 1995; originally published 1948), 3. Langston Hughes, "Ballad of Walter White," in *The Collected Poetry of Langston Hughes*, ed. Arnold Rampersad (New York: Vintage, 1995), 567.

30. N. Rehan and D. S. Tafida, "Multiple Births in Hausa Women," *BJOG: An International Journal of Obstetrics & Gynaecology* 87 (1980): 997–1004, doi: 10.1111/j.1471-0528.1980.tb04464.x.

31. Robin Andreasen, "Race: Biological Reality or Social Construct?" *Philosophy of Science* 67, Supplement. Proceedings of the 1998 Biennial Meetings of the Philosophy of Science Association. Part II: Symposia Papers (September 2000): S653–S666.

32. Rakesh Kochhar, Richard Fry, and Paul Taylor, "Wealth Gaps Rise to Record Highs Between Whites, Blacks, Hispanics," Pew Research Center and Demographic Trends, July 26, 2011, http://www.pewsocialtrends.org/2011/07/26/wealth-gaps-rise-to-record-highs-between-whites-blacks-hispanics/.

33. A 2011 study conducted in Boston concluded that some "Whites have now come to view anti-White bias as a bigger societal problem than anti-Black bias." Michael I. Norton and Samuel R. Sommers, "Whites See Racism as a Zero-Sum Game That They Are Now Losing," *Perspectives on Psychological Science* 6 no. 3 (May 2011): 215–218. doi: 10.1177/1745691611406922. "Whites see racism . . ." is one of those generic statements that I mentioned in the first chapter. It is, of course, consistent with the existence of millions of whites who don't see racism that way; indeed, recalling Sarah-Jane Leslie's example of mosquitoes and the West Nile virus, it's consistent with a majority of whites not doing so.

34. Alvin B. Tillery, Jr., *Between Homeland and Motherland Africa: U.S. Foreign Policy, and Black Leadership in America* (Ithaca: Cornell University Press, 2011); Bronwen Manby, *Citizenship Law in Africa* (New York: Open Society Foundation, 2010), 77.

35. Jeffrey Lesser, *Immigration, Ethnicity, and National Identity in Brazil, 1808 to the Present* (Cambridge: Cambridge University Press, 2013); Scott Morrison, " 'Os Turcos': The Syrian-Lebanese Community of São Paulo, Brazil," *Journal of Muslim Minority Affairs* 25 no. 3 (December 2005): 423.

36. "*Weil meine Seele doch nie Mohren lieben kann . . .*," http://www.theamoproject.org/.

37. Abraham, *op. cit.*, 198; Lochner, *op. cit.*, 178–179.

FIVE Class

1. Christopher Hussey, "High Cross Hill, Dartington, Devon: The Residence of Mr. W. B. Curry," *Country Life* 73 (February 11, 1933): 144. Hussey's review of the house is rather more respectful than this line suggests.

2. He's the Dunlop who begins a list in the ninth episode of the book, "Scylla and Charybdis": "Dunlop, Judge, the noblest Roman of them all, A.E., Arval, the Name Ineffable, in heaven height, K. H., the master, whose identity is no secret to adepts." Don Gifford with Robert J. Seidman, Ulysses *Annotated: Notes for James Joyce's* Ulysses, revised ed. (Berkeley: University of California Press, 1988), 197.

3. David Kynaston, *Austerity Britain, 1945–1951* (London: Bloomsbury, 2008), 322–323.

4. For accounts of Young's life, see Andrew McIntosh, "Michael in His Peer Group," in *Young at Eighty: The Prolific Public Life of Michael Young*, ed. Geoff Dench, Tony Flower, and Kate Gavron (Manchester, UK: Carcanet Press, 1995); Angela Lambert, "Profile: Lord Young of Dartington; Father of the Third Age," *The Independent* (January 20, 1996); Toby Young, "The Dream Maker," *The Guardian* (May 27, 2001); Toby Young, "Action Man," *The Guardian* (January 16, 2002); "Lord Young of Dartington," *The Telegraph* (January 16, 2002); and my principal source, Asa Briggs's biogra-

phy *Michael Young, Social Entrepreneur* (Basingstoke, UK, and New York: Palgrave, 2001).

5. E. P. Thompson, *The Making of the English Working Class* (New York: Vintage, 1966), 194, 9, 11. Careful exegetes of Marx will say that, while he posited two political classes, he parsed things somewhat more finely when it came to the full range of social categories.

6. Max Weber, *From Max Weber: Essays in Sociology*, ed. H. H. Gerth and C. Wright Mills (Abingdon, UK: Routledge, 1991), 180–187; and Marianne Weber, *Max Weber: Ein Lebensbild* (Heidelberg: Verlag Lambert Schneider, 1950), 78, 473.

7. P. N. Furbank, *Unholy Pleasure: The Idea of Social Class* (Oxford: Oxford University Press, 1985), 107. Furbank considered the concept of class to be not merely elusive but positively malign. See also his "Sartre's Absent Whippet," *London Review of Books* (February 24, 1994): 26–27.

8. The term for their relationship in Twi, the language of Asante, is *nua*, which is usually translated as sibling. But it is used to refer both to people with whom you share a mother and people with whom you share a maternal aunt: and my Auntie Vic was the child of my grandmother's sister. So in England she would have been called his cousin. They had been raised together in part because my grandmother had died when my father was young. But maternal cousins in Asante are close relatives—that's why you use the same word for them as you use for your siblings—and they often grew up together in the household of their mothers' senior brother in the past.

9. One Twi word for the matriclan, people related in the maternal line, is *bogya*, which is also the word for (literal) blood. So members of the Asantehene's Oyoko clan are of the same blood.

10. John Iliffe, *Honour in African History* (Cambridge: Cambridge University Press, 2005), 85. And cf. T. C. McCaskie, "The Consuming Passions of Kwame Boakye: An Essay on Agency and Identity in Asante History," *Journal of African Cultural Studies* 13 (2000): 55.

11. Frances Shelley, *The Diary of Frances Lady Shelley*, ed. Richard Edgecumbe (London: John Murray, 1913), 74.

12. Letter from Thomas Jefferson to James Madison, July 29, 1789, https://founders.archives.gov/documents/Jefferson/01-15-02-0307; and Thomas Paine, "Reflections on Titles," in *The Writings of Thomas Paine*, ed. Moncure Daniel Conway, vol. 1 (New York: G. P. Putnam's Sons, 1906), 46.

13. Joanne B. Freeman, *Affairs of Honor: National Politics in the New Republic* (New Haven: Yale University Press, 2002). John Adams unkindly referred to Hamilton as "the bastard brat of a Scottish peddler." John Patrick Diggins, *John Adams* (New York: Times Books, 2003), 87.

14. Thomas Jefferson, *The Works of Thomas Jefferson*, Federal Edition (New York and London: G. P. Putnam's Sons, 1904–5), vol. 12, http://oll.libertyfund.org/titles/808#lf0054-12_div_009.

15. Property qualifications for voting were abolished in Britain in the last year of the First World War, with the passage of the Representation of the People Act 1918, which also for the first time gave the vote to some women.

16. Alexis de Tocqueville, *Democracy in America: Historical-Critical Edition of De la démocratie en Amérique,* vol. 1, ed. Eduardo Nolla; trans. James T. Schleifer; a Bilingual French-English edition (Indianapolis: Liberty Fund, 2010), 85, http://oll.libertyfund.org/titles/2285#Tocqueville_1532 -01_EN_791, and footnote e, http://oll.libertyfund.org/titles/2285#lf1532 -01_label_1306.

17. David Herbert Donald, "Toward a Reconsideration of Abolitionists," in *Lincoln Reconsidered* (New York: Viking, 1956), 35–36.

18. Richard Sennett and Jonathan Cobb, *The Hidden Injuries of Class* (New York: W. W. Norton, 1972), 35.

19. Michael Young and Peter Willmott, *Family and Kinship in East London* (London: Routledge & Kegan Paul, 1957), 14.

20. See Kwame Anthony Appiah, *The Honor Code: How Moral Revolutions Happen* (New York: W. W. Norton, 2010).

21. Don Herzog, *Poisoning the Minds of the Lower Orders* (Princeton: Princeton University Press, 1998), 206.

22. This is a point made well in Bourdieu's discussions of what he calls "stratégies de condescendance" (strategies of condescension). See Pierre Bourdieu, "Social Space and Symbolic Power," *Sociological Theory* 7 no. 1 (Spring 1989): 14–25.

23. I was led to this passage by a mention of it in Herzog, *op. cit.,* 234.

24. See, e.g., Samuel B. James, *The Church and Society* (London: Houston & Wright, 1869).

25. Briggs, *op. cit.,* 111.

26. http://www.politicsresources.net/area/uk/man/lab45.htm.

27. See the Seventh Schedule of the 1949 Finance Act, http://www.legislation .gov.uk/ukpga/1949/47/pdfs/ukpga_19490047_en.pdf.

28. Quoted in Edward Shils, *The Order of Learning: Essays on the Contemporary University* (New York: Routledge, 2013; originally published 1997), 79. Young, too, cites this remark in *The Rise of the Meritocracy.*

29. See, e.g., Robert Putnam, *Our Kids: The American Dream in Crisis* (New York: Simon & Schuster, 2015); and, drawing on the UK Household Longitudinal Study, Nissa Finney, Dharmi Kapadia, and Simon Peters, "How Are Poverty, Ethnicity and Social Networks Related?" Joseph Rowntree Foundation, March 30, 2015, https://www.jrf.org.uk/report/how-are -poverty-ethnicity-and-social-networks-related.

30. Nancy Mitford, "The English Aristocracy," *Encounter,* September 1955, 5–11. In the years since, similar semisatiric ethnographies of class have emerged: e.g., Paul Fussell's *Class: A Guide Through the American Status*

System (New York: Summit Books, 1983), and Lisa Birnbach's *The Official Preppy Handbook* (New York: Workman Publishing, 1980).

31. There's no agreement in the social sciences about exactly how to define social capital, let alone on how to measure it, although Robert D. Putnam, notably, has tried. Putnam says, "Social capital refers to connections among individuals—social networks and the norms of reciprocity and trustworthiness that arise from them." Robert D. Putnam, *Bowling Alone* (New York: Simon & Schuster, 2000), 19. Pierre Bourdieu, more elaborately, suggests: "Social capital is the aggregate of the actual or potential resources which are linked to possession of a durable network of more or less institutionalized relationships of mutual acquaintance and recognition—or in other words, to membership in a group—which provides each of its members with the backing of the collectivity-owned capital, a 'credential' which entitles them to credit, in the various senses of the word." Pierre Bourdieu, "Forms of Capital," in *Handbook of Theory and Research for the Sociology of Education*, ed. J. C. Richards (New York: Greenwood Press, 1986), 241–258. Mike Savage offers a more straightforward definition: "your social networks, friendships and associations." Mike Savage, *Social Class in the 21st Century* (London: Penguin, 2015), 4.

32. So-called, as Gary Becker, the Nobel Prize–winning author of the classic book on the subject, put it, "because people cannot be separated from their knowledge, skills, health, or values in the way they can be separated from their financial and physical assets." Gary Becker, "Human Capital," in *The Concise Encyclopedia of Economics*, http://www.econlib.org/library/Enc/HumanCapital.html.

33. Savage, *op. cit.*, 168 (income, wealth, and social and cultural capital), 239 (elite universities versus others), 229 (proportion of graduates among social classes).

34. Catherine E. Harnois, *Analyzing Inequalities* (London: Sage, 2017), 176.

35. In the 1970s, there were efforts to identify an emerging professional-managerial cohort as a "New Class." See Barbara Ehrenreich and John Ehrenreich, "The Professional-Managerial Class," *Radical America* (March–April 1977); Alvin W. Gouldner thought that this New Class—which included "the technical intelligentsia" but also the critical, humanistic intellectuals who controlled the properties of the old capitalists but didn't own them—was the most progressive force in society, although he acknowledged that it was "elitist and self-seeking and uses its special knowledge to advance its own interests and power . . . it seeks special guild advantages—political power and incomes—on the basis of its possession of cultural capital." Alvin W. Gouldner, *The Future of Intellectuals and the Rise of the New Class* (New York: Continuum, 1979), 7.

36. Sennett and Cobb, *op. cit.*, 115.

37. J. D. Vance, *Hillbilly Elegy: A Memoir of a Family and Culture in Crisis* (New York: HarperCollins, 2016).

38. Tom W. Smith and Jaesok Son, "Measuring Occupational Prestige on the 2012 General Social Survey," National Opinion Research Center (NORC) at the University of Chicago, GSS (General Social Survey) Methodological Report No. 122, October 2014.

39. Plato *Theaetetus* 175a, trans. Benjamin Jowett. ". . . *cum referre negas, quali sit quisque parente natus, dum ingenuus . . . ,*" Horace *Satires* 1.6.

40. "*Si quid est aliud in philosophia boni, hoc est, quod stemma non inspicit,*" *Epistulae Morales ad Lucilium,* 44.

41. Michael Young, "Meritocracy Revisited," *Society* 35 no. 2 (January–February 1998), 378.

42. Michael Young, *The Rise of the Meritocracy* (London: Thames & Hudson, 1958), 18–19. In a footnote attached to the first use of this word, Young's sociologist of the future writes: "The origin of this unpleasant term, like that of 'equality of opportunity,' is still obscure. It seems to have been first generally used in the sixties of the last century in small-circulation journals attached to the Labour Party, and gained wide currency much later on."

43. *Ibid.*, 85–86. Young's mention of intraelite intermarriage has support from recent economic research into assortative mating. See, e.g., Gustaf Bruze, "Male and Female Marriage Returns to Schooling," *International Economic Review* (January 23, 2015), which finds that in Denmark, half the financial rewards of college come from the opportunity to marry a spouse with a higher income; and John Mare, "Educational Homogamy in Two Gilded Ages: Evidence from Intergenerational Social Mobility Data," *Annals of the American Academy of Political and Social Science* 663 (January 2016).

44. Barry E. O'Meara, *Napoleon in Exile; or, A Voice from St. Helena,* vol. 1 (London: Simpkin & Marshall, 1822), 405. (The original has *"talens."*)

45. Young, *Rise of the Meritocracy,* 25.

46. Reeves, *Dream Hoarders* (Washington, DC: Brookings Institution Press, 2017), 6, 12. And see the work of Raj Chetty *et al.* at the Equality of Opportunity Project, http://www.equality-of-opportunity.org/documents/. They define the motivation for their project as follows: "A defining feature of the 'American Dream' is upward income mobility: the ideal that children have a higher standard of living than their parents. Our work shows that children's prospects of earning more than their parents have fallen from 90% to 50% over the past half century."

47. Lee Anne Fennell, "Homes Rule," review of William A. Fischel, *The Homevoter Hypothesis: How Home Values Influence Local Government Taxation, School Finance, and Land-Use Policies* (Cambridge: Harvard University Press, 2001), *Yale Law Journal* 112 (December 2002), http://

chicagounbound.uchicago.edu/cgi/viewcontent.cgi?article=8029&cont ext=journal_articles; the demography of elite schools is studied in Raj Chetty *et al.*, "Mobility Report Cards: The Role of Colleges in Intergenerational Mobility," National Bureau of Economic Research Working Paper No. 23618, revised version, July 2017.

48. http://www.newhavenindependent.org/index.php/archives/entry/yale_law_commencement/.

49. "A joint study conducted by researchers at BeiDa and Australian National University indicated that women's occupation, status and wealth is almost completely determined by their father's occupation and status. For men, that determination is only about 80%." Ying Miao, "Interview with Professor David Goodman," http://cnpolitics.org/wp-content/uploads/2015/01/InterviewGoodman.pdf. In *The Son Also Rises: Surnames and the History of Social Mobility* (Princeton: Princeton University Press, 2014), Gregory Clark argues, on the basis of data from many societies, that "underlying social status in families regresses only slowly towards the mean, with a persistence rate of . . . 0.75." If this is true, it can take literally hundreds of years for the effects of differences in wealth and status to disappear.

50. Michael Young, "Down with Meritocracy," *The Guardian*, June 28, 2001.

51. Noel G. Annan, *Our Age: Portrait of a Generation* (London: Weidenfeld & Nicholson, 1990), 257.

52. Each year nearly 175,000 are enrolled in its courses; Oxford University, by comparison, has 275,000 living alumni altogether. http://www.open.ac.uk/about/main/sites/www.open.ac.uk.about.main/files/files/fact_figures_1415_uk.pdf.

53. Young, *The Rise of the Meritocracy*, 135–136.

54. Michael Young, *The Elmhirsts of Dartington* (London: Routledge & Kegan Paul, 1982), 156.

55. Ronald Dworkin, *Sovereign Virtue: The Theory and Practice of Equality* (Cambridge: Harvard University Press, 2000), 253.

56. *"Jeder Mensch hat ein eignes Maas, gleichsam eine eigne Stimmung aller sinnlichen Gefühle zu einander"* (Each person has his own measure, as it were an attunement of all his own sensory feelings to each other), Johann Gottlob Herder, *Ideen zur Philosophie der Geschichte der Menschheit*, chap. 7, sec. 1, in *Herders Sämtliche Werke*, ed. Bernard Suphan (Berlin: Weidmann, 1877–1913), 13:291. (We needn't follow him in thinking that it is only feelings that contribute to one's distinctive challenge.)

57. John Stuart Mill, *On Liberty and Other Writings*, ed. Stefan Collini (Cambridge: Cambridge University Press, 1989), 60.

58. Young, "Down with Meritocracy."

59. Young, *The Elmhirsts of Dartington*, 344.

60. Michael Dean, "Lord Young of Dartington," *The Guardian*, January

16, 2002, https://www.theguardian.com/news/2002/jan/16/guardian obituaries.books.

SIX Culture

1. Sir Edward Burnett Tylor, *Anahuac; or, Mexico and the Mexicans, Ancient and Modern* (London: Longman, Green, Longman & Roberts, 1861), 1. Tylor ended his book with a lament for old Mexico, as the country was gradually being impinged upon by its neighbor to the north: "it was our fortune to travel there before the coming change, when its most curious peculiarities and its very language must yield before foreign influences," *ibid.*, 330. Invaluable discussions of Tylor can be found in the work of anthropology's greatest historian, George W. Stocking, notably "Matthew Arnold, E. B. Tylor, and the Uses of Invention," *American Anthropologist* 65 no. 4 (August 1963): 783–799; and *Victorian Anthropology* (New York: Free Press, 1991). See also Peter Melville Logan, *Victorian Fetishism: Intellectuals and Primitives* (Albany: State University of New York Press, 2009); and the accounts collected here: http://web.prm.ox.ac.uk/sma/index.php/ articles/article-index/335-edward-burnett-tylor-1832–1917.html.

2. Matthew Arnold, *Culture and Anarchy* (Oxford: Oxford University Press, 2006), 5. Arnold pitted culture against the encroachments of "civilization," which, in his industrializing country, was obsessed with money and machinery, in his view. Civilization was the disease for which culture was the treatment. Norbert Elias famously asserted a general contrast in nineteenth-century thought between *Kultur* and *Zivilization*—the German concept being more particularist and spiritual; the French being more universalist and encompassing of economic as well as normative patterns—but his binary is perhaps more imposed than educed.

3. Edward B. Tylor, *Primitive Culture: Researches into the Development of Mythology, Philosophy, Religion, Art and Custom*, vol. 1 (London: John Murray, 1871), 1.

4. "Oh, East is East, and West is West, and never the twain shall meet, / Till Earth and Sky stand presently at God's great Judgment Seat; / But there is neither East nor West, Border, nor Breed, nor Birth, / When two strong men stand face to face, tho' they come from the ends of the earth!" Rudyard Kipling, "The Ballad of East and West," http://www.bartleby .com/246/1129.html. So the point of the poem is that people from East and West can come together, even though they come from unchangeably different places.

5. See Majid Khadduri, *War and Peace in the Law of Islam* (Clark, NJ: Lawbook Exchange, 2006), 52.

6. Herodotus *The Histories* 4.45. "οὐδ' ἔχω συμβαλέσθαι ἐπ' ὅτευ μιῇ ἐούσῃ γῇ οὐνόματα τριφάσιακέεται ἐπωνυμίας ἔχοντα γυναικῶν . . ."

7. Much of what I say here—including about the use of the word "Europenses"—I learned from reading David Levering Lewis's magisterial *God's Crucible: Islam and the Making of Europe, 570–1215* (New York: W. W. Norton, 2009). Another broad-gauged history I've found valuable is Hugh Kennedy, *Muslim Spain and Portugal: A Political History of al-Andalus* (London: Longman, 1996).

8. Edward Gibbon, *The Decline and Fall of the Roman Empire* (London: John Murray, 1887), 387.

9. Even this, however, is a bit of a simplification. In the middle of the eighth century, much of Europe was not yet Christian. Charlemagne was to spend three decades of bloody warfare, starting around 770 CE, seeking to convert the pagan Saxons to Christianity. The question of when "European," as a group identity, gained broader traction is taken up, if not entirely resolved, in Peter Burke, "Did Europe Exist Before 1700?" *History of European Ideas* 1 no. 1 (1980): 21–29. He notes, "If the first context in which people became aware of themselves as Europeans was that of being invaded by other cultures, the second was that of invading other cultures."

10. G. W. F. Hegel, "On Classical Studies," *On Christianity: Early Theological Writings,* trans. T. M. Knox and Richard Kroner (Chicago: University of Chicago Press, 1948), 324. The lecture was given in 1809. "The perfection and glory of those masterpieces," he continued, "must be the spiritual bath, the secular baptism that first and indelibly attunes and tinctures the soul in respect of taste and knowledge."

11. Mark R. Cohen, in *The Crescent and the Cross: The Jews in the Middle Ages,* 2nd ed. (Princeton: Princeton University Press, 2008), xvii, xix, suggests that "the 'myth of the Islamic-Jewish interfaith utopia' and the 'countermyth of Islamic persecution of the Jews' equally distort the past. . . . When all is said and done, however, the historical evidence indicates that the Jews of Islam, especially during the formative and classical centuries (up to the thirteenth century), experienced much less persecution than did the Jews of Christendom." And see David Nirenberg, *Communities of Violence: Persecution of Minorities in the Middle Ages,* 2nd ed. (Princeton: Princeton University Press, 2015).

12. A compelling account of Hasdai ibn Shaprut's career appears in Jane S. Gerber, *The Jews of Spain: A History of the Sephardic Experience* (New York: Free Press, 1992), 46–53.

13. Jerry Brotton, *The Sultan and the Queen: The Untold Story of Elizabeth and Islam* (New York: Penguin, 2016), 61.

14. James Reston, Jr., *Defenders of the Faith: Christianity and Islam Battle for the Soul of Europe, 1520–1536* (New York: Penguin, 2009).

15. See, for instance, Jan Helenus Ferguson, *The Philosophy of Civilization: A Sociological Study* (London: W. B. Whittingham, 1889), 316; William

Cunningham, *An Essay on Western Civilization in Its Economic Aspects,* vol. 1: *Ancient Times* (Cambridge: Cambridge University Press, 1898); and A. L. Kip, *Psychology of the Nations* (New York: Knickerbocker Press, 1902). In Germany, the culturally fraught use of the Occident, the *Abendland,* can be traced back a few generations earlier.

16. "My friend, apparently, was never the worse, but when next year his wife had an attack of the fever, there was shaking of heads among the wise." Chris Wingfield, "Tylor's Onion: A Curious Case of Bewitched Onions from Somerset," http://web.prm.ox.ac.uk/england/englishness -tylors-onion.html. The article quotes from a letter of Tylor's to an uncle in 1872, owned by Sarah Smith née Fox and transcribed by Megan Price. See also Chris Wingfield, "Is the Heart at Home? E. B. Tylor's Collections from Somerset," *Journal of Museum Ethnography* 22 (December 2009): 22–38.

17. Oswald Spengler, *The Decline of the West,* trans. Charles Francis Atkinson (New York: Oxford University Press, 1932), 12, n. 5. (The translation was originally published by Knopf in two volumes, appearing in 1926 and 1928.)

18. See, inter alia, Christopher GoGwilt, *The Invention of the West* (Stanford: Stanford University Press, 1995), 220–242; and David Gress, *From Plato to NATO: The Idea of the West and Its Opponents* (New York: Free Press, 1998). GoGwilt nimbly argues that the late-nineteenth-century emergence of the idea of the West "can be traced to the convergence of two distinct discursive contexts: the 'new imperialism' of the 1890s that gave wider currency to oppositions between East and West, and the influence of nineteenth-century Russian debates on Western European ideas of Europe."

19. Raymond Aron, *The Opium of the Intellectuals* (New York: W. W. Norton, 1962), 258. The first English edition of Aron's book appeared in 1957; it was originally published as *L'Opium des intellectuels* in 1955. Gertrude Himmelfarb, "The Illusions of Cosmopolitanism" in Martha C. Nussbaum, *For Love of Country?* ed. Joshua C. Cohen (Boston: Beacon Press, 2002), 75. Amartya Sen responded with a gentle rebuttal: "Because I have gained so much in the past from reading Himmelfarb's careful analysis of historical literature, I can only conclude that she simply has not yet taken much interest in the not insubstantial literature on these and related matters in Sanskrit, Pali, Chinese, and Arabic." Amartya Sen, "Humanity and Citizenship," in Nussbaum, *op. cit.,* 117.

20. Janheinz Jahn, *Muntu: African Cultures and the Western World,* trans. Marjorie Grene (London: Faber & Faber, 1961), 101. A longer discussion can be found in my "Europe Upside Down: Fallacies of the New Afrocentrism," *Sapina Journal* 5 no. 3 (January–June: 1993).

21. *"Aussi puis-je t'assurer qu'il n'y a jamais eu de royaume où il y ait eu tant de guerres civiles que dans celui du Christ."* Montesquieu, *Lettres persanes,* 29.

22. Raymond Williams, a century later, picked up on it when he encouraged us to think about culture not just as "the arts and learning" but as "a whole way of life," emphasis, again, on whole. See Williams, "Culture Is Ordinary" (1958), reprinted in *Resources of Hope: Culture, Democracy, Socialism* (London: Verso, 1989), 3–14, although the phrase turns up often in his work.

23. "Chicken Tikka Massala is now a true British national dish, not only because it is the most popular, but because it is a perfect illustration of the way Britain absorbs and adapts external influences. Chicken Tikka is an Indian dish. The Massala sauce was added to satisfy the desire of British people to have their meat served in gravy." Robin Cook, April 2000, when British foreign minister. https://www.theguardian.com/world/2001/apr/19/race.britishidentity.

24. Or, in its official statement, "*den Erhalt und den Schutz unserer christlich-jüdisch geprägten Abendlandkultur.*" Quoted in Christian Volk, "Why We Protest: Zur politischen Dimension transnationaler Protestbewegungen," in *Herrschaft in den Internationalen Beziehungen*, ed. Christopher Daase et al. (Wiesbaden: Springer, 2017), 160. Cf. Matthias Gretzschel, "Das Abendland–ein Mythos der Romantik," *Hamburger Abendblatt*, April 26, 2016, https://www.abendblatt.de/hamburg/kirche/article207470743/Das-Abendland-ein-Mythos-der-Romantik.html, and Hannes Schammann, "Reassessing the Opinion-Policy Gap: How PEGIDA and the AfD Relate to German Immigration Policies," in *Fortress Europe? Challenges and Failures of Migration and Asylum Policies,* ed. Annette Jünemann, Nicolas Fromm, and Nikolas Scherer (Wiesbaden: Springer, 2017), 139–158.

25. Suzann Gott, "Ghana's Glass Beadmaking Arts in Transcultural Dialogues," *African Arts* 47 no. 1 (Spring 2014): 10–29; Alexandra Robinson, "'Citizens of the World': The Earle Family's Leghorn and Venetian Business, 1751–1808," in *Slavery Hinterland: Transatlantic Slavery and Continental Europe, 1751–1808,* ed. Felix Brahm and Eve Rosenhaft (Rochester, NY: Boydell Press, 2016), 60–61.

CODA

1. E. M. Forster, *Pharos and Pharillon* (Richmond, U.K.: Hogarth Press, 1923), 9.

2. Naguib Mahfouz, *Miramar* (New York: Anchor Books, 1993), 8. I discuss these matters further in my "Presidential Address 2017—Boundaries of Culture," *PMLA* 132 no. 3 (May 2017): 513–525.

3. The Greek original is available at "The Official Website of the Cavafy Archive," http://www.kavafis.gr/poems/content.asp?id=3&cat=1.

4. T. S. Eliot, "The Function of Criticism," in *Selected Essays: 1917–1932* (New York: Harcourt Brace, 1932), 18.

Index